D0992577

EXPLORATIONS IN DOUGHTY'S *Arabia Deserta*

EXPLORATIONS IN

DOUGHTY'S

Arabia Deserta

EDITED BY STEPHEN E. TABACHNICK

The University of Georgia Press

Athens and London

© 1987 by the University of Georgia Press

Athens, Georgia 30602

All rights reserved

Designed by Barbara Werden

Set in Linotron Garamond No. 3

The paper in this book meets the guidelines for permanence and durability of the Committee on Production Guidelines for Book Longevity of the Council on Library Resources.

Printed in the United States of America

91 90 89 88 87   5 4 3 2 1

Library of Congress Cataloging in Publication Data

Explorations in Doughty's Arabia Deserta.

Bibliography: p.
Includes index.
1. Doughty, Charles Montagu, 1843–1926. Travels in Arabia Deserta. 2. Doughty, Charles Montagu, 1843–1926. 3. Arabian Peninsula. I. Tabachnick, Stephen Ely. II. Doughty, Charles Montagu, 1843–1926. Travels in Arabia Deserta.

DS207.D733E95 1987   915.3'044   86-11381

ISBN 0-8203-0899-4

CONTENTS

ACKNOWLEDGMENTS

I would like to thank the contributors for bearing with me through the difficult moments and delays that inevitably attend the preparation of a book of this nature and to ask their pardon for those times when editing of necessity became synonymous with nagging. I would also like to thank *my* editor, Karen Orchard, for a maximum of support. My wife, Sharona, provided both close reading of the text and spiritual aid when necessary, and my children, Daphne and Orrin, allowed me to work when that did not interfere with their plans. Librarians at the Ben-Gurion University, UCLA, and Tennessee Technological University confirmed my already high opinion of their profession by selflessly working for the good of this book. Finally, I would thank all those people, known and unknown to me, who helped the contributors with the work of getting their essays to me; and Dr. Frank Stapor and Mrs. Anne Schinbeckler for proofreading assistance.

ABBREVIATIONS OF SOURCES FREQUENTLY CITED

A   Thomas J. Assad, *Three Victorian Travellers: Burton, Blunt, Doughty.* London: Routledge and Kegan Paul, 1964.

F   Barker Fairley, *Charles M. Doughty: A Critical Study.* London: Jonathan Cape, 1927.

H   David G. Hogarth, *The Life of Charles M. Doughty.* London: Oxford University Press, 1928.

Ta Stephen E. Tabachnick, *Charles Doughty.* Boston: Twayne, 1981.

Tr Anne Treneer, *Charles M. Doughty: A Study of His Prose and Verse.* London: Jonathan Cape, 1935.

All quotations from *Travels in Arabia Deserta* are from the New York: Dover, 1979 edition and are cited only by volume and page number(s) in parentheses in the text.

A NOTE ON SPELLING AND PUNCTUATION

Since the use of more than one system of transliterating Arabic words would be confusing, the spelling of these words in the contributors' texts has been standardized on Doughty's own spelling as revealed in the "Index and Glossary of Arabic Words" in *Arabia Deserta*, but without any diacritical marks. The reader should also be aware that what look like typographical errors in the quotations from *Arabia Deserta* are not errors: Doughty uses on many occasions an eccentric personal system of punctuation that has been faithfully retained wherever possible.

EXPLORATIONS IN DOUGHTY'S *Arabia Deserta*

STEPHEN E. TABACHNICK

Art and Science in
Travels in Arabia Deserta

RECEPTION

In 1802, William Wordsworth predicted that "The remotest discoveries of the chemist, the botanist, or mineralogist, will be as proper objects of the poet's art as any upon which it can be employed."[1] Commenting on this passage in the introduction to their recent collection, *Nature and the Victorian Imagination*, U. C. Knoepflmacher and G. B. Tennyson write, "And yet the fusion between the artist and the objectifying man of science never came about" in the nineteenth century.[2] Wrong. It did come about at least once in that century, perhaps once in English literary history, in the form of Charles Montagu Doughty (1843–1926) and his great *Travels in Arabia Deserta* of 1888. In spite of recent claims for the virtues of Darwin's *Origin of Species* (1859) as a work of art as well as a scientific text,[3] only in the case of *Arabia Deserta* can it truly be said that the art of the book is worthy of its most important scientific explorations and discoveries.

For Doughty was equally a scientific and literary explorer of magnitude. A geologist by training, he had studied at Caius and Downing colleges, Cambridge, and conducted an examination of Norwegian glaciers before embarking, almost haphazardly, on his Middle Eastern travels, motivated by a desire for knowledge but also for self-exploration.[4] *Arabia Deserta* is expectedly full of geological, geographical, archaeological, anthropological, and linguistic observations and concludes with a geological appendix setting forth Arabia's rock structure. Yet it remains art of a very high order. In Doughty's description of the eruption of Vesuvius in 1872, we

see how he unites the scientific observer and incomparable prose stylist in
Arabia Deserta:

> I approached the dreadful ferment, and watched that fiery pool heaving
> in the sides and welling over, and swimming in the midst as a fount of
> metal,—and marked how there was cooled at the air a film, like that of
> a floating web upon hot milk, a soft drossy scum, which endured but
> for a moment,—in the next, with terrific blast as of a steam-gun, by
> the furious breaking in wind of the pent vapours rising from the infer-
> nal *magma* beneath, this pan was shot up sheetwise in the air, where,
> whirling as it rose with rushing sound, the slaggy sheet parted di-
> versely, and I saw it slung out into many great and lesser shreds. The
> pumy writhen slags fell whissing again in the air, yet soft, from their
> often half-mile high parabolas, the most were great as bricks, a few
> were huge crusts as flag-stones. The pool-side spewed down a reeking
> gutter of lavas. (1:466–67)

Doughty wrote several long poems—*The Dawn in Britain* (1906–7), *The
Cliffs* (1909), *The Clouds* (1912), *The Titans* (1916), *Mansoul* (1920; revised
1923)—after *Arabia Deserta,* but never again was he able to approach the
poetic yet scientifically precise power of a passage like the above. Even his
relatively successful dramatic poem, *Adam Cast Forth* (1908), falls short.
If, as he wrote his biographer, D. G. Hogarth, he felt he "was as much
Geologist" as Christian in Arabia (H, 130), he was at least as much poet as
scientist, conceiving of his book as "only nominally 'prose'" (H, 177) and
producing in effect an epic prose poem of nineteenth-century Arabia.

Yet Knoepflmacher and Tennyson neglect Doughty completely, and not
one of the authors in their massive collection even mentions him. In fact,
the reader interested in Doughty soon discovers that it is difficult if not
impossible to find a single anthology of Victorian writers or articles about
Victorian nonfiction that acknowledges, much less quotes, one of the
most important monuments of Victorian intellect and art prose—*Arabia
Deserta.*[5] Similarly, modern scientific studies of Arabia are silent aside
from casual footnotes or brief mentions of Doughty's book.[6] But greatness
does not always conform to easy success formulas, and despite its scholarly
neglect in recent times, Doughty's massive work remains, one hundred
years after its publication, a magisterial Presence whose understanding
requires the combined insights of literary criticism, linguistics, archae-

ology, anthropology, geology, history, and geography. Hence this collection, the first attempt ever undertaken to see *Arabia Deserta* whole.

Doughty's twin literary and scientific goals caused trouble with his publisher, Cambridge University Press, as Professor W. Robertson Smith, author of *Lectures on the Religion of the Semites* (1889) and one of Doughty's strongest advocates, wrote him: "They are prepared to spend money on Arabia but not on your experiment in English" (H, 119). In fact, at least partially because of the tension between its literary and scientific elements, *Arabia Deserta* may be the most troublesome great book ever written—troublesome for Doughty himself, for his publishers, for his reviewers, and for readers and scholars in his own time and in ours.

He had to hew it out of the rock by struggling twenty-one long months in a hostile human and physical environment to gather the raw material for it, suffering from opthalmia, bilharzia, and the lack of money and a passport document almost all the way: this greatest of all travel books is actually the record of a traveller's nightmare! *Arabia Deserta*'s forty chapters divide naturally into nine plot sections which detail the difficult adventures of Khalil, as Doughty called himself in Arabia, beginning on 10 November 1876 when he left Damascus clothed as a Syrian doctor to join the pilgrim caravan to the Holy Cities. In this first or pilgrimage section of the book (volume 1, chapters 1–3), he records in a Chaucerian manner his difficulties as a Christian among the pilgrims, as well as the sights, sounds, customs, and lore of the caravan. In chapters 4 through 7 we witness a new phase of Khalil's existence in Arabia: his semidisappointing exploration of the Medain Salih Nabataean monuments—the ostensible primary object of his journey—and his difficulties in getting along with the inhabitants of the *kella,* or caravan way station, which he inhabits during this period; the personalities of Haj Nejm, the gatekeeper, and Mohammed Aly, the tower guardian, magically transform from affability to violence and back again, much to Khalil's surprise and shock. The third plot section (volume 1, chapters 8–13) details Khalil's stay with Sheykh Zeyd of the Fejir or Fukara Beduin as Khalil decides not to go back to Damascus with the returning *Haj,* or pilgrim caravan. Khalil learns Beduin ways at first hand, serving as a go-between to reclaim Zeyd's disaffected wife, Hirfa, and the light-hearted style of narration shows Khalil's pleasure in the life of the desert. By May 1877, however, he is ready to leave Arabia, his goals fulfilled; but delays and illness prevent this, and, unknowingly, he finds himself committed to another full year's stay.

Chapters 14 through 21 of volume 1 tell of the four summer months that Khalil spends with various Beduin tribes, including his suffering caused by near-famine conditions, a harrowing experience of near-blindness in Teyma, and trouble with Horeysh, one of a series of treacherous guides. The fifth plot section, beginning with the end of chapter 21 of volume 1 and extending through the first part of chapter 3 of volume 2, constitutes one of the dramatic high points of the whole journey, when Khalil finds himself in conversation with Mohammed Ibn Rashid, feared ruler of northern Arabia, in his capital city, Hayil. We learn the tragic history of this prince, whom Doughty decides is a worthy man despite his recourse to assassination, and also witness the mores of an Arabian court. But Khalil's stubborn refusal to show obeisance to the emir, combined with his refusal to at least appear to become a Moslem, and the emir's own suspicion of British colonial intentions in the Near East eventually result in his expulsion from the town on 20 November 1877, just one year after the beginning of his Arabian adventure.

Khalil often expresses a desire to see Kheybar, the focus of legends about ancient Jewish habitation. Chapters 3 through 8 of volume 2 reveal his attainment of this goal in spite of a difficult guide, Ghroceyb, and the terrible anticlimax he suffers there: instead of a legendary city, he finds a poor village subject to a chronic fever and a brutal and corrupt Turkish commandant, Abdullah, who keeps Khalil a virtual prisoner from the end of November until the middle of March. The friendship of Mohammed en-Nejumy makes his life more bearable, but this whole section is a Gothic episode, replete with marvelous but frightening *jin* tales, superstition, and darkness, until the enlightened pasha of Medina commands Abdullah to release Khalil and send him back to Hayil. Here there will be no rest for a weary Khalil because, as we learn in chapters 9 through 11 of volume 2, Mohammed Ibn Rashid's chamberlain refuses to forward him to Bahrein as he desires and instead sends him back to Kheybar! Trouble with guides who desert him and an attack by the inflamed population of Boreyda conclude this section of the plot on a characteristically difficult note, but we should remember that even now, as always, Khalil goes on cataloging information as carefully as ever and never loses his interest in seeing as much of the Peninsula as possible.

Deeper penetration of the country causes deeper problems for Khalil as he comes into contact with the stricter, or Wahaby, variety of Islam, and the reader feels this growing tension and exhaustion, especially toward the end of the second volume. Chapters 12 through 16 tell of Khalil's apparent salvation in the town of Aneyza, in which he is at first well received by the ruler, Zamil, and the wealthy merchants Abdullah el-Kenneyny and Abdullah el-Bessam, and then of his distress as he is suddenly expelled from this oasis of rest because of the incitement of the town's preachers. The biting tone of the narration of these events reveals a man pressed to the limit, but final escape is still far off. The climactic section of the book (chapters 16 through 18 of volume 2) describes Khalil's most frightening adventure: near Mecca, which he is forbidden as a Christian to enter, he is threatened by the mad sheykh Salem and his cohort, Fheyd, who take Khalil's own proffered pistol (this must be the most unique Western-style "showdown" in all literature!) and are barely restrained from killing him. But help appears in the form of Maabub, servant of the sherif of Mecca, and Khalil has the satisfaction of seeing the sherif pronounce judgment upon Salem when they arrive at Tayif. Although Khalil is ready to accept the sherif's offer to see Wady Duwasir and even to attempt the dangerous Empty Quarter (not crossed by a European until Bertram Thomas's feat of 1931), he is simply too sick to do so. *Arabia Deserta* ends abruptly, ironically, and magnificently as Khalil, a true prince of the spirit who has triumphed over all obstacles, dressed as an Arab prince, descends to the port of Jidda, where he will be warmly received by the same British bureaucracy that had refused to grant him a passport—thus causing much of his trouble—at the beginning of the book. The date is 2 August 1878.

Doughty's hardships during the journey were followed by spiritual hardships with publishers and societies in England. He spent almost four years (circa June 1879 to May 1883) writing his manuscript while being totally ignored by the Royal Geographical Society, which, when it did finally invite him to speak on 26 November 1883, was less than appreciative of his results, partially because of ineffective delivery on his part. (Yet in 1912 this same society awarded Doughty its highest honor for his discoveries!) Four commercial publishing houses rejected the project. Cambridge University Press accepted it on 6 February 1885 (only after expressing concern about Doughty's style and his total refusal to allow tampering with it) and proceeded to lose the large sum of 393 pounds on the work when Doughty, an inexperienced author, made too many expensive proof corrections and the book failed to sell many copies at the high price of 3 guineas (H, 126–27).

First reviewers and readers immediately recognized *Arabia Deserta*'s scientific merit. But outside of a few serious artists like Wilfrid Blunt, Robert Bridges, and Edward Burne-Jones, who were engaged in similar artistic experiments, reviewers and readers seem to have regarded a journey through its more than half a million brilliant but flinty words with something of the same trepidation that Khalil felt at the prospect of a trip through the lava fields of northern Arabia. This review from the *Times* of London is typical in its imbalance between scientific praise and artistic denigration:

> No doubt this region has been visited by previous travellers, but none, we venture to think, have done their work with so much thoroughness or with more enthusiasm and love. . . . Mr. Doughty's contribution to the geology of Arabia and its wonderful volcanic remains is in itself of great value. . . . [However] the fact is that Mr. Doughty has lived so much among Semites that unwittingly he has become as one of themselves, as far, at least, as mode of expression goes. His style is much like that of the Bible, with just an occasional suggestion of unintentional travesty. It lacks, however, all the directness and simplicity of the matchless biblical narrative, and places his work under a distinct disadvantage. While much of it abounds with interest, much of it can be read only with great effort. (6 April 1888, 13)

When Doughty, in a typically reticent mood (he tells us very little of himself directly in *Arabia Deserta,* not even how Khalil looks), destroyed the manuscript in his garden (preserving, however, thirteen manuscript notebooks and many cartons of "word notes" or personal vocabulary cards, similar to a dictionary-thesaurus),[7] he created problems for any scholar interested in tracing the development of his intellect and literary art. And his insistence on regarding his masterpiece as a mere digression from his calling as the author of long and dreary "epics" of England has only helped obfuscate his reputation as the great artist of *Arabia Deserta* as well.

Yet as the book approaches the one hundredth anniversary of its publication, it remains as disturbing as ever, especially in its refusal to just go away. Ever since a relatively inexpensive, shortened (330,000 words) form edited by Edward Garnett appeared with the title *Wanderings in Arabia* (1908), *Arabia Deserta* has been resurrected, if for a narrow audience. The World War I exploits of T. E. Lawrence reawakened English interest in the Near East, leading to a full, unabridged reissue in 1921 with Lawrence's brilliant and enthusiastic introduction, and then to all of the various editions, in several languages, enumerated by Philip O'Brien for the first time ever in the primary bibliography in this volume. From 1921 until 1971, when the unabridged original went out of print in England (Penguin continues to publish a second 130,000-word abridgment by Garnett, *Passages from Arabia Deserta*), Jonathan Cape Ltd. managed to sell a respectable 21,000 copies (Ta, 172). Today, the full-size edition remains in print only in the United States through Dover Books, which reports that it is doing well.[8] And Doughty would have the satisfaction of knowing, were he alive today, that a copy of the 1888 edition, which sold poorly, now fetches prices in excess of $300 according to the most recent book price indexes.

Intrepid scientific and literary readers seem to have discovered that while few books are so demanding, to the extent that the successful reader of *Arabia Deserta* feels, with Khalil himself, like the survivor of a long and difficult journey, few books so amply repay the effort of exploration. T. E. Lawrence, who was, perhaps providentially, born in the same year as the book's publication and who subsequently became its most practical user, both as an intelligence agent among the Beduin and as the author of his own great Arabian epic, *Seven Pillars of Wisdom,* points to *Arabia Deserta*'s dual nature when he describes it as "a bible of its kind. . . . the first and indispensable work upon the Arabs of the desert" and also as "a great record of adventure and travel (perhaps the greatest in our language)" (1:17, 27). Other critics have focused on the book's double power, the scientific and the artistic. Leonard Woolf, for instance, writes that it "has all the fascination of the greatest" travel exploits and yet "is a work of the highest art." Similarly, Peter Brent remarks that *Arabia Deserta* is "the one indispensable classic which Arabian exploration has added to the canon of travel literature," and Wilfrid Blunt, himself a noted Arabian traveller and poet (Blunt, however, never achieved Doughty's fusion of science and art in the travel book), remarked that Doughty's methods helped save his life in an encounter with the Senussi sect in North Africa and also that *Arabia Deserta* "is the greatest prose work of the XIXth Century" in English.[9]

As the essays in the second half of this collection show, *Arabia Deserta* will always retain its importance in any scientific discussion of what Arabia was like in the nineteenth century; but as they also show, it has been naturally superseded by more precise and/or modern studies in several areas, particularly geology. Once valued mainly for its science, it will inevitably become increasingly valued primarily for its art, perhaps fol-

lowing Burton Hatlen's theory that literary critics become interested in
certain works of prose only when these works grow less important or
useful in scientific areas.[10] In fact, although it has been cited only ten
times in natural science articles in the last thirty years, *Arabia Deserta* has
been mentioned at least thirty-five times in social science and humanities
articles during the last ten years alone, and the only complete books and
dissertations on Doughty, outside of Hogarth's biography, have been written by literary critics.[11]

The essays in the second half of this collection constitute the very
first full-length attempts to assess *Arabia Deserta* in the various natural
and social science fields upon which it touches, but in the literary area we
can quote a long series of very impressive—and often forgotten—testi-
monies to the book's value. Far from a curiosity of literature, as it is
sometimes regarded by English professors, *Arabia Deserta* has been seen as
centrally important by many of the foremost practitioners of the literary
art from the time it was published to the present day. It was one of
William Morris's very favorite books toward the end of his life,[12] and W.
B. Yeats, who read it three times, very likely based most of his desert
poetry, including the famous "Second Coming," on it.[13] Wyndham Lewis
has praised its "archaic but delightful jargon,"[14] while T. S. Eliot, who
justly attacks Doughty's *Titans* for lack of agreed tradition and con-
creteness, calls *Arabia Deserta* a "great work" and says that it, along with
the novels of James and Conrad, may indicate the future directions of
English prose.[15] D. H. Lawrence read it twice,[16] and Aldous Huxley
thought Doughty in *Arabia Deserta* "A most splendid, archaic stylist."[17]
Perhaps the most influenced by Doughty's book, aside from T. E. Lawrence, was the novelist Henry Green, who writes that Doughty is a "genius" and a "composer of great prose"[18] and whose own style reflects some
of Doughty's mannerisms, according to both John Russell and Michael
North in their books on Green.[19] Louis MacNeice reports that W. H.
Auden was reading *Arabia Deserta* in 1928,[20] and Rex Warner has expressed his esteem for the book. Henry Miller lists it among the books he
would most like to read.[21] More recently, John Bickerson ("Binx") Bol-
ling, the hero of Walker Percy's *The Moviegoer* (1961), has a one-book library consisting of *Arabia Deserta,* and an academic critic has named it
"one of the greatest travel books in English."[22] Others, including this
writer, would go farther and pronounce it the greatest travel book of all
time. But what does such praise mean? And, in view of it, how did it ever

come about that Doughty's book remains widely unknown today, especially among students of English literature?

THE ANATOMY OF NEGLECT

When we consider the neglect of Doughty's masterpiece, particularly by academics (it remains outside the university natural and social sciences and literature curriculum and generally languishes in a "kind of revered obscurity," in Ruth Gay's words),[23] we cannot fall back on currently fashionable and standard ideological and other explanations involving the author's class, race, sex, or publishing economics. Written by a solidly respectable (and even nationalistic) white male member of the upper class with excellent family connections, *Arabia Deserta* was published by a major university press, received many and good reviews (at least for its scientific contributions), was immediately recognized by avant-garde artists for its style, and has remained in print in one form or another at least since 1921. None of the essays in Robert von Hallberg's recent theoretical collection *Canons* (University of Chicago Press, 1984), could explain the reasons for *Arabia Deserta*'s omission from the academic and popular consciousness, because the contributors in typical fashion pay more attention to why certain books have been canonized rather than to why others have been allowed to sink without trace, and even when they do consider such cases they fall back on the standard reasons listed above.[24]

But as soon as we think about why even great books are *not* sometimes given their due, rather than about why the known classics have achieved their celebrity, we find that Doughty's work has been the victim of some of the most insidious reasons for neglect. First, we discover what may be termed the more general reasons. *Travels in Arabia Deserta* unites science and art and cuts across many recognized fields of study. Academics, with their understandable but not particularly praiseworthy passion for compartmentalization and classification, are uncomfortable with a book that evades neat categorization and are ill-equipped to deal with it. A literary scholar will downplay the book's scientific contribution because he will not be able to assess it, and the opposite holds true for a scientific reader, who will not know what to do with the book's "strange" style. Then, the book deals with and reflects a culture—the Arabic—that most Western scholars, like most popular readers, know little about. Doughty's language is not more (if not less) unique than that of any other great artist in prose or as demanding for the nonspecialist as the work of most nine-teenth-century scientific writers. The problem is simply that Doughty's work makes use of Arabic rather than German or French expressions and syntax and thus reveals the narrow ethnocentricity of readers who refuse to rise to his demand to open themselves to the linguistic and thought patterns of a non-European culture. Literary scholars, for instance, regularly discuss the works of Old and Middle English writers, Puritan sermonists, and difficult Modernists who are at least as hard to understand as Doughty: *Arabia Deserta* is certainly far more accessible to the twentieth-century reader than *Finnegans Wake,* or even *Ulysses.*

Finally (under general reasons for neglect), teachers face the practical problem, difficult to admit, that *Arabia Deserta*'s one thousand–plus pages do not fit conveniently into the quarter (or even semester) system, making it difficult to present to a class. And although Garnett's second abridgment, *Passages from Arabia Deserta* (1931), is suitable for a usual course in terms of length, it unavoidably omits many of Doughty's best touches, including the wonderful *jin* tales and full Gothic atmosphere of the Kheybar section, and the brilliant denouement and final, ironic sentence, "On the morrow I was called to the open hospitality of the British Consulate" (2:574), not to mention many of Doughty's more choice execrations of Arab society.

Second, we have what might be regarded as the natural and social scientists' excuses for ignoring the book. The fact that *Arabia Deserta* has been cited in articles on animal husbandry, geography, nutrition, geology, and opthalmology during the past thirty years and the value seen in the book by almost all the contributors of the scientific essays in this volume show that it has some present applications in many fields. Nonetheless, scientists can plead with some justice—as Shagam and Faul do in their essay—that the book has been superseded and that even for its own time Doughty's work is less than perfect, largely because of the difficult conditions under which he had to undertake it. Beyond the difficulties caused by his need to guard his life constantly, however, scientists point to what is one of Doughty's greatest strengths and weaknesses—his refusal or inability to arrive at general formulations based on the data he collects. Wagstaff, Shagam and Faul, Hammond, Winder, and Fernea all point to the value of many of Doughty's isolated observations and the rich mine of data he has collected, but the reader will sometimes detect a certain muted or overt impatience with Doughty's failure to unite his perceptions in a grand theory concerning a given field. What the literary scholar like Rogers, Bevis, Deledalle-Rhodes, or Tabachnick is likely to praise as "ambiguity" or suggestiveness can become for the scientist a lapse in Doughty's professional equipment, rendering his book a "source" but not a study. But even if we credit such well-based objections to Doughty's work, can we justify the fact that these objections were never aired in full-length scientific pieces or assessments of Doughty until a hundred years after his work appeared? And is it not true that even those most critical of Doughty, such as Shagam and Faul, still find many things, such as his local cartography and his exploratory observations, to praise? Fernea, in fact, is very emphatic about the advantages of Doughty's nontheoretical method. Thus, like general readers and humanists, scientists have much to apologize for in their failure to mention or think about Doughty's contribution outside of a few brief footnotes and obituaries.[25] Suffice it to say that the job of exploring northern Arabia could not have fallen to a man better equipped to record *all* the country's facets, rather than just one specialized aspect of it. However lacking Doughty's account may sometimes be in specific areas, it arouses wonder owing to its very comprehensiveness and breadth.

Literary scholars, who provide the third main category of reasons for neglect, may justifiably claim that they have paid more attention to *Arabia Deserta* than anyone else, even if they almost never teach or anthologize the book and have allowed large blocks of time to pass between publications about it. In fact, they have less justification than the scientists, for good works of art cannot be superseded.

Unfortunately, Doughty was essentially a one-book author (although many critics have called attention to *Adam Cast Forth,* his powerful dramatic coda to *Arabia Deserta*), and literary critics in particular are fond of tracing an author's development across manuscripts or several works. But perhaps the most important reason for neglect, particularly by literature teachers, paradoxically offers the most hope for the active, permanent resuscitation of Doughty's reputation. For *Arabia Deserta* is a classic of travel literature, and travel literature was not even recognized as a genre worthy of study by critics enamored of the novel, poetry, and drama until about ten or fifteen years ago. Not only *Arabia Deserta* but Kinglake's *Eothen,* Lawrence's *Seven Pillars of Wisdom,* Thesiger's *Arabian Sands,* and even Richard Henry Dana's *Two Years Before the Mast* have never achieved their proper position in literary or other university studies. But now that is changing.

Until recently, travel literature was regarded as "intellectual background" or source material for the work of "genuine" artists, as Martin Day has pointed out with justified exasperation.[26] Thus, such studies as J. L. Lowes's famous *Road to Xanadu* (1927), Robert Cawley's *The Voyagers and Elizabethan Drama* (1938), and even Samuel Chew's classic *The Crescent and the Rose* (1937) substituted for any systematic attempt to look at travel literature itself as art, rather than at its influence. In this atmosphere, it is not surprising that the two books that pioneered the analysis of Doughty as literary artist—Barker Fairley's *Charles M. Doughty: A Critical Study* (1927) and Anne Treneer's *Charles M. Doughty: A Study of His Prose and Verse* (1935)—met with little understanding. While Fairley and Treneer erred in trying to make claims for the admittedly impossible poetry, thus diluting their praise of *Arabia Deserta* and undermining confidence in their judgment, their work should have produced more attention to the book than F. R. Leavis's dismissive comment, "it will remain a respected but little-read minor classic,"[27] which has become a self-fulfilling prophecy.

Only with the arrival of Northrop Frye's *Anatomy of Criticism* (1957) was the way theoretically cleared for the equal appreciation of all genres, including the autobiography and the travel book. And this movement forward, even while only barely recognized by such "bibles" as the *Norton Anthology of English Literature* (which devotes a scant few pages to travel literature) and the *Oxford Anthology of English Literature* (which is no better in this respect), has been increased with the advent of recent French criticism, which would include all discourse and indeed all sign-systems as worthy objects of literary analysis (perhaps too generously). With these developments, critics have begun to understand that as the world of canonical fiction, poetry, and drama grows a smaller and more cramped place owing to the ministrations of the largest critical machine ever known, travel literature affords much virgin territory for their explorations. Thus, Percy Adams's exhaustive bibliography of academic work on seventeenth- and eighteenth-century travelogues as well as his important study, *Travel Literature and the Evolution of the Novel,*[28] Joanne Shattock's annotated listing of scholarly studies on the nineteenth- and twentieth-century travellers,[29] the widespread and favorable recognition accorded Paul Fussell's *Abroad,*[30] and the continuing vigor of the journals *Terrae Incognita* and *Exploration* and the Modern Language Association Special Session on Travel Literature (the first special session ever founded, apparently, but unfortunately not the most aggressively pursued) testify to a great expansion of recent research in this field that is gradually making its way into university course offerings.[31] Perhaps academics will at last catch up with the general public, for whom travel books have been popular favorites since at least the eighteenth century (recent examples include Paul Theroux's *Great Railway Bazaar* and William Least Heat Moon's *Blue Highways*). We hope this collection, as part of these general intellectual trends, will help clear the way for full academic and popular recognition of Doughty's classic travel book.

THE ELEMENTS OF TRAVEL LITERATURE

Recent investigations in travel writing help us understand how Doughty's book fulfills all the demands of its genre and more, and why travel literature is particularly congenial to Doughty's blend of science and art. What emerges from these studies is that travel writing, at least since the eighteenth century, appears to occupy a middle ground in prose writing between the essay, with its personal opinion and factual underpinning, and the mainstream autobiography, with its focus on the development of the self in society. It is perhaps best described as a form of autobiography (and Hogarth in 1927 already uses the phrase "autobiography of travel" [H, 132]) in which the self is temporarily brought into contact with an alien culture (of country, religion, class, language, or region) and thus highlighted in isolation or abrasive contact rather than in a greater or lesser degree of harmony against the backdrop of a familiar society. In short, travel literature (as opposed to guidebooks and travel journalism) consists of well-written, first-hand accounts of actual journeys in which the writers both describe what they saw, felt, and did and meditate on its significance for themselves and their societies.

   From that basic definition, we derive the four elements of travel literature which any analysis of a given work must consider:

   1. *Fact:* "actual journeys . . . describe what they saw, felt, and did." If we are to understand the other culture itself, as well as the dynamics of an author's eyewitness contact with it, we must have a completely accurate—if selected—rendering of the journey undertaken, conditions found, people met, and the outlines of the other culture as the author understands it. Without this factual base, a travel book becomes a form of novel, an imaginary or fictional journey, like *Gulliver's Travels* or Jan Morris's recent *Letters from Hav.*[32] However delightful, such novels do not serve one primary purpose of all travel accounts: to provide a source of information and

comparison of impressions for subsequent travellers and even scientists. Travel literature is a genre well rooted in the documentary and subject to the claims of verification as no fiction is. Joyce's Dublin, however well ballasted with facts, cannot be trusted by a geographer or historian as an accurate picture of the city because we cannot know where fiction begins and facts leave off;[33] Doughty's Hayil, despite his moralizing, is so trusted, as J. M. Wagstaff's, Robert Fernea's, and Bayly Winder's essays demonstrate. However the world views of travel writers differ, they must offer highly verifiable accounts.

2. *Opinion:* "meditate on its significance for themselves and their societies." As Harold Spender commented about *Eothen* a long time ago, "Facts must be interpreted as well as observed."[34] And Martin Day, referring to the speculative and artistic qualities of the literary travel book, points out that it bears the same relation to a mere guidebook as genuine poetry does to "Thirty Days Hath September."[35] We want to know what writer-travellers think of the other culture and even of travelling, life, and the universe itself, and we enjoy agreeing or disagreeing with their thoughts and perceptions whether or not we have been to the area of the world they describe; there are no "digressions" in a good travel book.

3. *Shaping art:* "well-written . . . accounts." As Paul Fussell has pointed out, to be considered literary, a travel book must show its author's interest in writing as well as in travelling. The travelogue permits any type of organization or approach, but must display special qualities of style, characterization, drama, and structure if literary readers are to become interested in it. Thus, travel writers' portraits of the people they met must be based on truth, if the truth as they saw it rather than the view from inside a character's head, as in a novel; but they must write of these people in such a way as to engage our interest.

4. *Personality:* "first-hand accounts . . . significance for themselves." We expect a truthful but personal memoir of the journey, not a third-person narrative history or a journalistic assemblage of facts which attempts to suppress the personality of the writer in order to pretend to objectivity. As a form of autobiography, travel writing must make the writer-traveller's personality interesting and engaging however directly or indirectly, carefully or haphazardly, it emerges from the book. If we have no interest or trust in the people doing the travelling, why should we be interested in learning how the other culture reacts to them and they to it?

In short, what we ask as readers of the travel book is that it reveal both the other culture and the traveller's personality in contact with it in as lively, informative, entertaining, and believable a way as possible.

Arabia Deserta AS TRAVEL AUTOBIOGRAPHY

As a way of accounting for its felt power, let us now see how well *Arabia Deserta* fulfills the theoretical demands of its genre.

1. *Fact.* Just how much does the book tell us about the land, people, and history of Arabia? The essays in the second section of this volume answer that question very clearly, most of them for the first time ever. In spite of its imperfections or scientific failures of technique, Doughty's work is not simply a recapitulation of what was already known in his time or a travel book in the usual sense of a retreading of a known area, but a work of primary investigation, an *exploration,* a record of the search for all the then-unanswered questions about Arabia. Doughty never allows us to forget that he was a scientist by training: almost every page of *Arabia Deserta* contains precise specifications of the rock structure and topography of Arabia, sometimes interspersed with archaeological probings or anthropological and linguistic observations, sometimes with metaphysical speculations about the nature of being. *Arabia Deserta* thus has something of the Victorian encyclopedic quality of *Moby Dick* about it; but unlike Melville, who confines his science to whaling and his disquisitions about it to sharply defined chapters, Doughty leaps back and forth in single paragraphs, making a very close weave between science and speculation:

> As for me who write, I pray that nothing be looked for in this book but the seeing of an hungry man and the telling of a most weary man; for the rest the sun made me an Arab, but never warped me to Orientalism. Highland Arabia is not all sand; it is dry earth, nearly without sprinkling of the rains. All the soft is sandy; besides there is rocky moorland and much harsh gravel, where the desolate soil is blown naked by the secular winds. (1:95)

At an important moment when he could have died at the hands of the wild sheykh Salem, Khalil worries about the fate of his aneroid barometer (2:529). As lacking as his geology may be in the view of Shagam and Faul, Doughty knew more about science than did Melville and did establish for the first time, as they point out, that Arabia's rock structure is similar to that of Sinai. Their challenging revisionist essay, which reveals among other things the geological superiority of the work of his contemporary Oscar Fraas to Doughty's, represents an exception—if a very well grounded one—to the general scientific praise Doughty has received. For instance, the anonymous reviewer for *Nature* wrote that "Mr. Doughty was a careful observer, and he has not only made important additions to our geographical knowledge of Arabia, but also to our geological knowledge of it" (28 June 1888, 195).

In fact, appreciation of Doughty's achievements in the factual realm, even before the writers in the present volume rendered their up-to-date and more precise estimates, has been unequivocal, and we see a certain continuity of response among older and more recent scientific readers. Thus Hogarth writes that "So much and such expert testimony has been borne to the book's fidelity to fact that no more need be adduced here" (H, 134). In his *Brittanica* article on Doughty, H. St. John Philby (the second Westerner to cross the Empty Quarter, in 1931) calls him "the greatest of all Arabian travellers" and in his *Arabia of the Wahhabis* Philby confirms the details of Doughty's journey by recording the testimony of Beduin who remembered him even after half a century. In his essay in this volume, Bayly Winder confirms not Doughty's story of his own travels, but rather his comments on Arabian history and his picture of nineteenth-century Arabian society. He finds that, although *Arabia Deserta* is only "one of many" useful works in establishing " 'facts' about Arabian politics, tribes, chronologies, and dynasties," still "no single work paints an overall picture of nineteenth-century Arabian society that tells us more." He thus seconds, from a perspective of half a century's further accumulation of knowledge about Arabia, something of Hogarth's claim that Doughty's book "remains without peer among literary portrayals not only of Arab society but of any alien society in the world" (H, 134). There is something very democratic and infinitely touching about Doughty's recording of the personal histories of common people, like Amm Mohammed or the wicked Abdullah es-Siruan, which would otherwise have gone unrecorded, and which aligns Doughty with historians of our own day as well as of his.

Doughty's reports in the German periodical *Globus* in 1880, 1881, and 1882[36] established his priority in solving the problem of the true nature and flow of the Wady Hamd and Wady er-Rummah watercourses, describing the volcanic tracts between Tebuk and Kheybar, and revealing the nature of Kheybar and its environment, according to Hogarth (H, 101). J. M. Wagstaff in this volume reassesses this older estimate of precise discoveries and then explores the area of Doughty's skills and uses for the geographer today. He finds, for example, that

> As well as bringing out an acceptable regionalization of northwestern Arabia in terms of terrain and ultimately geology, *Arabia Deserta* reveals Doughty's sense of the relationships between physical conditions and the pattern of human activity. It is thus possible to recognize regions in the fullest sense understood by nineteenth-century geographers.

According to Wagstaff, Doughty's main value for geographers nowadays lies in what is termed "perception geography" as well as in historical geography. He allows us to understand the city of Hayil, for instance, as it appeared to a sensitive and careful observer in the late nineteenth century, and thus gives us a point of comparison for learning how things have changed since. In its telescopic view of the past, *Arabia Deserta* will remain timeless as a geographer's source book.

Doughty's *Documents épigraphiques recueillis dans le nord de l'Arabie* (1884), containing his "squeezings" of Nabataean inscriptions, and his personal account of his Nabataean discoveries in the Medain Salih section of *Arabia Deserta* have proven his value to archaeologists as well as to historians, geographers, and, to some degree, geologists. The contemporary *Nature* reviewer quoted earlier writes that "The inscriptions he obtained at Medain Salih and elsewhere have been published by the French Government, and important inferences have been drawn from them." In fact, his inscriptional work was quickly repeated if not quite equalled in his own time by the subsequent travellers Julius Euting and Charles Huber, but as Philip Hammond points out, Doughty's book remains an invaluable mine of source material. Doughty had the advantages of a slow pace, almost unlimited time, an amazingly observant eye, and, perhaps most of all, the compulsion to record without omissions every fact observed. Doughty's book has helped Hammond himself probe the mysteries of the Nabataean ruins around Petra, and he remarks that "If the Nabataeans were 'Arabs,' then Doughty's work must be seen by Nabataean researchers in terms of T. E. Lawrence's recommendation: 'in a few of its pages you learn more of the Arabs than in all that others have written' (1:27)." Hammond points to the vast untapped resources that remain in Doughty's book not only for the archaeologist but for those interested in the historical flora and fauna of the region as well. His insight is confirmed by George Conn, who writes in his anthology *The Arabian Horse in*

Fact, Fantasy and Fiction that *Arabia Deserta* "has long been known as the Arabian horseman's Bible";[37] and citations in recent works on animal husbandry in the desert show that Doughty may well be a prime authority on sheep and camel raising, too.

As Shagam and Faul have demonstrated, Doughty was remiss in failing to read the work of Oscar Fraas and Louis Lartet on geology either before or after his travels, although it was available. A similar example of what Harold Bloom has called "the anxiety of influence," or the tendency on the part of later writers to be cavalier toward their predecessors because of fear or envy, is the fact that Doughty's work is barely mentioned, if at all, in Alois Musil's many thick volumes about his Arabian explorations, H. R. P. Dickson's massive work on the Beduin, and Wilfred Thesiger's *Arabian Sands*.[38] The essays in the scientific section of this volume set the record straight, but perhaps the single most impressive testimony to Doughty's continuing usefulness in the factual arena is simply the knowledge that in both World Wars I and II, British intelligence regarded his book as primary source material on the topography and anthropology of Arabia.[39]

Of all the factual areas covered by Doughty's encyclopedic work, however, none is more difficult to assess in terms of accuracy than the anthropological comments. For Doughty is not a twentieth-century anthropologist trained in the relativity of cultures and the ability to suppress his own reactions to cultural phenomena that are unfamiliar, but rather a very personal if careful observer of facts, and here the trouble begins: Doughty gives us what he sees in precise detail, but he also indicates what he thinks of it, much to the distaste of many modern readers. Is he or is he not accurate in his description of Arab culture? How can another culture be described objectively, or is this impossible? Robert Fernea, who has worked in the same area (Hayil) that Doughty visited and wrote about in a lengthy section of *Arabia Deserta,* tackles these very difficult questions with the equipment of the modern anthropologist. His findings, in keeping with the tendencies of recent social science research, may surprise some readers. Precisely because Doughty was confrontational in his dealings with the Arabs and made no efforts to conceal his prejudices from them or from the reader, his book constitutes ethnology of great value, according to Fernea. Doughty's sometimes antagonistic stance brings out his opponents' personalities and beliefs in a way that a more diplomatic approach would not have done; and he also lets us see his own biases in the open, where we can allow for them. And Doughty, alone among ethnologists in Arabia, found the appropriate language to allow his subjects to speak on their own, without the distortions caused by translations into more standard English. Thus, Doughty actually lets us see how many Arabians thought and acted with greater accuracy than many other and more recent anthropological writers have achieved.

Fernea's essay, like Wagstaff's, Hammond's, and Winder's, reveals the determination on the part of the contemporary social sciences to learn how to value and use sensitive individual perceptions as opposed to a perhaps spurious "objectivity," which was the ideal of the 1950s. In effect, they attempt to find a way to come to terms not only with the straightforward observations afforded by Doughty, but with what forms the second element common to literary travel books and which he displays in abundance: opinion, or interpretation of the facts perceived.

2. *Opinion.* As truculent as Doughty sometimes is when describing Islam or condemning a particular Arab custom, he is only doing the expected in a travel book, if a bit more vehemently than usual, as when he writes that "The nations of Islam, of a barbarous fox-like understanding, and persuaded in their religion, that 'knowledge is only of the koran,' cannot now come upon any way that is good" (1:142). One of the great freedoms granted by the travel book even in our more diplomatic age is the expression of what writers really think about the cultures they observe. They are not under the anthropologist's presumed obligation to at least consider a relativistic position or to pretend to objectivity. Thus, their comments can and do range from the most prejudiced, in which another culture or a whole ethnic or national group is condemned *en masse,* to the most relativistic, in which the habits of another culture are preferred to one's own. We see both tendencies in the work of Wilfred Thesiger, the last great Anglo-Arabian explorer and travel writer:

> being fond of Arabs, it was probable that I could never really like Kurds.[40]

> I went there with a belief in my own racial superiority, but in their tents I felt like an uncouth, inarticulate barbarian, an intruder from a shoddy and materialistic world.[41]

A dislike of all Kurds comes together with a respect for the Beduin as our superiors. Even though readers will most probably not agree with Thesiger's unabashed tendency toward group characterizations and even rankings, they must admit that these opinions—for that is what they must be

called—keep them interested in Thesiger's books. And Doughty's incon
sistent comments on the Arabs (and Turks, and Jews, and Persians, and
Eastern Christians, and English), some negative, some positive, continually force our attention and interest, even if often in the same manner
as the rub of sandpaper against our skin.

In stating in a blanket manner that the Arab nations cannot be worth
anything because they follow Islam, Doughty offends against good taste
and toleration, not to mention logic and historical fact: Islam did not
prevent the Arabs from leading the world in science and enlightened government one thousand years ago. But if we see Doughty's statement and
other similar comments in his book as reflections of pique brought on by
his many difficulties and his own deeply held Christian beliefs, we learn to
expect and make allowance for them as we read. Janice Deledalle-Rhodes
tackles the issue of Doughty's true attitude toward the Arabs—no easy
matter, given his many favorable as well as unfavorable comments about
them—by comparing his attitudes to those of many other nineteenth-
century Anglo-Arabian travellers as revealed in their travel accounts. She
finds that Doughty's very contradictions, so unlike the consistent and
stereotypical views of other travellers, are the guarantee of his sincerity
and honesty in reporting his feelings. More than that, his many arguments with the Arabs actually prove his respect for them, for he, alone
among nineteenth-century European travellers to Arabia, thought enough
of his opponents' opinions to dispute them. Despite his differences with
the Arabs on the subject of religion and the many prejudices he brought
with him from England, he listened to the Arabs' opinions and responded
more or less logically to their objections to his. Finally, as she points out,
we have the fact that he made not just one but many friends in Arabia and
went out of his way to keep in touch with them in later life and to record
their kindnesses in *Arabia Deserta*. Thus, Doughty actually represents a
transformation of nineteenth-century European mentality toward other
cultures in the direction of equality and mutual respect.

In *Arabia Deserta*, Doughty responds not only to the other culture, but
to nature itself. His cosmological meanderings are all the more intriguing
because Doughty hints at his opinions concerning the universe rather than
stating them openly, as he does in the case of his cultural reactions:

We look out from every height, upon the Harra, over an iron desolation; what uncouth blackness and lifeless cumber of vulcanic matter!—

an hard-set face of nature without a smile for ever, a wilderness of
burning and rusty horror of unformed matter. What lonely life would
not feel constraint of heart to trespass here! the barren heaven, the
nightmare soil! where should he look for comfort?—There is a startled
conscience within a man of his *mesquîn* [pitiful] being, and profane, in
the presence of the divine stature of the elemental world!—this lion-
like sleep of cosmogonic forces, in which is swallowed up the gnat of
the soul within him,—that short motion and parasitical usurpation
which is the weak accident of life in matter. . . . There is here but a
small black solitary bird of slender form . . . a cheerful neighbour to
mankind. Many a time the passenger hears at unawares her short descant ringing upon the waste moors, in perplext desert ways, in the awe
and the Titanic ruins of desolate mountains, with a silver sweetness, as
it were the voice to his soul of some benign spirit. (1:451–52)

In an earlier important article in *Victorian Studies*, Richard Bevis has
shown how Doughty was attracted to the barren wastes of the world in
order to find the God of the geologist Lyell there, hard at work on the face
of the land in a way visible to humanity. In his essay in this volume, Bevis
persuasively and instructively demonstrates how Doughty transmutes
eighteenth- and nineteenth-century ideals of the sublime in nature into
his own kind of simplicity, bareness, and austerity. For all its apparent
strangeness, Doughty's thought looks forward to the twentieth-century
artistic doctrine of minimalism.

Beyond the sublime and the titanic, we find another element in a passage like the above: we hear and see not only emptiness and the overpowering force of nature's lifeless elements here, but the marvel and gift of
fragile life in its midst. Doughty frequently calls attention not only to the
immense lifelessness of the universe, but to the mystery of consciousness
in its center:

The summer night's delightful freshness in the mountain is our daily
repast; and lying to rest amidst wild basalt-stones under the clear stars,
in a land of enemies, I have found more refreshment than upon beds and
pillows in our close chambers.—Hither lies no way from the city of the
world, a thousand years pass as one daylight; we are in the world and
not in the world, where Nature brought forth man, an enigma unto
himself, and an evil spirit sowed in him the seeds of dissolution. And,
looking upon that infinite spectacle, this life of the wasted flesh seemed

to me ebbing, and the spirit to waver her eyas wings unto that divine obscurity. (1:520)

Even in the otherwise unpleasant atmosphere of Kheybar, where Khalil was held prisoner for months, he hears a special voice of life and being amidst the inanimate world:

Oh, what bliss to the thirsty soul is in that sweet light water, welling soft and warm as milk, [86° F.] from the rock! and I heard the subtle harmony of Nature, which the profane cannot hear, in that happy stillness and solitude. Small bright dragon-flies, azure, dun and vermilion, sported over the cistern water ruffled by a morning breath from the figgera, and hemmed in the solemn lava rock. The silver fishes glance beneath, and white shells lie at the bottom of this water world. I have watched there the young of the thób shining like scaly glass and speckled: this fairest of saurians lay sunning, at the brink, upon a stone; and ofttimes moving upon them and shooting out the tongue he snatched his prey of flies without ever missing. (2:219–20)

Even in the midst of a rhapsodic communion with nature, he remembers to measure the temperature of the water precisely and to use exact scientific language ("saurians"). This alerts us to an important aspect of Doughty's speculations: he believes that by observing and measuring natural phenomena humans will ultimately be able to explain them, whether the question be the formation of all matter or the appearance of life in the universe. Scientific measurement and the corresponding Ruskinian doctrine of "Truth to Nature," meaning the close imitation of natural details in art, come together in Doughty's mind and his book. Behind all the gathering of data, we feel a constant, questing impulse for answers accompanied by a sense of awe as complete as any recorded. But, of course, the method does not work: even the closest observations do not inevitably lead to answers to the great questions. Thus, we leave *Arabia Deserta* as Doughty does, in awe over the contrast between the limitless desert and the solitary, finite consciousness of the traveller, but without any formulation of the relationship between the two or idea of how life could have arisen from inanimate elements in the first place. Doughty's contemporaries, such as Charles Kingsley, author of the *Water-Babies* fantasy (1863), and the Victorian "fairy painters," were not satisfied by their inability to go beyond this cosmic block and so invented worlds in which answers could be

given. Doughty, in his own poetry, frequently wrote of the Shakespearean
fairy Oberon, one of the Victorians' favorite fantasy-creatures. But in
Arabia Deserta, his "incredible journey" is real and he limits himself to
facts and wonderings.

The result is, that for all his science and his sophisticated artistic consciousness, Khalil has no intellectual answers, but rather like the Beduin
is reduced by nature to the elemental, lowest common denominator of
being, as Middleton Murry once commented superbly.[42] In the desert,
Khalil, the tribesmen, and the wild animals become one in their attempt
to survive against the vast and merciless world of matter. And Doughty as
writer captures this fellow-feeling in his book. Doughty's ultimate opinion about society and nature, glimpsed in these quotations, is that, under
their many differences, all living things are one. Tabachnick's essay shows
how Doughty mixes animal and human imagery to make this point,
among others. Below all the diverse data and fragmentary details in
Doughty's book, the sensitive reader perceives this deep, almost mystical
unity of fellowship, also heard in Friedrich von Schlegel's lines from "Die
Gebüsche":

> Durch alle Töne tönet
> im bunter Erdentraum
> ein leiser Ton gezogen
> für den, der heimlich lauschet.

> (In all Sounds there sounds
> through Earth's varied Dreams
> a gentle Sound apparent
> to him, who listens closely.)

3. *Shaping art.* In his preface to *The Nigger of the Narcissus,* which appeared only ten years after Doughty's book, Joseph Conrad writes that
"My task which I am trying to achieve is, by the power of the written
word to make you hear, to make you feel—it is, before all, to make you
see. That—and no more, and it is everything."[43] In a remarkably similar
statement in the second preface to *Arabia Deserta,* Doughty writes: "The
haps that befel me are narrated in these volumes: wherein I have set down,
that which I saw with my eyes, and heard with my ears and thought with
my heart, neither more or less" (1:33). And in the third preface he transfers these sense perceptions from writer to reader: "While the like phrases

of their nearly-allied and no less ancient speech, are sounding in our ears, and their like customs, come down from antiquity, are continued before our eyes; we almost feel ourselves carried back to the days of the nomad Hebrew Patriarchs" (1:35). Like Conrad, Doughty wants, through his art, to make us hear what he heard and see what he saw. Most previous commentary has focused on Doughty's auditory power, his ability to capture Beduin speech and older English and Arabic rhythms to the extent that we feel we are hearing another language through Doughty's English; but his ability to capture sights, to allow us to *see* what he is describing, has not been equally noticed. Yet his choice of metaphor in his preface to the first edition is clearly visual, for he calls *Arabia Deserta* "a mirror, wherein is set forth faithfully some parcel of the soil of Arabia" (1:29).

Doughty's penchant for precise measurement and his desire to be absolutely faithful to the facts at first suggests the photograph, particularly the photographs in Louis Vaczek and Gail Buckland's fascinating *Travellers in Ancient Lands: A Portrait of the Middle East, 1839–1919* as a suitable analogy for the visual side of his art.[44] Like the photographs in that volume, Doughty's book is precise regarding details of topography, customs, features of people met, and the actual facts of events that overtake Khalil. Of Zeyd's wife, Hirfa, for instance, he wrote to S. C. Cockerell that "I have spoken of her as she was absolutely, in my sight, without adding or detracting anything: as I have also of every other person mentioned in the *Arabia Deserta* volumes" (H, 52). His notebooks in the Fitzwilliam Museum, Cambridge, testify to his attempt to record events accurately, despite their many gaps and brief entries for what become, in *Arabia Deserta*, lengthy incidents.[45] And, of course, the testimony of modern anthropologists and scientists confirms his factual accuracy regarding Arab life, as the essays in this volume prove.

In fact, a photograph like Gertrude Bell's "cold winter's day" (Vaczek and Buckland 1983:80), or those of Bonfils and W. H. I. Shakespear (ibid.:81), or indeed any of the Beduin portraits in Vaczek and Buckland's chapter 4 remind us to some degree of Doughty's descriptions in *Arabia Deserta*. Especially in Bonfils's work we see something of Doughty's description of Zeyd:

> such a male light Beduin figure some master painter might have portrayed for an Ishmaelite of the desert. Hollow his cheeks, his eyes looked austerely, from the lawless land of famine, where his most nour-

ishment was to drink coffee from the morning, and tobacco; and where the chiefest Beduin virtue is *es-subbor,* a courageous forbearing and abiding of hunger. (1:143)

But Doughty's very syntax, his combination of English and Arabic, his biblical allusion, and his subtle focus on Zeyd's cheeks and eyes take us away from the stark, direct portrayal of things as they are that we find in the Bonfils photographs and other early examples of Middle Eastern photography. Rather, Doughty's artistic methods are those of a "master painter," to use his own metaphor, who employs detail and realism only as a basis for a more shaped and subtle portrayal of reality. Whether he knew it or not (and he most likely did not, given his cavalier ignorance of the work of his contemporaries in all fields), Doughty was following in his art John Ruskin's injunction in *Modern Painters:*

> to go to Nature in all singleness of heart and walk with her laboriously and trustingly, having no other thoughts but how best to penetrate her meaning and remember her instruction; rejecting nothing, selecting nothing and scorning nothing; believing all things to be right and good, and rejoicing always in the truth. Then when their memories are stored and their imaginations fed, and their hands firm, let them take up the scarlet and gold, give reins to their fancy and show in what their heads are made of.[46]

As in Ruskin's doctrines, science and art come together in Doughty's book. A precise, accurate, deeply observed factual basis becomes the taking-off point for artistic vision, as memory, selection of detail, and style of portrayal soon transcend the purely photographic. Doughty portrays Hirfa's looks, actions, and statements exactly as they were remembered by him, but chooses to express these things in a biblical-medieval style that reflects his own vision of Beduin life.

The proper visual analogy for Doughty's art, then, is painting, with its ability to combine precise and accurate fact with selection, lighting, and colors and its ultimate subordination of the thing perceived to the artist's desires. But to whose paintings can we compare Doughty's art? We think immediately of the Orientalist painters of Doughty's own century; but if we survey the work collected in MaryAnne Stevens' fine *The Orientalists: Delacroix to Matisse, The Allure of Africa and the Near East* we search with difficulty for someone like Doughty.[47]

In the French painter Jean-Léon Gérôme, for instance, we find a control of detail as perfect as anything in a photograph or in Doughty's precise measurements of heights and temperatures, but this is combined with a constant, deliberate emphasis on "exotic" scenes only: dervish prayers, prostitutes, harems, slave markets. As Albert Boime comments, "Eroticism is a constant topic of concern in Gérôme's work, existing both as subject and context . . . he labors hard to transmute raw sexuality into rarefied sensations essentially linked to antiquity or Near Eastern settings. . . . Gérôme's paintings of slave markets and women at the bath are obsessive reveries hinting at Victorian frustrations and fantasies."[48] Other European painters in the Near East, such as Fromentin, Delacroix, Deutsch, and John Frederick Lewis, share Gérôme's taste for the sensational and the erotic, combined with a perfect, photographic technique that makes their selective Western fantasies of the East seem real. But storms, lion hunts, harems, and intercepted *billets doux* do not represent a complete expression of Near Eastern any more than of Western life. And in fact Doughty bitterly dismisses these heightened painterly and literary views of "romance, exotic beings, haunting memories" (in Boime's words) when he writes in *Arabia Deserta* that in Arabia there is "so little (or nothing) of '*Orientalism*' " (1:631) and completely rejects "tales rather of an European Orientalism than with much resemblance to the common experience" (1:96). We find in Doughty only one brief moment of eroticism, when he spies a black slave's body through her robes (1:421), but this takes up one paragraph out of the thousands in the book. And Doughty never hesitates to show us the dirt and disease that he saw in the East (as when he writes the famous dictum, "The Semites are like to a man sitting in a cloaca to the eyes and whose brows touch heaven" [1:95]), while we never see these things in the Orientalist painters (and writers) except when, as in Delacroix's *Pest House of Gaza,* the painter wishes to portray exotic horrors against the mixed glories of Napoleon's Near Eastern campaign.

Of all the Orientalist painters, one of the most honest, accurate, and least interested in sensationalism of any kind is the Scottish artist of past architectural glories, David Roberts. In such pictures as his *Karnak, The Temple of Baalbek,* and *Mosque of the Metwalis,* however, we see clearly his Romantic view of the past, which overshadows the small human figures of the present. But Doughty, who is a biblical and medieval Romantic, is less interested in architectural grandeur than Roberts: the Medain Salih

monuments, for instance, which are the primary goal of his journey, are
for Doughty the work of "Semites, expeditious more than curious, and
naturally imperfect workmen" (1:156) and when Khalil visits the monuments at el-Hejr a third time, the narrator calls them "rat holes" set
against "those ghastly grinning ranges of the Héjr" (1:553), as Hogarth
has pointed out. Even the most impressive building he sees, the Ibn
Rashid palace of "ochre and jiss" (1:638), is far less overpowering than any
Roberts palace or ruin and clearly subordinate to the life it contains.

We find few painterly parallels to Doughty among the Orientalists.
And yet, if we take a mighty passage like the following description of
desert heat—a favorite Orientalist topic—we *see* the heat as in few
paintings:

> The summer's night at end, the sun stands up as a crown of hostile
> flames from that huge covert of inhospitable sandstone bergs; the desert
> day dawns not little and little, but it is noontide in an hour. The sun,
> entering as a tyrant upon the waste landscape, darts upon us a torment
> of fiery beams, not to be remitted till the far-off evening.—No matins
> here of birds; not a rock partridge-cock, calling with blithesome
> chuckle over the extreme waterless desolation. Grave is that giddy heat
> upon the crown of the head; the ears tingle with a flickering shrillness,
> a subtle crepitation it seems, in the glassiness of this sun-stricken
> nature: the hot sand-blink is in the eyes, and there is little refreshment
> to find in the tent's shelter; the worsted booths leak to this fiery rain of
> sunny light. Mountains looming like dry bones through the thin air,
> stand far around us. . . . Herds of the weak nomad camels waver dis-
> persedly, seeking pasture in the midst of this hollow fainting country,
> where but lately the swarming locusts have fretted every green thing.
> (1:367–68)

Doughty uses the present tense to give us an immediate apprehension of
the heat and moves us, like a good painter, from the crowned, all-domi-
nating tyrant sun to the near-total absence of life, as humans are reduced
from kingship to mere consciousness by the heat. Everywhere we find a
silent desolation and a landscape of one color—fire. Ironically, the sun's
beams are portrayed as rain. No wonder that we see only an occasional
black tent or desolate camel dotting the landscape dispiritedly, or that the
mountains seem like dry bones. And yet, there are no actual bones bleach-
ing in the desert here, as in Gustave Guillaumet's *The Desert* (Stevens

1984:83): with typical truthfulness, Doughty comments, "I saw not anywhere the reported strewed skeletons of camels nor mounds of sand blown
upon their fallen carcases" (1:96). Because of Doughty's sharp eye for detail, obsessive, almost hallucinatory focus upon the heat, and imaginative
shaping of scene, this passage has a concrete tactility and precision that
enable us to feel what he is talking about.

When, immediately after this passage, Doughty narrates the change to
the freshness of evening, we see—and hear and feel, too—what he
experienced:

> The lingering day draws down to the sun-setting; the herdsmen, weary
> of the sun, come again with the cattle, to taste in their menzils [camps]
> the first sweetness of mirth and repose.—The day is done, and there
> rises the nightly freshness of this purest mountain air: and then to the
> cheerful song and the cup at the common fire. The moon rises ruddy
> from that solemn obscurity of jebel like a mighty beacon:—and the
> morrow will be as this day, days deadly drowned in the sun of the
> summer wilderness. (1:368)

Now, as in the work of an old Dutch painter, we see the gathering of
humanity and animal life, the return to a human level of song, and the
warmth of the fire and light of the moon rather than the silent, merciless
flames of the sun, as abundantly flowing coffee replaces the sun's fiery rain,
so much like drowning. *Desert: Day* and *Desert: Night* might be appropriate titles for these two contrasting companion pieces.

But Doughty's painterly qualities are not confined to broad landscapes
and human groups; he is equally good at portraiture. In a few strokes he
reveals a man's character—in this case the ruler Ibn Rashid's—to the core:

> Mohammed the Emir appeared to me, when we came into the light,
> like a somewhat undergrown and hard-favoured Beduwy of the poorer
> sort; but he walked loftily and with somewhat unquiet glancing looks.
> (1:644)

> His skin is more than commonly tawny, and even yellowish: lean of
> flesh and hollow as the Nejders, he is of middle height: his is a shallow
> Nejd visage, and Mohammed's bird-like looks are like the looks of one
> survived out of much disease of the world,—and what likelihood was
> there formerly that he should ever be the Emir? (1:640)

In these Goyaesque comments of light and shadow, we see Doughty's method of drawing character via several superimposed remarks, what might be called a "spatial" method, as of layers of oil paints gradually built up to create an in-depth portrait. Khalil's final remark on Ibn Rashid, " 'He is a worthy man' " (2:543), comes hundreds of pages after the descriptions above and takes us, like the sherif of Mecca, aback with surprise since we do not expect such a belated and positive summation. In Mohammed Ibn Rashid, Doughty shows us a very uncertain, very haughty, and yet very worthy man; there are few really simple portraits in Doughty's book, owing to his layered method.

Many painters and travel writers have portrayed the "nobility" of the Beduin, which forms the reverse side of the "fanatic" Arab stereotype. The following is a passage from Gray Hill's *With the Beduins,* which in its externality is comparable to a typical Orientalist painting of the Beduin, such as Frederick Goodall's *Early Morning in the Wilderness of Shur,* for instance:

> Ali Diab looks about sixty, and is a man of very remarkable appearance. A high Roman nose, shaped almost like an eagle's beak, sunken cheeks, heavy eyebrows, "an eye like Mars to threaten and command,"—and a peaked beard, give him a most haughty, aristocratic look. One might take him for some medieval warrior king, stern even ruthless, accustomed to command and be obeyed, and yet capable of generous acts.[49]

Hill's portrait is intelligent, yet conventional; he makes the stereotyped comparison between sheykh and "medieval warrior king," but the picture is entirely and uncritically positive, and we have no sense of Ali Diab's unique personality.

Compare Hill's description of Ali Diab with Doughty's completely individual portrayal of Motlog, sheykh of the Fukara:

> he was a personable strong man and well proportioned, of the middle stature, of middle age, and with a comely Jewish visage; and thereto the Arabian honour of a thick black beard, and he looked forth with manly assurance under that specious brow of his sheykhly moderation. A fair-spoken man, as they be all in fair weather, full of the inborn Beduin arts when his interest was touched. Simple in his manners, he alone went with no gay camel-stick in his hand and never carried a

sword; by which politic urbanity, he covered a superfluous insolence of the noblemen, which became him well. When the mejlis [daily council] assembled numerous at his booth, he, the great sheykh and host, would sit out with a proud humility among the common people, holding still his looks at the ground; but they were full of unquiet side-glances, as his mind was erect and watching. (1:292)

Although we would question Doughty's use of the word "all" to generalize about Beduin fair-speaking, his observant eye and truthfulness result in an insight into Motlog's *image* as a ruler and his manipulation of the arts of command that is lacking in Hill's idealization of Ali Diab. Doughty sees Motlog and sees through him too, and the result is an honest, rather than a romanticized, portrait that allows us to treat Motlog as a human being, not a noble god.

If the Orientalists, then, provide us with few parallels to Doughty, the Pre-Raphaelites are closer to the mark. William Rogers provides a very persuasive and comprehensive argument—including the first Doughty-Carlyle comparison ever—for regarding Doughty as an integral part of his period in art and culture rather than a notorious exception to it. Like Carlyle and the Pre-Raphaelites, Doughty felt reverence for the medieval period and wanted to make the Bible live again; indeed, he conceived of *Arabia Deserta* as a new Bible that would turn England back from Victorian English to Doughty's conception of a language fit for honest communication with God and man—pre–King James English, with strong northern roots.

In the visual realm, the artist closest to Doughty's outlook and even style is William Holman Hunt, the Pre-Raphaelite who journeyed to the Holy Land in order to paint biblical scenes authentically and who believed that art should serve truth and justice. In writing of a wild Arabian mountain goat, "his colour purple ruddle or nearly as that blushing before the sunset of dark mountains" (1:665), Doughty uncannily (or perhaps he saw the painting, since it appeared in 1855), captures the colors in Hunt's *The Scapegoat,* which was actually painted on the Dead Sea. In that much-misunderstood picture, Hunt has many of the qualities that we also find in *Arabia Deserta:* (1) the authentic colors of the area, which anyone familiar with it immediately recognizes; (2) the use of a real goat as a model; (3) a perfection of detail; and (4) a heavy air of spirituality verging on a certain queasiness but never quite becoming repellent, as seen particularly in the painting's frame. Doughty, too, is absolutely faithful to fact and authenticity, observes every detail carefully, and in his writing remains the artist of the precise word and sentence rather than the larger literary structures such as the page and paragraph; and he transforms himself as Khalil into a martyr or "scapegoat" who proves the Christian doctrine of turning the other cheek and makes his book into a Bible, stopping just short of a repulsive, too-heavy air of sanctity. And, as in Hunt's *The Finding of the Saviour in the Temple* (1860), Doughty in the following passage combines a medieval vernacular with religious allusion:

> "What wot any man," exclaimed Strongbrawns, "that I was not one come to spy their place, and the Frengies would enter afterward to take the country?" This honest host fed us largely in his great tent of a sheep boiled (such here is their marvellous abundance) in buttermilk. For Israel ascending from Sinai this was a land that flowed with milk indeed. (1:75)

Both the Old and New Testaments are never far from Doughty's mind (see Ta, 33–38), but the expression here, as in the strange stasis of the figures and background in Hunt's painting, is medieval—"wot," "Strongbrawns," "honest host," not to mention the very syntax of the excerpt.

The high definition of Doughty's syntax and diction in this passage as in all others in *Arabia Deserta* reminds us that, however visual his style may be, it is still of course verbal and based entirely on words. Edward Levenston, in his essay in this collection, subjects Doughty's style to a modern, formal linguistic analysis for the first time ever. He shows in detail the precise devices Doughty employs, revising previous views, including even Walt Taylor's classic work on *Arabia Deserta*'s Arabic and older English elements, and ultimately demonstrates how Doughty's manner becomes his matter and how Doughty treats the reader as a bilingual person. But he arrives at the conclusion, supported by all previous critics, that Doughty's style in the book is uniformly distinctive, a fantastic *tour de force* when we consider its thousand-plus pages. The analyses of Levenston and Rogers advance the work of earlier critics such as Fairley, Treneer, Taylor, McCormick, and Tabachnick by adding more information and fresh details and insights to our knowledge of a style that will continue to enchant and to some degree evade those who try to analyze it. Doughty's biblical, Pre-Raphaelite, and Arabic-inspired stylistic mirror seems to capture Arabia's sights and sounds better than any other medium according to many knowledgeable critics, but it also reflects the genius of a man and writer and traveller unlike any other.

4. *Personality.* How is Khalil, *Arabia Deserta*'s hero, like and unlike the man Charles Doughty, upon whom he is based? Even though *Arabia Deserta* makes every effort to be faithful to the facts of Doughty's personality no less than to the facts of Arabia, every autobiographer must select characteristics and shape his self-character in literary terms; thus, an autobiographical self-portrait is very rarely a precise photographic likeness and more usually resembles a rich, deep, and ambiguous self-portrait in oils. Since Doughty is writing an "oratorical autobiography of travel" in which Khalil serves as an example of Christian forbearance and British honor and the narrator points for us the morals of Khalil's behavior and that of the Arabs who react to him so variously,[50] we find certain differences between the man in Hogarth's biography and the "world wanderer" Khalil, whether or not Doughty consciously decided to have these emerge. But first, Doughty's life as we now know it.

In Hogarth's indispensable but external biography, which tells us very much about Doughty's life but very little about the inner man, Doughty appears honest, reliable, patriotic, and humanistic. Born in Theberton, Suffolk, in 1843, he was soon orphaned and brought up, with his brother (who became a relatively mundane lawyer), by an uncle. Refused permission to join the Royal Navy because of a slight speech impediment, Doughty soon dreamed of other, perhaps compensatory activities that would bring him glory: the writing of a poem about Britain's national birth. At Cambridge, as a student of geology, he probed the origins of man and the earth, following the theories of Lyell and Darwin but continuing to believe in a God who is manifest in the world through natural forces. He studied Norwegian glaciers and wrote a pamphlet (1866) about them, and then, upon graduation, disappeared into the libraries for a few years to gather material for his epic. He embarked on wanderings around Europe and North Africa. Finally, from Greece, he made his way to the Holy Land and Sinai, stopping at Damascus, where he spent a year studying Arabic. Then, from 1876 to 1878, the great adventure recorded in *Arabia Deserta* took place, and from Arabia he sailed for India and then returned to England. The rest of his life—with some time out for travel to Damascus to collect his papers and residence in Italy, which he loved— was spent publishing his scientific results and writing *Arabia Deserta*, getting married, and then, aided by a precarious inheritance, composing a series of long, insufferable poems which have understandably not caught on. The poems are unpleasantly blood-thirsty, but, more important, lack *Arabia Deserta*'s sympathy-despite-itself for the opponents of Christendom as well as Khalil's strange blend of Pauline humility and zealousness. Even Doughty's wife, apparently, could never reconcile herself to the narrow-minded and bloody battle passages which her husband would read aloud in the house.[51] Doughty enjoyed increasing respect, if not great fame, as traveller and author (Honorary D.Litt., Oxford, 1908; R.G.S. Gold Medal, 1912; *Honoris Causa,* Cambridge, 1920; Honorary Fellowship, British Academy, 1922), but nothing in his writing or his life was again to approximate *Arabia Deserta*'s amazing story and equally amazing artistic power. In fact, toward the end of his life Doughty appeared rather an absurd figure, as recorded in this newly discovered "portrait" by the litterateur Edmund Gosse, dated 25 June 1914:

> Today my colleague . . . brought the author of "Arabia Deserta" to lunch with me at the House of Lords. He was "rewarding" beyond all hope. His personal appearance is that of a man of 50, tho' he is really just 70. He has copious curly hair and full beard of a uniform warm light brown colour, just beginning to grizzle; a strong, square skull and full forehead, a good deal wrinkled. His eyes are large, and he has the curious habit of suddenly opening his eye-lids very wide, so that they glare at you like lamps. He seemed to be very shy, very fierce and very much in earnest. His voice is strangely weak, almost a whisper, and is on this account disconcerting. He recalled to me, in some measure, William Morris, but more phantasmal, in a way more absurd. Doughty is, in fact, slightly absurd. He has curious falsetto inflexions in his voice, and a sort of elderly-lady-like dignity. . . . He rather startled me by asking me whether I could secure the Nobel Prize for him. . . . He was more interesting, but more reluctant, in talking about Arabia; with some difficulty I persuaded him to give us some curious particulars of the Bedouin life.[52]

Arabia was in fact the only interesting thing Doughty was ever involved in; and fortunately both Khalil and Doughty in his prime share certain stiff-necked qualities of greatness which later degenerated, apparently, into the sad eccentricity that Gosse records. Just as Khalil refused steadfastly to compromise his integrity by pretending to be a Moslem, even when under great duress, so Doughty refused to have a single word of his

English revised by H. W. Bates, the secretary of the Royal Geographical Society, when his lecture was due for publication: "as an English scholar I will never submit to have my language of the best times turned into the misery of today—that were unworthy of me" (H, 109). Also, Doughty and Khalil, despite what Hogarth says about Doughty's humanitarian agnosticism, share a profound Christian faith which we see emerging at various points in *Arabia Deserta* (1:176, 181, 486, 493; 2:179, 406, 423) and in Doughty's poetry, where God is always on Britain's side in wars, Joseph of Arimathea is mawkishly sentimentalized, and Jesus takes clear precedence over other holy men.[53] This faith both causes Khalil trouble in Arabia and enables him to overcome all difficulties by turning the other cheek, even to the extent of handing over his pistol to Salem and Fheyd, his enemies. And then, both Doughty and Khalil are men of their time, committed to empiricism and scientific progress; reliable men of their word who, from all accounts (including *Arabia Deserta*), do what they say they will.

But Doughty and Khalil are also different, for the man who acts in *Arabia Deserta* is intended to be an Everyman, transcending time and place and reduced to the common denominator of all men and beasts: the need to survive. In contrast to the swashbuckling Richard Burton of his *Personal Narrative of a Pilgrimage to Al-Madinah and Mecca* (1855), the scholarly J. L. Burckhardt of *Notes on the Bedouins and Wahabys* (1831), the whimsical Alexander Kinglake of *Eothen* (1845), or the complicated, contradictory T. E. Lawrence of *Seven Pillars of Wisdom* (1926), Doughty has chosen to stress one great quality in his self-image Khalil: self-effacement. We see one aspect of this primary trait in Khalil's absent-mindedness, which impels his friend Amm Mohammed to comment:

> "But who . . . can imagine any evil of Khalîl? for when we go out together, he leaves in one house his cloak or his driving-stick, and in another his agâl [head-cord]! he forgets his pipe, and his sandals, in other several houses. The strange negligence of the man! ye would say he is sometimes out of memory of the things about him!" (2:224)

Doughty can also stoically downplay Khalil's very real troubles, as a daunting moment of illness is passed over in one brief but memorable sentence: "Ah! what horror, to die like a rabid hound in a hostile land" (2:483). And Khalil can be both supremely forgiving and even kind: he actually bids his brutal jailer at Kheybar, Abdullah, a polite farewell and helps the Kheybarians who despise him to build a good well. He can be crafty when the situation demands it, but far more often chooses modestly yet unwaveringly to speak the truth that he is a Christian even to the most xenophobic opponent.

With some amazement we arrive at the end of the book and realize that we still do not know how Khalil looks, outside of one incident in which Arab women are amazed by his red beard; the narrator never describes him physically, any more than he tells us Khalil's reasons for travelling in Arabia. When we finish the work, each of us must answer its opening question to Khalil, " 'what moved thee, or how couldst thou take such journeys into the fanatic Arabia?' " (1:39) for himself. The stoic author and character provide few direct answers, and these must emerge for each reader individually out of contact with the book.

And if Khalil loses his temper occasionally, who would not have, in his situation? All too human, perhaps, is his desire to see Islam humiliated as he was humiliated by a series of inconstant guides, superstitious towns-people, and suspicious sheykhs and rulers; all too human is his inability to see his own prejudices against Islam, Eastern Christianity, and Judaism in the same light as his companions' prejudices against Christians. When we see him in Tayif at the end of the journey, however, he is clearly a man who has paid his dues, whatever his own failings:

> The tunic was rent on my back, my mantle was old and torn; the hair was grown down under my kerchief to the shoulders, and the beard fallen and unkempt; I had bloodshot eyes, half blinded, and the scorched skin was cracked to the quick upon my face. (2:539–40)

This is not the Doughty who arrogantly asks Gosse for the Nobel Prize, or who comments proudly in the "Map of Arabia" entry in the index and glossary that "every chartographer of those parts of Asia has founded upon my labours; which I trust to be such that no time shall overthrow them" (2:643). Fond (and false!) hopes.

If we remember Doughty, it is not for his false pride and his blood-thirsty poetry, but rather as the weary and sick Khalil who finally descends to the sea at Jidda; the same Khalil who, as a "world's wanderer," selflessly seeks the answers to the geological, geographical, anthropological, lin-guistic, archaeological, and historical mysteries of Arabia and who in his moment of greatest danger from Salem is most worried about the possible breakage of his barometer; the Khalil who, faced with the possibility of having to kill his tormentors, chooses to surrender rather than corrupt his soul with murder. It is Khalil the modest yet steadfast prince of the spirit who remains with us against an unforgettable background of human failure, be it Turkish, British, or Arab. As in the case of all great authors, Doughty's art has proven far more interesting and permanent than his life. Doughty is gone, Khalil abides. One hundred years after the publication of *Arabia Deserta,* it continues to loom like Vesuvius over all previous and subsequent travel books. And given the uniqueness, precision, and majesty of its story of Khalil and Arabia, it probably always will. The essays in this volume, even when they are critical, will help the reader understand why.

NOTES

1 Preface to *Lyrical Ballads,* in *The Norton Anthology of English Literature,* ed. M. H. Abrams et al. (New York: Norton, 1979), 2:172.

2 Berkeley: University of California, 1977, xix.

3 See Gillian Beer, *Darwin's Plots* (London: Routledge and Kegan Paul, 1983). Perhaps a better case could be made for Darwin's *Voyage of the Beagle,* a sensitive travel diary combining close observation and lucid style.

4 On Doughty's motivation, see the essays by Bevis in this volume and in *Victorian Studies* 16 (December 1972): 163–81, and Ta, 64–90.

5 A complete listing of all the books that should at least list Doughty but do not is impossible. But here are a few prominent examples: G. B. Tennyson and Donald Gray, *Victorian Literature: Prose* (New York: Macmillan, 1976) does not even mention Doughty in the index let alone in its table of contents, while Charles Harrold and William Templeman, *English Prose of the Victorian Era* (New York: Oxford, 1968), another standard anthology, is similarly silent. George Levine and William Madden's collection of critical essays, *The Art of Victorian Prose* (New York: Oxford, 1968) also does not contain a single reference to Doughty.

6 The only actual *assessments* of Doughty's work that one finds in the scientific literature, outside of the contemporary reviews of *Arabia Deserta,* seem to be D. G. Hogarth's comments in *The Penetration of Arabia* (New York: Frederick A. Stokes, 1904) and in his biography of Doughty, his son W. D. Hogarth's article in the *Dictionary of National Biography,* C. M. Pastner's anthropological study, "Englishmen in Arabia: Encounters with Middle Eastern Women," *Signs* 4 (Winter 1978): 309–23, and a number of brief obituary notices: *Nature* 117, 6 February 1926, 204; *Geographical Journal* 67 (April 1926): 381–84, and 72 (December 1928): 555–58; *Geographical Review* 16 (April 1926): 333; *Revue Archéologique* 23 (1926): 346, reprinted and translated in *American Journal of Archaeology* 31 (January 1927): 99; *Islam* 16 (1927): 122–25. He is also discussed in some popular or more general books on Arabian travellers; these are listed in the bibliography of secondary works.

7 For a superb study of the notebooks, see H, chaps. 3 and 4. On the composition of *Arabia Deserta,* consult H, chap. 6, Ta, 42–48, and Ruth M. Robbins, "The Word Notes of C. M. Doughty," *Agenda* 18 (1980): 78–98.

8 "When we publish a book like this, we do a small first printing of a few thousand copies and hope to sell it out in a few years. Our first printing, issued in 1980 [sic], will be sold out fairly soon, and we find that we are still selling several hundred sets of *Travels in Arabia Deserta* every year. We consider this a reasonable sale for a book like this, and I have no doubt that we will issue a new printing when the time comes." Letter of 26 September 1984 from John W. Grafton, assistant to the president of Dover Books, to S. E. Tabachnick.

9 *My Diaries* (London: Secker, 1932), 273. Leonard Woolf's comments appear in his review of *Arabia Deserta* in *The Nation and the Athenaeum,* 27 October 1923, 155. For Peter Brent's comment, see his *Far Arabia* (London: Weidenfeld and Nicolson, 1977), 135.

10 Burton Hatlen, "Why Is *The Education of Henry Adams* 'Literature,' While *The Theory of the Leisure Class* Is Not?" *College English* 40 (February 1979): 665–76.

11 Source: *Science, Social Sciences,* and *Arts and Humanities Citation Index.*

12 May Morris, Introduction to vol. 8 of *The Collected Works of William Morris* (New York: Russell and Russell, 1966), xxij.

13 See S. B. Bushrui's excellent "Yeats's Arabic Interests," in *In Excited Reverie: A Centenary Tribute to William Butler Yeats, 1865–1939,* ed. A. N. Jeffares and K. G. W. Cross (London: Macmillan, 1965), 280–314, for full information on Yeats's extensive interest in Doughty and T. E. Lawrence. I thank Dr. Kelly Hood of the Tennessee Technological University English Department for this reference.

14 *Blasting and Bombardiering* (Berkeley: University of California, 1967), 242.

15 See "Mr. Doughty's Epic," *Manchester Guardian,* 24 July 1916, 3, for Eliot's attack on *The Titans,* and his "Contemporary English Prose," *Vanity Fair* 20 (July 1923): 58, for his high praise of *Arabia Deserta.* I thank Dr. Richard Shusterman of the Ben-Gurion University Foreign Literatures Department for these references.

16 Billy T. Tracy, "D. H. Lawrence and the Travel Book Tradition," *D. H. Lawrence Review* 11 (1978): 274.

17 This remark (and Huxley's high praise of T. E. Lawrence's style) is reported by Patrick Foulk in his Huxley memoir, "Memories of a Timeless Man," *Horizon* 23 (1980): 71.

18 Henry Green, "Apologia," *Folios of New Writing* 4 (Autumn 1941): 44, 47.

19 John Russell, *Henry Green* (New Brunswick: Rutgers, 1960), 44–49; Michael North, *Henry Green and the Writing of His Generation* (Charlottesville: University of Virginia, 1984), 58–61.

20 North, *Henry Green,* 58.

21 See Henry Miller, *The Books in My Life* (Norfolk, Conn.: New Directions, 1952), 320.

22 See Douglas Grant, "Barker Fairley on Charles Doughty," *University of Toronto Quarterly* 26 (1967): 221.

23 Ruth Gay, "Charles Doughty: Man and Book," *American Scholar* 50 (Autumn 1981): 527.

24 See my review of this book, *American Book Review* 7 (May–June 1985): 6–7.

25   For these, see note 6 above. But two recent scientific articles that cite him, thus
     proving the current value of his work, are A. E. Dorman, "The Camel in Health and
     Disease," *British Veterinary Journal* 140 (1984): 616–33, and C. N. Raphael and H.
     T. Shaibi, "Water-Resources for At Taif, Saudi-Arabia—A Study of Alternative
     Sources for an Expanding Urban Area," *Geographical Journal* 150 (July 1984): 183–
     91.

26   Martin S. Day, "Travel Literature and the Journey Theme," *Forum* (Houston) 12
     (1975): 38.

27   F. R. Leavis, "Doughty and Hopkins," *Scrutiny* 4 (December 1935): 317.

28   Percy Adams, "Travel Literature of the Seventeenth and Eighteenth Centuries: A
     Review of Recent Approaches," *Texas Studies in Literature and Language* 20 (Fall 1978):
     488–515; *Travel Literature and the Evolution of the Novel* (Lexington: University Press
     of Kentucky, 1983).

29   Joanne Shattock, "Travel Writing Victorian and Modern: A Review of Recent Re-
     search," *Prose Studies* 5 (May 1982): 151–64. This entire issue of *Prose Studies* is
     devoted to "The Art of Travel."

30   New York: Oxford, 1980.

31   See my "Little-Travelled Roads: Travel Literature in the Curriculum," forthcoming in
     Exploration.

32   New York: Random House, 1985.

33   For critical discussion of this complex and interesting topic, see Peter Laslett, "The
     Wrong Way through the Telescope: A Note on Literary Evidence in Sociology and in
     Historical Sociology," *British Journal of Sociology* 27 (September 1976): 319–42; J.
     Rockwell, *Fact in Fiction* (London: Routledge and Kegan Paul, 1974); and Douglas
     Pocock, ed., *Humanistic Geography and Literature* (London: Croom Helm; Totowa,
     N.J.: Barnes and Noble, 1981).

34   Harold Spender, Introduction to Alexander Kinglake, *Eothen* (London: Dent; New
     York: Dutton, 1908), viii.

35   Day, "Travel Literature," 38.

36   37 (1880): 201–3; 39 (1881): 7–10, 23–30; 40 (1881): 38–41; 41 (1882): 214–18,
     249–52.

37   New York: Barnes and Noble, 1959, 5.

38   Alois Musil, *Oriental Explorations and Studies,* nos. 1–6 (New York: American Geo-
     graphical Society, 1926–28); H. R. P. Dickson, *The Arab of the Desert* (New York:
     Macmillan, 1950); Wilfred Thesiger, *Arabian Sands* (Harmondsworth: Penguin,
     1976; first published 1959).

39   For World War I, the testimony comes from H, 184, and from T. E. Lawrence, who
     writes that *Arabia Deserta* "became a military text-book, and helped to guide us to
     victory in the East" (1:27). In her article, "Doughty's Mirror of Arabia: His Travels in
     Arabia Deserta," *Moslem World* 33 (July 1943): 47, Mary Z. Brittain recalls how
     Lawrence, then in British intelligence in Cairo, persuaded her missionary father to
     give him his copy of *Arabia Deserta,* apparently the only one available anywhere in the
     city at that time. Hogarth too tells of this incident (H, 184). Lawrence's own large
     paper copy (one of only six printed) of *Arabia Deserta* (London: Medici and Cape,
     1921) is now in the Humanities Research Center, The University of Texas, Austin.

For World War II the evidence is even more direct, in the form of Hugh Scott et al.'s geographical manual, *Western Arabia and the Red Sea,* B.R. 527 (Restricted), Geographical Handbook Series (London: Naval Intelligence Division, 1946), in which Doughty is listed in the bibliography and quoted at several points.

40 Thesiger, *The Marsh Arabs* (Harmondsworth: Penguin, 1976; first published 1964), 21.

41 Thesiger, *Arabian Sands,* 38.

42 John Middleton Murry, "Charles Montagu Doughty," *Times Literary Supplement,* 11 February 1926, 85.

43 *Joseph Conrad's Prefaces to His Works,* ed. Edward Garnett (New York: Books for Libraries, 1971), 52.

44 Boston: New York Graphic Society, 1983.

45 On this point, see Ta, 42–44.

46 Quoted in Jeremy Maas, *The Victorian Art World in Photographs* (New York: Universe, 1984), 93. Maas's *Victorian Painters* (New York: G. P. Putnam, 1969) is also a superb reference for the painters of this period, including the Orientalists and the Pre-Raphaelites.

47 Washington: National Gallery; London: Weidenfeld and Nicolson, 1984.

48 Albert Boime, "Gérôme and the Bourgeois Artist's Burden," *Arts Magazine* 57 (January 1983): 66.

49 London: Fisher Unwin, 1891, 44.

50 See Ta, 52–53, for a discussion of the genre of Doughty's book, and Ta, 48–52, for an analysis of its literary personae, including Doughty as artist, narrator, and Khalil. See also Robert Fernea's essay in this volume on this point.

51 Information courtesy of Ruth M. Robbins, who knew Doughty's wife; given to me during our conversation on 27 July 1978 at the Gonville and Caius College Library, Cambridge. This library houses Doughty's manuscripts, including his "word notes," while his notebooks are held in the Fitzwilliam Museum, Cambridge, as noted earlier.

52 Quoted in Paul F. Mattheisen, "Gosse's Candid 'Snapshots,'" *Victorian Studies* 8 (1965): 329–54.

53 See Ta, 33–38, 46, 124–25, 146.

PART ONE

Arabia Deserta *as Art*

WILLIAM N. ROGERS II

Arabia Deserta *and the Victorians: Past and Present*

Early in *Travels in Arabia Deserta* Doughty candidly characterized his narrative as "the seeing of an hungry man and the telling of a most weary man" (1:95), "neither more nor less" than what he saw and heard (1:33)—laconic understatements of the sort characteristic of the Anglo-Saxon writers whom he had studied and admired. The reality is that he laboriously set down in *Arabia Deserta* a far from "plain tale" of mere seeing and telling. His massive rendition of an alien landscape, woven of well over 500,000 exactly chosen words, postulates an ideal reader able to evaluate copious data about the cartography, geology, flora and fauna, anthropology, archaeology, and human history of desert Arabia while at the same time capable of appreciating a craggily self-hewn prose style that conveys the wanderings of a Christian traveller amid a people largely hostile to his faith. The one completely ideal reader for such a text was none other than the writer himself; his real-life, too humanly limited readers have had to make what they can of a book that Doughty conceded elsewhere in his first volume and again with typical understatement to be "not milk for babes" (1:29). But even beyond *Arabia Deserta*'s complex but nonetheless overt interplay of "personal narrative" and scientific comprehensiveness there is a further, less obvious intention that for Doughty was of soul-cleansing importance for late-Victorian England, something which he acknowledged some fourteen years after the book's 1888 publication by writing that "My main intention was not so much the setting forth of personal wanderings among a people of Biblical interest, as the ideal endeavour to continue the older tradition of Chaucer and Spenser, resisting to my power the decadence of the English language: so that whilst my work should be the mere verity for Orientalists, it should be also my life's contribution, so far to literature."[1] *Arabia Deserta* at one level presents a bold, dangerous, and even foolhardy adventure, at another intends to be full of "verity" for "Orientalists" and scientists, and at still another seeks nothing less than to suggest an alternative to "the Victorian English" that the writer abhorred.[2] By such a reform of English he would be contributing to a reform of England itself, since "all impotent and disloyal vility of speech . . . is no uncertain token of a people's decadence."[3]

Criticism in its fifty-some-year efforts to deal with *Arabia Deserta* has paid much attention to its inner patterns and stylistic modes, but has had considerably less to say about the book's relation to the ideas and writers of the Victorian age (such as "decadence," which was a pervasive late-nineteenth-century concern), as these might provide a context for the particularities of Doughty's achievement. Our patchy knowledge of Doughty's early life and reading has undoubtedly had a good deal to do with this. There is no biography of Doughty more recent than Hogarth's pioneering effort of 1928 and no collection of his letters; the only record of his reading from the crucial ages of twenty-five to twenty-seven is a list of some fifty titles he ordered in the Bodleian Library from 1868 to 1870.[4] Dating mostly from the sixteenth and seventeenth centuries, these include Bosworth's dictionary of Anglo-Saxon and such writers as Chapman, Skelton, Lilly, and Wycliffe; the most recent book is a copy of Bishop Percy's *Reliques of Ancient English Poetry* of 1765. This seemingly confirms the stereotype of Doughty as a nineteenth-century "sport"—someone whose sole literary mentors were Chaucer and Spenser and even the Anglo-Saxons. Yet such an "antiquarian" list by no means proves that Doughty had even in his young manhood cut himself off entirely from the literature of his own times. Such giants of the preceding generation as Carlyle, Ruskin, Dickens, and Thackeray, to name only a few, could hardly have been completely overlooked during his youthful reading.

It is certainly true, however, that from his university years on Doughty's relation to the literature of his own times grew increasingly tenuous and even hostile. He concentrated on geology at Cambridge and read older English texts in the immediately subsequent years, learned foreign languages during his time of "studious travel,"[5] spoke Arabic exclusively for two years, and wrote much of the initial version of *Arabia Deserta* while living in Italy. He was thus during some of the crucial formative and creative years of his life quite disengaged from spoken English and from the contemporary literary life of England. This fact, partially imposed by circumstances, became a fixed characteristic as the years went by and he devoted himself hermetically to the composition of poetry. He came to pride himself on his deliberate isolation from the writers of his time, some of whom, even the major figures, he undoubtedly scorned as practitioners of "an illiberal remissness of language which is not known in any barbarous nation" (1:592). Typical of his old age was his reaction in 1909 to a critic who claimed that Doughty's *The Cliffs* derived from Hardy's *The Dynasts:* he angrily denied the connection and disclaimed any knowledge whatever of Hardy, of whom, he said, he would continue to remain ignorant.[6]

Taking Doughty at his own estimation and focusing on the exoticism of his achievement, Edith Batho and Bonamy Dobrée in 1938 denied Doughty's relation to the literary culture of his age. They found his writings to be "entirely outside the tradition of Victorian prose or poetry."[7] In recent years some critics have, however, argued that Doughty must be seen as securely lodged in the literary culture of Victorian England. For Stephen E. Tabachnick, Doughty "represents a variation on the basic interests of his period," and his book, "far from an anomaly, remains a brilliantly novel variation on the tradition of its own age."[8] In line with this critical tendency I intend in this essay to suggest in some general and specific ways how Doughty's achievement in *Arabia Deserta* might be aligned with various impulses and traditions, both scientific and literary, of the Victorian age. To see the book in its connectedness with its own time and place will, I hope, position Doughty less as a strangely atemporal being or a grand eccentric in a vaguely defined late-century "aesthetic movement" and more as a partaker of a central, mid-Victorian tradition akin to that of other writers.

At the most general level *Arabia Deserta* is pervaded by a characteristic Victorian obsession with past time—geologic, human, and linguistic—that coexists easily with a progressive, scientific, and humanitarian spirit which is also a major aspect of the English nineteenth century. The concern with past time is quite consistent with Doughty's adoption at Cambridge of geology as a field of study—then considered progressive and advanced—since geology is in fact a field which must immerse itself very much in the history of the distant past if it is to understand the ongoing processes shaping the planet. But geology was not a "pure" science for the Victorians, one devoid of implications for the workaday world. If many Victorians found geology giving a clear view into aspects of the past that had previously been seen only through the haze of myth and religion, they found in that clarity immense and disturbing implications. The geologists, "with their dreadful hammers," as Ruskin wrote, had attacked the literalism of traditional religious faith through bringing into question the time-scale of creation in Genesis. In his mid-century *In Memoriam* Tennyson reacted to this apparent contradiction between science and revealed religion by becoming a kind of poet laureate of geology; it was only after an anguished emotional and intellectual struggle that he finally arrived at a religiosity imbued with evolutionary implications not devoid of hope. But Doughty, whose *Arabia Deserta* is quite free of the typical Victorian dramatization of the struggle of "faith" with "doubt," maintained simultaneously both a scientific and a religious outlook. Richard Bevis has gone so far as to argue that a kind of "spiritual geology" was the prime motivation for Doughty's wanderings—the effort to discern through the naked rocks of Arabia the intentions of a God whose biblical revelations appeared less complete than they had to previous generations.[9]

Also compelling for the Victorians were the records of past "human generations"—especially those, Doughty wrote, pertaining to "Biblical research" (1:31)—of the sort that Doughty found etched in sandstone at Petra and Medain Salih. His intense curiosity about the Hejr monuments is one of the several reasons Doughty cites for his plunge into the Arabian fastness. It was there with a scrupulous attention to detail that he recorded in words and sketches all that he could gather of the stone facades and carvings that testified to the ancient Nabataeans' cultural attainments—so much greater than those of the nineteenth-century Beduins. The traveller's tenacious effort here was very much in accord with the new sciences of anthropology and archaeology that were developing rapidly during the decade of his wanderings in Europe and the Near East, years when E. B. Tylor, the founder of modern anthropology, published such important works as *Primitive Culture* (1871) and *Anthropology* (1881). A sharpened sense of the human past, historic, prehistoric, and even mythic, found diverse literary expression through the nineteenth century and into the early twentieth in a profusion of historical novels owing much to Scott's example, and in the time-pervaded Wessex novels of Hardy, Kipling's *Puck of Pook's Hill* (1906), which delved into the origins of England and its national myths, and Doughty's own *The Dawn in Britain* (1906–7) with its epic struggles of Britons and Romans.

Doughty's wanderings were also motivated by a rarely presented chance

to live with and observe the Beduins, a people whose way of life con-
stituted something of a living replica of the nomadic, patriarchal life of
the Old Testament. This anthropological-religious impulse is characteristic in a Victorian like Doughty who strove to understand Christianity
more fully in the context of its historical seedbed, just as both David
Friedrich Strauss and Ernest Renan had done in their books embedding
Jesus in Near Eastern history and culture.[10] In another and larger framework these excursions into past time indicate that in the nineteenth century a verifiable sense of historic place and chronology came to extend
beyond the confines of the northern Mediterranean basin with its familiar
classical civilizations of Greece and Rome. The time sense encompassed
the older and much less well known civilizations of Egypt and the Near
East. Doughty's singlehanded archaeological endeavors in Arabia were a
heroic expression of the European scientific engagement with the Eastern
past that, among many others, drew A. H. Layard to Nineveh, Heinrich
Schliemann to Troy, and Arthur Evans to Crete.

Arabia Deserta possesses as well another temporal and spatial emphasis
of the mid to late nineteenth century: an awareness of the lands of northern Europe and, for the English, of the northern heritage of England, in
effect a much-delayed assertion of the importance of the northern culture
over the long religious and cultural dominance of southern Europe. A
clear expression of this is when Doughty connects Arabia and his own
English national past, even though one of his artistic principles in *Arabia
Deserta* is to avoid comparisons and allusions that would draw the reader
away from the scenes at hand.[11] It seems fully appropriate for him to
align the Beduin description of the Red Sea—the "Sea of the glooming
(West)"—with the words of "our Saxon king, Alfred, in his book of Geography: 'Ireland is dim, where the sun goeth on settle'" (1:462). As
well, the geologic starkness of the highlands of Arabia suggested to
Doughty the similar starkness of the North, even in the Norway he had
visited to explore and report on the Jöstedal-brae glaciers.[12] However, a
completely pervasive reminder in *Arabia Deserta* of Doughty's attitude
toward the North is simply his handling of the English language to emphasize its rugged pre–Norman French origins. His frequent references to
"the divine Muse of Spenser and Venerable Chaucer" (1:31) are testimony
of his desire to reach an English more plastic and less formed—one altogether more vigorous and alive than "the Victorian English" of the present. In his own way he is a "deconstructionist" of the language as he finds

renewed meaning and power in its basic elements. Herbert Grierson exaggerated somewhat when he observed of the language of Doughty's poetry that "the writer uses the English language as if he had found it lying about and was the first to use it without regard to any tradition of idiom and structure," but this description does convey a sense of how Doughty's prose at times strikes the reader as something newly formed and unique. [13] His creative use of the language is strongly in agreement with his steady orientation to the past in general and, more specifically, to the past of the English language before "tradition" had dictated rules and standards of correct usage and decorum.

An awakening interest in the North and the original cultures of Britain can be traced back at least to the eighteenth century in such writers as Gray, "Ossian," and Bishop Percy. Scholarly work on Anglo-Saxon began as well in that century and was already well established by the 1830s. [14] A romanticism with a heightened and positive sense of the North came together in Walter Scott's historical novels, which set in motion an enduring Victorian interest in the northern past. One among many novels with a medieval setting, *Ivanhoe* (1819) was greatly influential in presenting a reading of English history that contrasted the solid and virtuous Anglo-Saxons with the devious and exploitative Normans, representatives of the to-be-scorned South. The nineteenth-century English-language writer, however, who played the greatest role as disseminator of the northern past and of German culture of his times is Thomas Carlyle. An awareness of and insistence on Germany and the mythology of the North runs through his entire career: his earliest works were translations and studies of German literature (1828–31); *Sartor Resartus* (1833–34) bodies forth German idealism in a German setting; Odin is the "Hero as Divinity" in *On Heroes, Hero-Worship, and the Heroic in History* (1841); and his last major work took for its hero Frederick the Great (1858–65).

In the 1840s and 1850s Carlyle was at his peak as an immensely influential—and controversial—figure on the Victorian literary and intellectual scene. He had no unquestioning disciples, but he was the thinker whose example of moral authority reached more of the other "Great" Victorians than any other. John Stuart Mill attended Carlyle's London lectures on heroes and hero-worship in 1840; Dickens dedicated *Hard Times* to him in 1854; the young Matthew Arnold in 1849 acknowledged his importance by singling him out as one of the prime "moral desperadoes" of the age; and even the hard-headed biologist T. H. Huxley turned to *Sartor*

Resartus in 1860 as a way of coping with the loss of a son. One with whom all felt they had to reckon, he is a man who "reminds us of the moral dimension of all actions, and . . . calls upon the reader to ponder such concepts as justice, evil, blessedness, purpose, and the duty of man."[15] In Doughty these are also recurring imperatives, and while such ideas were in the Victorian air, particularly that of duty, the probability is that the young Doughty of the late 1850s and early 1860s, like his near-contemporaries, read Carlyle's work and was influenced by it or at least found in it a confirmation and strengthening of ideas and attitudes he already held. A difficulty in establishing an unquestioned Carlyle-Doughty connection is that Doughty's writings and such of his correspondence as is available yield no direct references to Carlyle and his writings. A verbal and thematic emphasis in *Arabia Deserta* does, however, provide some evidence of an awareness of a familiar Carlylean idea. It occurs when Doughty writes at length and in largely negative terms about "the personage of Mohammed" and his religion, a subject that Carlyle had discussed at length in *On Heroes, Hero-Worship, and the Heroic in History* when he chose "Mahomet" as "The Hero as Prophet." These are Doughty's words:

> Mohammed is man, an householder, the father of a family; and his is a virile religion: also his people walk in a large way, which is full of the perfume of the flesh purified; the debate betwixt carnal nature and the opinion of godliness is not grievous in their hearts.—In the naturally crapulent and idolatrous Europe man himself is divine; *every age brings forth god-like heroes.* And what seek we in religion?—is it not a perfect law of humanity?—to bind up the wounds, and heal the sores of human life; and a pathway to heaven. (2:406–7; my emphasis)

The occurrence of the phrase "every age brings forth god-like heroes" used in connection with a Carlylian "hero" such as Mohammed is some tangible evidence that Doughty was aware of Carlyle. This suggests the usefulness of examining the nodes of ideas and moral emphases that both Carlyle and Doughty share—those involving religion, the medieval ideal, style, and a stance of sincerity coincident with the role of the prophet-sage.

"A RELIGION WITHOUT THEOLOGY"

Doughty, who would not dissimulate and renounce his Christianity while in Arabia despite all pressures to do so, proudly bore an opprobrious classification as a *Nasrany*. He emerges in *Arabia Deserta* as an English Christian Everyman, apparently seeing his Englishness and Christianity inextricably bound together and himself as representative of the English nation. His training in geology, which called into question the received Mosaic chronology, coexisted easily with a religious faith that throughout *Arabia Deserta* is presented as unwavering and impervious to doubt. It was a "broad" Christianity, not tied to any one sectarian position—"a perfect law of humanity . . . and a pathway to heaven," as he describes what men "seek" in religion (2:407). Nondoctrinal, it is the "common religion of humanity" (2:68) to which he appeals when denouncing the Mecca-centered slave trade. Out of the ecumenical and humanitarian nature of his religion flows his criticism of Islam, in his view an exclusive and jealous religion that hardens its heart against the outsider.

Carlyle was for the Victorians the rugged prophet-priest of a religiosity established outside the confines of conventional doctrine and sacramental ritual, but they were fully aware that this "religion without theology" was not easily arrived at. Its authority came in part from the fact that it was earned only after painful wanderings in a wilderness of religious negation and indifference. Carlyle's struggle with and for faith is dramatized in what was something of a holy text for many of his contemporaries—*Sartor Resartus*. Carlyle's German protagonist, Diogenes Teufelsdröckh, has his childhood religion swept aside by rationalism, wanders in doubt and negation, and finally regains his faith in a burst of nondoctrinal insight associated with the vast forces of nature: "What is Nature? Ha! why do I not name thee GOD? Art not thou the 'Living Garment of God'? O Heavens, is it, in very deed, HE, then, that ever speaks through thee; that lives and loves in thee, that lives and loves in me?"[16] This overwhelming insight causes him to look on man thereafter with new eyes, "with an infinite Love, an infinite Pity." In turn he is led to a philosophy of Action and Duty, quoting Goethe's *Wilhelm Meister:* " 'Doubt of any sort cannot be removed except by Action.' " " '*Do the Duty which lies nearest thee,* which thou knowest to be a Duty! Thy second Duty will already have become clearer.' "[17]

In *Sartor Resartus* "The Everlasting Yea" encapsulates much of what religion became for those Victorians who had been exposed to the so-called higher criticism of the Bible and the disturbing conclusions of geology and the other sciences. Doughty's religion is very much one of duty and responsibility—a faith that set him, stiff-necked, against the Arabians and provided motivation for the lifetime task of renovating and restoring the English language to a long-lost elemental purity. As with so much of the secularized religion of Victorian intellectuals Doughty's religion, like that of Carlyle, is strong on duty and responsibility but vague on sacramental matters and the afterlife. Perhaps the essential core of Doughty's faith (and Carlyle's) is summed up in Arthur Hugh Clough's poem "Qui Laborat, Orat" of the mid 1840s in which the "only Source of all our light and life" will "In worldly walks the prayerless heart prepare; / And if in work its life it seem to live, / Shalt make the work a prayer."[18] The new religion is one even harder than the old—there is always work in the fields of the Lord, never play: work is prayer.

THE MEDIEVAL IDEAL

As it was expressed by such writers as Scott, Cobbett, Carlyle, Disraeli, Ruskin, and Morris, among others, English medievalism is both pervasive and elusive. On the one hand it can simply designate another aspect of the characteristically eclectic nineteenth-century style in art, architecture, or interior decoration—the trappings and emblems of the medieval past, particularly of northern Europe, resuscitated in the present. On the other it can posit a serious political, social, and religious alternative to the brutal realities of the "cash-nexus" dominating the age. Alice Chandler's *A Dream of Order* generalizes in these terms about the thorough-going medievalism that came to be idealized as a life-sustaining alternative to an inhumane present:

> All humanitarians realized that the condition of England demanded change. Those who were conservatives, as all medievalists tended to be, saw in the medieval ideal of the guided society a rough sketch of the changes to be made. Religion, a deep spiritual faith, was one of the values it offered both the English and Continental medievalists—the same faith that was being sought in Romantic poetry. Paternalism was another advantage. Man was a "poor, bare, forked, animal" according to the conservatives' fearful yet pitying view. The Middle Ages provided him with adequate food and shelter and, more important, with the ties and traditions that by making him content would eliminate the danger of revolt. [19]

Doughty falls into the orbit of medievalism through focusing on the language of his beloved Chaucer and Spenser as an ideal. This impulse brings him together with other writers at least tinged with what might be called a "verbal medievalism." William Morris and G. M. Hopkins, both contemporaries of Doughty, each in his own way looked to the medieval past for words and rhythms that would differentiate their styles from a Tennysonian smoothness and euphony that they believed had grown attenuated. Carlyle's medievalism also involved him on occasion in looking into the Anglo-Saxon origins of modern English words as yet another way of making vivid his radical criticisms of the contemporary social order.

In regard to the question of a usable societal past it appears that Doughty and Carlyle diverge most strongly in their medievalism. Carlyle's *Past and Present* (1843) is his most sustained excursion into full-blown medievalism and one of the most complete nineteenth-century expressions of what might be termed a societal medievalism. Looking to the past for faith and leadership, he juxtaposed the medieval and modern worlds, finding in the organic society of the Middle Ages and the "heroism" of Abbot Sansom a glowing, life-enhancing ideal to posit against the atomistically selfish "hard times" of the present. Abbot Sansom exercises firm, paternalistic, even autocratic leadership, but he gets work done, provides well for a dependent community, and is committed to service to a spiritual ideal and order. For Carlyle this heart-whole faith of the past stands in starkly favorable contrast to the spiritual emptiness and narrow self-interest of present-day England with its acquiescence to the indifferent laws of the marketplace.

There is nothing in *Arabia Deserta* akin to this idealizing of a community of faith of the distant past. Doughty responds favorably to individual Beduins and town-dwellers—"medieval" in some ways—and recognizes the essential humanity they share with him, but he in general castigates their religion and society. Many other nineteenth-century writers tended to look favorably on so-called hard primitives (that is, rough-hewn folk such as the Highlanders of Scotland), but Doughty stands obdurately opposed to the harsh way of life and prescientific thought of the people with whom he lives. He remains a man of science and progress, opposing his "science" and rationality to what he finds to be the credulity and fatalism of both the Beduins and city-dwellers of Arabia. From the standpoint of literary artistry it is this sustained conflict between Khalil the *Nasrany* and the Arabs that is of course a prime factor lending drama to and building tension in Doughty's extended narrative.

This divergence about the social order of the past—as distinct from an attitude toward the language of the past—would seem to divide Carlyle and Doughty so sharply as to negate any claims of influence. But Carlyle's full attitude toward past and present goes well beyond a unilinear idealization of a monastic hero of the Middle Ages. Born after the beginning of the Industrial Revolution, Carlyle realized that the future for England could not reside in a reimposed medieval agrarianism. He allowed room for the economic and technological realities of his own time and place. "Carlyle was influenced by the Saint-Simonians . . . a society at once conservative and dynamic—founded on religion and yet directed toward social progress, allowing for change but rejecting revolution," Alice Chandler writes.[20] Therefore *Past and Present* does not end in the Middle Ages but advances to the nineteenth century to consider the industrialist Plugson of Undershot, the sort of man who could lead England with confidence through the uncharted waters of the future. Carlyle transferred the ideally paternalistic leadership of the Middle Ages to the present and found its embodiment in an enlightened industrialist. "Carlyle's most original contribution to the development of English medievalism," Chandler asserts, "is in adapting the idea of the paternal leadership of society to an industrial age."[21]

To look at Doughty and Carlyle from the perspective of "medievalism" is to realize how wide a net the designation casts. In *Arabia Deserta* Doughty will have no truck with idealizing the society of the past, whether in England or Arabia; he never, in fact, offers any speculations about the nature of an ideal society and certainly does not use the societal achievements of the past to castigate the present. The bold exception to his unwillingness or inability to play the social prophet is in the area of language, where he locates the "best" of language in the past, reverencing throughout his life the language of Chaucer and Spenser. Through renovating the language of his England he suggests the possible renovation of English moral life itself; but this is as far as he will go. Doughty is not a social theorist, a man willing and able to envision the specifics of a desired future, as Carlyle will do to a degree; he is purely a writer. And even in his literary works consciously planned structure is not his strength. *Arabia Deserta* has, as Barker Fairley points out,[22] a most effective narrative sequence, but it is, of course, one given by the rhythms of his wandering themselves, not invented by Doughty; *The Dawn in Britain,* his long-meditated poetic epic, is weakened by its overall narrative design while remaining effective in individual sections.

Carlyle, in contrast, is a man of passionate political and social concerns who looks to the past for a social ideal, which he then translates to the present in the form of Plugson of Undershot. In the case of language Carlyle is a conscious modernist, creating a style quite in keeping with the revolutionary changes that broke up the stable society of the eighteenth century. Both writers are nonetheless drawn together under the heading of medievalism through their characteristic English tendency toward a progressive conservatism or a conservative progressivism. They both exhibit a typical post–French Revolution fear of revolution with its wholesale, inchoate efforts to remake society from the ground up; they extract what they consider the best from the past; they burn with a righteous indignation and sincerity when confronting human stupidity and lack of charity, whether those are found in "medieval" Arabia or modern-day England.

STYLE

Doughty's prose contrasts sharply with the smooth-flowing, carefully articulated lines of such contemporary master-stylists as Newman and Ruskin, whose Latinate and King Jamesian language sustains itself easily over long and involved paragraphs tightly linked one to the other. Another sharp contrast is with Matthew Arnold, whose urbane and lightly ironic stance toward his readers is far from Doughty's stance of rugged, homespun independence and hammer-hard ironic insistence. Much closer to Doughty's stylistic ideals—his concern with the individual sentence and exact word over the smoothly developed paragraph—are the two great nineteenth-century originals: the passionate and deliberately difficult Carlyle and Browning, both of whom frequently presented the rhythm of a human voice under the pressure of emotion. Through this they necessarily entered into the territory of language that was elliptical, fragmented, and even ugly. Engaged alertness was both elicited and demanded from their readers, a quality equally demanded by Doughty.

When Trelawney Saunders of the India Office defended Doughty's style in a paper Doughty had written for the Royal Geographical Society in 1884, he referred to Carlyle's precedent in creating an unconventional English, although he hastened to qualify this by writing that he thought "it an injustice to [Doughty] to have [his] style compared with [Carlyle's] barbaric dialect."[23] In the subsequent century this stylistic linkage with Carlyle—proposed and then hastily withdrawn by Saunders—has not, however, been pursued by those who have written on Doughty, although much effort has been spent in trying to find antecedents for a style that has compelled respectful but often somewhat puzzled attention. I think this comparison is worth pursuing, even though limitations of space prevent a point-by-point aligning of the full modulations of both styles.

Doughty's style cannot be easily categorized, as S. E. Tabachnick has shown through his intriguing analyses of the multiple "registers" of Doughty's prose. These are seen as ranging from a highly crafted and artificial first sentence to a plain style that renders geographic and other scientific detail to a romantic exchange of dramatic dialogue when Khalil faces Wahaby inquisitions.[24] To pick any one sentence or group of sentences from this massive work for "characteristic," representative qualities is dangerous, given the book's wide stylistic modulations. For my purposes, however, the following passage, which comes when Doughty confronts the lava wastes of upland Arabia, is apposite. It is one of his relatively rare set-pieces but in its rhythms is certainly not unrepresentative:

> We look out from every height, upon the Harra, over an iron desolation; what uncouth blackness and lifeless cumber of vulcanic matter!— an hard-set face of nature without a smile for ever, a wilderness of burning and rusty horror of unformed matter. What lonely life would not feel constraint of heart to trespass here! the barren heaven, the nightmare soil! where should he look for comfort?—There is a startled conscience within a man of his *mesquîn* being, and profane, in presence of the divine stature of the elemental world!—this lion-like sleep of cosmogonic forces, in which is swallowed up the gnat of the soul within him,—that short motion and parasitical usurpation which is the weak accident of life in matter. Anâz appeared, riding as it were upon the rocky tempest, at twelve miles distance;—I despaired of coming thither, over so many vulcanic deeps and reefs of lavas, and long scalding reaches of basalt rolling stones. (1:451–52)

The passage's similarities with Carlyle's "dialect" include a sudden shift of perspective through the asking of rhetorical questions and the piling up of short syntactic units. Both writers' styles are short-winded, marked by heavy internal punctuation; both are consciously "northern" in courting rugged, rather harsh effects that slow down the pace of reading and make the reader focus on specific phrases, sentences, and even words. For his part Carlyle was thoroughly conscious of the revolutionary implications of his style, as he made clear in responding to his friend John Sterling's

complaint that the style of *Sartor Resartus* was in parts "positively barbarous":[25]

> Do you reckon this really a time for Purism of Style; or that Style (mere
> dictionary Style) has much to do with the worth or unworth of a Book?
> I do not: with whole ragged battalions of Scott's-Novel Scotch, with
> Irish, German, French, and even Newspaper Cockney (when "Liter-
> ature" is little other than a Newspaper) storming in on us, and the
> whole structure of our Johnsonian English breaking up from its founda-
> tions,—revolution *there* as visible as anywhere else![26]

Doughty, too, saw his style as a challenge to the prevailing—and, in his
view, degraded—use of language in his times. He and Carlyle strove to
reawaken and reanimate readers lulled by writing that too assiduously
cultivated euphony and seamless texture. All the "elemental" resources of
"northern" English were marshalled to confute a "southern," Latinate me-
lodiousness and an ideal of civilized, unruffled urbanity.

SINCERITY AND THE PROPHET-SAGE

Going beyond congruencies of faith and style is what can be called the
integrity of Carlyle and Doughty—the sense they convey of an absolute
sincerity of belief and engagement in their matters of concern. Above and
beyond what has so far been specified about them in terms of similarities
between their religious points of view, stylistic emphases, and differences
about the past is a common stance of moral rectitude. Carlyle's fundamental ideas are not difficult to grasp, else they would not have had the broad
impact they had on so many diverse contemporaries. Rooted in the harsh
Scottish Calvinism of his youth, but with predestination and hellfire removed, they contain a belief in God manifested in Nature, assert the
necessity of Duty and Hard Work, and retain a certain Calvinistic skep-
ticism about the value of Art. A nondoctrinal theism linked with an ethic
of duty and work was a religio-social idea that meshed well with the spirit
of his age, which was one that found the conclusions of the critical intellect inescapable but which could not confront the full implications of such
critical thought as it challenged long-hallowed beliefs. These Carlylian
belief-ideas were important in themselves, but what gave him such an
immense impact and authority were the sagelike tones of complete
sincerity he uttered in presenting them.[27] Here was a man speaking with

the urgency and authority of the wise man of the tribe. What set him apart so strikingly from the other well-known Victorian writers was his style: assertive, exclamatory, questioning, denunciatory, foreign-sounding because of its borrowings from German, wide-ranging in allusion, juxtaposing the cosmic with the trivial and ephemeral—a voice of passionate, intense engagement expressed by someone in touch with sources of knowledge and insight beyond logical demonstration. Representative of his prophetic utterance at its wildest are these sentences that describe Diogenes' initial step away from a consuming despair about the human condition, a state prior to the conversion process:

> Full of such humor, and perhaps the miserablest man in the whole French Capital or Suburbs, was I, one sultry Dogday, after much perambulation, toiling along the dirty little *Rue Saint-Thomas De l'Enfer,* among civic rubbish enough, in a close atmosphere, and over pavements hot as Nebuchadnezzar's Furnace; whereby doubtless my spirits were little cheered; when, all at once, there arose a Thought in me, and I asked myself: "What art thou afraid of? Wherefore, like a coward, dost thou forever pip and whimper, and go cowering and trembling? Despicable biped! what is the sum-total of the worst that lies before thee? Death? Well, Death; and say the pangs of Tophet too, and all that the Devil and Man may, will or can do against thee! Hast thou not a heart: canst thou not suffer whatsoever it be; and as a Child of Freedom, though outcast, trample Tophet itself under thy feet, while it consumes thee? Let it come, then; I will meet it and defy it!"[28]

A further significant point of connection between Carlyle and Doughty lies in the assumption of the role of the sage, a stance that brings to the reader's mind the distant biblical past with its angry, passionately engaged prophets. The role is not insisted on in Doughty the way it is in Carlyle: Doughty less often *tells* the reader what to think about matters of faith and conduct compared to the Scottish sage, although he does on occasion. But in another sense the sagelike mantle is pervasive in Doughty's tonality, which projects a remoteness and distant atemporality. Like all the other nineteenth-century sages, Doughty has certain assumptions about life and conduct that he shares with his readers but about which he is not disposed to argue or to prove in any rigorously logical way. His charges about the language of Victorian England once again should be considered in this connection. In drawing attention to the "remissness" and "vility" of the

contemporary speech corroding the national essence, he presents an opposing English redolent of the past of Chaucer and Spenser. The use of Arabic
elements in the language of *Arabia Deserta* is also part of this effort at
finding a vitality in the etymological foundations of language, according
to Walt Taylor.[29] But this is as far as he goes: he will not argue his case at
length and is not concerned how the language of the past can practically
be brought into the mainstream of nineteenth-century English life. The
prophet-sage brings a message home implicitly through his hundreds of
thousands of exactly chosen words. That is either sufficient or insuffi-
cient—the prophet-sage has had his say.

From the beginning of *Arabia Deserta* Doughty stresses his plainspoken-
ness, his truth telling, the fact that he would have his readers say of him
"PROSIT VERITATI" (1:29). He makes much of his sincerity, the fact that
he is not a fireside-bound, overfed "man of letters" but a weary, solitary
man with no ax to grind except that of "humanity" and England's moral
health. For Carlyle the "sincerity" of his heroes is continually emphasized:
"I should say sincerity, a deep, great, genuine sincerity, is the first characteristic of all men in any way heroic."[30] "If a book come from the heart, it
will continue to reach other hearts; all art and author craft are of small
amount to that."[31] "It is not to taste sweet things, but to do noble and
true things, and vindicate himself under God's Heaven as a God-made
Man, that the poorest son of Adam dimly longs."[32] "Not a mealy mouthed
man! A candid ferocity, if the case call for it, is in him, he does not mince
matters!"[33] In turning to Doughty's own language these qualities of truth
telling and of the prophet-sage are fully evident. One telling example
occurs when Doughty reflects on the fact that "I have heard it from credi-
ble Moslems, that *nearly no Haj passes in which some unhappy persons are not
put to death as intruded Christians."* His indignation mounts as he warms to
the subject:

> A trooper and his comrade, who rode with the yearly Haj caravans,
> speaking (unaffectedly) with certain Christian Damascenes (my familiar
> acquaintance), the year before my setting out, said 'They saw two
> strangers taken at Mona in the last pilgrimage, that had been detected
> writing in pocket-books. The strangers being examined were found to
> be "Christians"; they saw them executed, and the like happened most
> years!' Our Christian governments too long suffer this religious brigan-
> dage! Why have they no Residents, for the police of nations in Mecca?

Why have they not occupied the direful city in the name of the health of nations, in the name of the common religion of humanity, *and because the head of the slave trade is there?* (2:68)

Khalil again and again puts his life at risk before the Arabs through his unwillingness to dissimulate his Christianity or to cease arguing against the slave trade. In so doing he comes to exemplify the heroism and faith that Carlyle and others found wanting in the England of the nineteenth century; he is also the one sagelike Victorian to undergo the extreme trials that the Old Testament prophets occasionally suffered—truly wandering in the wilderness, an outcast scorned.

Doughty's role of an Everyman of England's past is expressed in his heroism, his plainspoken faith, and most pervasively in his language itself, which has a newly minted quality—a presence of an "elemental" English that at the same time modulates to a plain style capable of recording scientific data according to the scrupulous standards of the nineteenth century. Doughty's example is one of a latter-day hero who braves all difficulties of travelling and book making, pursuing his way successfully because of his faith and sincerity. When Carlyle wrote of the "Hero as Man of Letters" he considered this form of the hero as a prevailing contemporary one since "the true university of this day is a Collection of Books," "Books are our Church too," and "Literature is our Parliament too."[34] If, as Carlyle also writes, "The strong man will find *work,* which means difficulty, pain, to the full measure of his strength,"[35] then Doughty is very much a modern-day Hero as Man of Letters, a man who carries with him a faith, not an "argumentative theology," since "a man lives by believing something: not by debating and arguing about many things."[36] He uses the pen, not the sword, to win converts for his "faith." Of course not to be forgotten is Doughty's deep involvement with the purely factual, with bringing back from Arabia a trove of scientific information; but the figure of Doughty-Khalil and the language of *Arabia Deserta* move beyond the scientific into a realm of the spiritual and prophetic that aligns Doughty most solidly with Carlyle of all the Victorians who sought to influence the moral life of England.

What is so characteristic of Doughty in the context of his age is the bringing together of the progressive and scientific with the mantle of the sage-prophet. This sets him apart from the central concerns of the aesthetic movement with its emphasis on style and form over content—away from

Pater with his emphasis on "getting as many pulsations [of aesthetic experience] as possible into the given time [of one's life]."[37] For Doughty, although style is important, it is important because it is linked to the overall moral state of England, and it is that concern that links him much more strongly with the Great Victorians—and most especially Carlyle—than with the aesthetic movement of the 1880s and 1890s, despite the fact that *Travels in Arabia Deserta* appeared in 1888. One should not allow a perception of Doughty's initially perceived exoticism of subject matter and concern with style to blind one to the fact that in his deep and central concerns he is a Victorian in a sense much pervaded by Carlylian values, creating a work that contributes much in the scientific spirit of the age, while simultaneously asserting a spiritual and moral purpose to counteract a merely physical, mechanistic view of the universe. A mid-Victorian balance informs *Travels in Arabia Deserta* from beginning to end.

NOTES

1 Letter to D. G. Hogarth, 1902, quoted in H, 114.
2 Letter to D. G. Hogarth, 1913, quoted in H, 115.
3 *The Dawn in Britain,* intro. by Ruth M. Robbins (London: Jonathan Cape, 1943), 687–88.
4 H, 206–7.
5 H, 9.
6 Letter of 14 June 1909, quoted in H, 172.
7 Edith Batho and Bonamy Dobrée, *The Victorians and After, 1830–1914* (New York: McBride, 1938), 176.
8 Ta, 42.
9 See Richard Bevis, "Spiritual Geology: C. M. Doughty and the Land of the Arabs," *Victorian Studies* 16, no. 2 (December 1972): 163–81.
10 Strauss's *Leben Jesu* appeared in 1835; Renan's *Vie de Jesus* in 1863.
11 I argued at length in my dissertation, "Arabian Involvement: A Study of Five Victorian Travel Narratives" (Berkeley, 1971), that one of the elements that gives *Arabia Deserta* its particular intensity and purity is precisely the fact that, unlike other Victorian travel writers, Doughty consciously strove to rid his text of material that would distract the reader from the Arabian experience or specifically bind his text to one historical time and place.
12 The lands of the North and South coalesced in his mind even toward the very end of his Arabian wanderings when the topography on the way to Mecca "brought the Scandinavian *fjelde,* earlier well-known to me, to my remembrance" (2:515).
13 Quoted in Batho and Dobrée, *The Victorians,* 176.
14 For a clear account of the emergence of Anglo-Saxon from obscurity, see Carl T. Berkhout and Milton McC. Gatch, eds., *Anglo-Saxon Scholarship: The First Three Cen-*

turies (Boston: G. K. Hall, 1982), especially Gretchen P. Ackerman's essay "J. M. Kemble and Sir Frederic Madden: 'Conceit and Too Much Germanism,'" 167–81.

15 G. B. Tennyson, "Thomas Carlyle," in *Victorian Literature: Prose* (New York: Macmillan, 1976), 24.

16 Thomas Carlyle, *Sartor Resartus,* ed. Charles Frederick Harrold (New York: Odyssey, 1937), 188.

17 Ibid., 196.

18 Walter E. Houghton and G. Robert Stange, *Victorian Poetry and Poetics,* 2nd ed. (Boston: Houghton Mifflin, 1968), 356.

19 Alice Chandler, *A Dream of Order: The Medieval Ideal in Nineteenth Century English Literature* (Lincoln: University of Nebraska, 1970), 150.

20 Ibid., 131.

21 Ibid., 147–48.

22 See F, 44–76.

23 Quoted in Ta, 47.

24 See Ta, 57–63.

25 Letter to Carlyle, 29 May 1835, quoted in Carlyle, *Sartor Resartus,* 310.

26 Letter to Sterling, 4 June 1835, quoted in ibid., 317.

27 In *The Victorian Sage: Studies in Argument* (London: Macmillan, 1953) John Holloway includes—along with Carlyle—Disraeli, George Eliot, Newman, Arnold, and Hardy.

28 Carlyle, *Sartor Resartus,* 166–67.

29 See Walt Taylor, *Doughty's English,* S.P.E. Tract, no. 11 (Oxford: Clarendon Press, 1939).

30 Carlyle, *Sartor Resartus,* and *On Heroes and Hero Worship,* Everyman's Library (London: Dent, 1908), 280.

31 Carlyle, *On Heroes,* 300.

32 Ibid., 304.

33 Ibid., 306.

34 Ibid., 390, 392.

35 Ibid., 404.

36 Ibid., 402.

37 Conclusion to *The Renaissance,* in Tennyson, "Thomas Carlyle," 1129.

RICHARD BEVIS

Desert Places: The Aesthetics of Arabia Deserta

In his preface to the 1921 edition of *Travels in Arabia Deserta*, T. E. Lawrence pays generous tribute to "a book not like other books, but something particular, a bible of its kind. . . . We call the book 'Doughty' pure and simple, for it is a classic. . . . The book has no date and can never grow old" (1:17). Now, at its centenary, more scholars and general readers than ever before, as well as a gratifying continuation of reprints, testify to its durability. Not only is the book aging well; it actually seems to be growing with time, rising out of the rubble of modern prose like the "Aueyrid mass," an adamantine lava field which "now stands six hundred fathoms aloft, like a mighty mountain, which was in old time even with the floor of the now low-lying sandstone plains!" (1:465).

Doughty was, among other things, an inspired writer on topography, one whose evocations of landscape were based on painfully acquired information about *jebels* (mountains), *wadis* (riverbeds), and drainages, "pains which I took the more willingly, that my passing life might add somewhat of lasting worth to the European geography" (1:469). Balancing the rhapsodical passages that testify to the feelings that Arabia Deserta can inspire are the lists of place-names in a given watershed and the carefully drawn map of northwestern Arabia presented to the Royal Geographical Society in 1883 and included with good editions of the complete *Arabia Deserta*. My own purpose with his book is analogous to Doughty's with the landscape: to examine salient features, to see where important streams had their source, and to sketch some of their ramifications.

One of the great cultural phenomena of the European and American nineteenth century was the way art and intellect and energy reached out toward the waste, empty reaches of not only the physical universe but of the imagination as well, leading to what Robert Martin Adams has called "the literary conquest of the void." In *Nil* (1966), he chronicles the preoccupation of (for examples) Poe and Melville in America and Flaubert, Baudelaire, and Leconte de Lisle in France with exotic varieties of the Nothing that is Something, yet these writers are only, as it were, the tip of the iceberg. Increasingly skilled explorers, mariners, and climbers were pushing across oceans and ice floes toward both poles, crossing larger deserts and scaling higher peaks. Writers as gifted and diverse as Ruskin and Hardy, Burton and Doughty devoted major efforts to describing the fascination of places that had generally been regarded as useless, dangerous, and ugly. Composers in tone poems and artists on canvas evoked arid steppelands, icy summits, ocean reaches, and Arctic perils. Geologists, biologists, and astronomers reported voluminously on the human and philosophical interest of regions uninhabited by man. Books by authors who were not themselves explorers helped spread this taste: Meredith's volumes of "Earth" poetry, H. G. Wells's *The Time Machine,* Jules Verne's *Le Sphinx des glaces.* Indeed, a fair amount of modern and early modern literature is inexplicable without reference to this development; confronted with the peculiar bleakness of *The Waste Land,* the barren vision of St. Exupéry's *Terre des hommes,* the implications of Frost's "Desert Places," you see how the void has encroached upon us.

Besides Adams's *Nil,* whose primary concern is belles lettres, literary criticism has made some partial attempts to survey this territory. M. H. Nicolson's *Mountain Gloom and Mountain Glory* shows how the Augustan fear of mountains as deformed became the Romantic exaltation of them as sublime, but there she leaves the story. A recent collection, *Nature and the Victorian Imagination,* documents the fascination of the Alps and the poles, but (surprisingly, I think) omits the impact of deserts on the public who welcomed Kinglake's *Eothen,* Bartlett's *Forty Days in the Wilderness,* Burton's *Pilgrimage to Mecca,* Palmer's *Desert of the Exodus,* Gertrude Bell's *Persian Pictures,* and so on. Yet it can be shown that Doughty's classic derives from the aesthetic tradition chronicled by Nicolson and that it is attuned to a frequency of the Victorian imagination, besides having its own distinctive sound, one with increasing resonance in our century.

At the simplest, broadest level of his penchant for large barren landscapes, Doughty, like other desert writers, feels and writes of aesthetic emotions generated by what Addison called "The Great," which he described as "stupendous works of nature" (that is, deserts, "huge heaps of mountains," and "a wide expanse of waters"), possessing a "rude kind of magnificence" that creates in the beholder "a pleasing astonishment at such unbounded views" and a "delightful stillness and amazement in the soul." Addison theorized that the pleasure of Great phenomena is partly a freedom from restraint ("a spacious horizon is an image of liberty"), partly an overloading of the imagination analogous to the effect of mathematical puzzles or cosmic paradoxes on the mind: "Such wide and undetermined prospects are as pleasing to the fancy as speculations of eternity and infinitude are to the understanding."[1] Doughty almost regularly sees Arabia in terms of just these "speculations"; the "illimitable empty wastes" of the nomads are "full of eternal silence," the desert sky at night is an "infinite spectacle," the Beduin have lived thus "from the beginning," and so on.

Addison's prescient passage helped to found a main line of English aesthetics that runs through Burke and Byron to Ruskin, Hardy, and Doughty. Even his categories of landscape have cohered remarkably, with some additions. Edmund Burke, who uses "the great" as a synonym for "the sublime," thought deserts less sublime than mountains because less fearful, but posterity—when it actually reached the desert—overruled him in favor of Addison while endorsing Burke's emphasis on pain and fear. It was Byron who best combined these two pioneer theories of Great aesthetics in his passage on the "cold sublimity" of the Alps in *Childe Harold:* "All that expands the spirit, yet appalls, / Gathers round these summits."[2]

Inheriting the theory at approximately this point, the Victorians expanded and split it. Adventurers such as Burton attested to the sublimity of deserts, and illustrated reports of polar expeditions led to a recognition of an "Arctic Sublime," as Chauncey Loomis has shown.[3] The Great, however, became more ambiguous; whereas Ruskin (and most of the mountaineers) continued the Coleridge-Byron line of exaltation, Hardy picked up from Shelley a sadder and more sombre version of sublimity, which he darkened further on the basis of his readings in evolutionary science and higher criticism as well as his studies in astronomy. In 1878, the year Doughty returned from Arabia, Hardy published *The Return of the Native,* whose main character is a piece of waste landscape. Egdon Heath, "grand in its simplicity," dwarfs the human actors who move upon it and possesses a "chastened sublimity" that the author finds well suited to his age and probably a clue to future standards of natural beauty: "The new Vale of Tempe may be a gaunt waste in Thule: human souls may find themselves in closer and closer harmony with external things wearing a sombre-

ness distasteful to our race when it was young."⁴ *Travels in Arabia Deserta*
is a remarkable confirmation that the new/old "aesthetics of Thule" was
not merely an eccentric's hallucination—the more remarkable in that
Doughty insisted some thirty years later that he had not *heard* of Hardy.
Independently, then, he devoted his magnum opus to a portrayal of the
"chastened sublimity" of a "gaunt waste" that dwarfs Egdon Heath and to
a narration of the lives and sufferings of those who endure it.

Doughty worked in the tradition of the Great as modified by Victorian
pessimism. We have noted that Doughty was put in mind of infinity and
eternity by his "vast wilderness," just as Addison had predicted; that is,
travel in Arabia was for him a quasireligious experience.⁵ Devoutness he
discovered was easier at night, but the "astonishment" and "amazement"
of soul specified by Addison were emotions he felt in viewing the *harras* or
remembering Vesuvius. His reaction to an imposing landform was actually glandular: "Yonder vulcanic flood lies brimming upon the crystalline
mountains: a marvel . . . to make the forehead sweat!" (2:566). Moreover, the topographic categories nominated by Addison as Great all figure
in the narrative; Doughty's Arabia is a composite—*montana* and *oceana* as
well as *deserta*. Some of his strongest reactions are to vistas or crossings of
desert mountains or massifs, which are frequently imaged as "coasts" or
"headlands" into which the dry ocean projects "bays." The Beduin become
"land-navigators" seeking the "unstable village port" of their encampment
(1:393), lava fields become "floods," "waves," or "reefs," with edges "like
the ice-brink of a glacier" (2:239), a sandstone mesa is seen as "an island
with cliffs" (2:249), and so forth. To these first greatnesses Doughty adds
the heavens, especially the night sky, which for the Victorians had become
part of the sublime, and on occasion he brings them all together at once.

> The . . . watch-fire made a pleasant bower of light about us, seated on
> the pure sand and breathing the mountain air, among dim crags and
> desert acacias; the heaven was a blue deep, all glistering with stars,
> *that smiled to see*
> *the rich attendance on our poverty:*
> we were guests of the Night, and of the vast Wilderness. (2:561)

But *Arabia Deserta* is a nineteenth-century embodiment of the Great, in
darker tones. Addison's "pleasing" and "delightful" emotions, whose in-
adequacy was recognized as early as Burke, have virtually disappeared.

Pleasure and delight indeed seem too shallow and simple in the presence
of this "great and terrible wilderness" (1:274); something like Burke's
pain and fear or Byron's dismay and terror are what Doughty feels before
"the immense mountain blackness, terrible and lowering, of the Harra"
(1:123). To the student of Lyell's geology, Arabia is a "Titanic desolation"
(1:427), as Egdon Heath was a "Titanic form" in Hardy's eyes. The emotional connotations are not those of (deistic) religious reverence for God's
handiwork, but of awe at the primordial power of Titans and volcanoes.

In *Arabia Deserta*, then, there are literally dozens of references to strong
emotions in response to various kinds of Great landscape and to glimpses
of the infinite and eternal through them, but they are overshadowed by a
much larger number of allusions to desolation, barrenness, and emptiness,
an iteration that does not so much destroy the idea of Great aesthetics as
redefine it by shifting the emphasis. Of course deserts, high mountains,
polar wastes, and even oceans are—for chauvinist *homo sapiens*—mostly
desolate and empty, but it makes a great deal of difference to a book how
frequently and in what terms the author calls the reader's attention to
these qualities. It is at this point that *Arabia Deserta*, while remaining
recognizably Victorian, begins to find its own distinctive voice.

In the beginning "desolate" is used straightforwardly enough—"Commonly the Arabian desert is an extreme desolation where the herb is not
apparent for the sufficiency of any creature" (1:95)—but soon it becomes
an ominously intense and pervasive quality. A ruined *kella* or waterhole
fort seems "High and terrible . . . in the twilight in this desolation of the
world" (1:120); a barrier cliff appears "an horrid sandstone desolation, a
death as it were and eternal stillness of nature" (1:172); a locust plague is
"a desolation of the land that is desolate" (1:538). Before long, in a characteristic transfer, Doughty turns this quality of external nature into a metaphor of an inner state. "How often in my dwelling in that hostile country
have I felt desolate," he exclaims (1:216), but not only *there:* he would
wish to "live peaceably in the moral desolation of the world" (1:305). At
times the usage might be either natural or metaphorical or both. Banished
to a sparse "palm ground" outside Aneyza, he spent "more than three
weeks in this desolation" (2:473).[6]

An associated theme is that of decay: "Arabia in our days has the aspect
of a decayed country. . . . she is forsaken and desolate" (1:154). The decay
is that of human arts, but these include agriculture and so touch nature.
Thus Syria is a "bald country, which might again be made fruitful"

(2:400); and one whole side of Gofar is ruinous, its "once fruitful orchard-grounds . . . now like the soil of the empty desert," its house-walls broken, its wells abandoned: "a died-out place" (1:634–35). When Doughty marvels, "how far are they now from these arts of old settled countries in Nejd!" Abdullah admits, " 'Wellah, the Arabs (of our time) are degenerate from the ancients, in all!' " (2:420–21). The two kinds of erosion, "that abandonment of human arts and death of nature which is now in Arabia" (1:581), become linked at the levels of feeling and image, however logically the mind may distinguish them.

More prominent still is the stress placed on the emptiness of the land. Again, Great landscapes are by their nature empty, yet we do not take it for granted that travellers will become obsessed by the fact. "The vast emptiness of the desert pervades the book," notes Martin Armstrong.[7] Actually emptiness takes many forms in *Arabia Deserta*, ranging from the all-pervasive hunger to anarchy. As the *khala*, "The empty solitary waste where they were never in assurance of their own lives" (1:177), it is constantly before the reader. Doughty and his hosts do not ride off into sunsets but into "the emptiness": absolutely "waste desert," a "land under no rule" (2:635) where, if they met him alone and unprotected, the Arabs say they would kill him (1:319). The largest *khala*, Robba el-Khaly, the Empty Quarter, "they believe to be void of the breath of life!" (2:558). Emptiness may have a certain grandeur—"in the immensity of empty Arabia" it is strange to encounter a familiar face (2:534)—or it may crawl inside, as the Arabs' "incessant weariness and . . . very emptiness of heart" (1:355). Emptiness is in the realization that "no other life, it may be, is in the compass of a hundred miles about us" (1:348) and in the vacuity of sun-blasted days, so that dusk becomes "the fall of the empty daylight" (1:303). Here Doughty sounds like a case study from Adams's *Nil,* though a remark such as "The Arabs are barren-minded in the emptiness of the desert life" (2:302–3) suggests that the metaphor of void ties in to other metaphors for him.

"Where man is not, nature is barren," runs Blake's epigram. He might more accurately have written, "Where nature is barren, man is not," but in either case barren and empty form a natural pair. That *Arabia Deserta* would be full of references to barren lands seems obvious enough, yet Doughty need not have made barrenness the thematic heart of the book, as he does. "Nothing is interposed between our senses and the barren, yet austerely beautiful reality," wrote John Middleton Murry;[8] had he stopped before "yet" the sentence would have been equally true. Every few pages, more than a hundred times in all, Doughty calls our attention to the "great barrenness" of the "inhuman desert," a "sorry landscape" in which "man's life seems cast away," or to the "iron wilderness" of the *harras,* or the "dreadful aspect" of the "uncouth hostile mountains" and "vast sand wilderness" near Mecca (1:68, 72, 268, 348, 425; 2:307). Many of these allusions, though strikingly phrased, are no more than colorful geographical or geological writing with a dash of pathetic fallacy; but others are too emotional, metaphorical, or philosophical to be passed off as science. Like other desert travellers (Burton, for example), Doughty perceives the Arabs' desert mountains as "the carcase of the planet" (2:515), the naked *Ding an sich:* that is part of their fascination. He lets his own emotion slip out into the landscape (the "weary wilderness") and then finds the land getting inside him: "my mind was full to see so many seamed, guttered and naked cinder-hills of craters in the horrid black lavas before us" (2:247).

Barrenness in the book is as full of variety as "the waste soil of Arabia" itself in Doughty's eyes (1:619). It can be an inversion of Mother Nature, like bestiary tales of animals who devour their young: "an unfostering soil of sun-stricken drought, which corrodes all life . . . a land which eateth up the inhabitants thereof" (1:477); or it is a ravaging disease, a "dire waste of nature" itself (2:196). At times we seem to move in a setting for a poem by T. S. Eliot: "Here is a dead land" (1:95; cf. 1:505). Nor is it only the *land* that is barren: so are the climate, the sunshine, and the atmosphere, so is the Aarab's life (1:245), so even is the "heaven" above the *harras:* "What lonely life would not feel constraint of heart to trespass here! the barren heaven, the nightmare soil! where should he look for comfort?" (1:452). All of which inevitably raises the question of his motivation: what was he doing here? For the moment it is enough to acknowledge that in this "deep wilderness of dearth and misery" Doughty spent— voluntarily, for the most part—nearly two years of his life, periodically praising the nomad existence.

Yet this is still not all the barrenness in *Arabia Deserta,* probably not even the most important, certainly not the most original, type. To this point Doughty is still arguably a Victorian travel writer who has accepted a darkened, postevolutionary version of Great aesthetics, a "chastened sublimity," and who differs from his predecessors in quantity and intensity of reference more than in kind. But he goes much farther, and in what follows I hope to show that he transcends his age and anticipates important aspects of modernism. If Doughty grows out of the nineteenth century, he also outgrows it.

Earlier, we saw Hardy claiming a correspondence between the mood of Egdon Heath and the spiritual state of modern man. Similarly, Doughty suggests a relation between Arabia Deserta and those who try to live upon it; that is, between geology and anthropology. Roughly speaking, for every reference to barren land, there is one to barren people *of* the land. Here we must try to distinguish between *bareness,* a quality Doughty often admires, and *barrenness,* always a regrettable dearth. The Edomites, whose "wisdom" teaches them to keep "their habitations . . . so simple, void of unnecessary things" (1:82), live bare lives, while Doughty's first host, Zeyd, blighted in his heart, miserable in his hospitality, and unable to beget upon Hirfa, lives barrenly: his bareness is not wisdom but necessity. As with the other themes, the forms are many in which barrenness afflicts the Arabians. They may be literally barren, childless, like Zeyd and Hirfa, Mohammed Ibn Rashid, and the whole village of Kheybar (2:33, 128); or they may be figuratively so in any number of ways. Some are barren of invention, like the Teymites who cannot make decent walls or wells; some are barren of speech, like the "impertinent tongues" in Motlog's tent (1:559) and the wretched cameleer at el-Ayn; and many are barren of energy or occupation. At Petra, "Heavy is their long day of idleness . . . some of them I have seen toss pebbles in their hard fists, to drive the time away" (1:79). The denizens of the *kella* at Medain Salih live lives of stunning ennui, while the nomads of the open desert show a "fatal indolence" about pursuing a "weak enemy" that has taken a tenth of their livestock (1:392).

The whole portrait of the Beduin—the major characters in the book—is of a burned-out people: "their spirits are made weary with incessant apprehension of their enemies, and their flesh with continual thirst and hunger. The necessitous lives of the Aarab may hardly reach to a virtuous mediocrity; they are constrained to be robbers" (1:285–86). What with "squalid ignorance" and the "pining daily carefulness of their livelihood," many become "wild men"; virtue must navigate a "strait possibility" (1:302). As poor as if "disinherited of the world," yet "they can wait wretchedly thus, as the dead, whilst a time passes over them" (1:355). Their very names—Beduwy, "inhabitant of the waste," Beni Sokhr, "sons of limestone"—link them to the surrounding natural desolation, but Doughty cannot always summon up his Christian charity for their afflictions. Meeting some Beni Aly on the desert, he comments, "These were as all the other Beduw whom I have known, a merry crew of squalid wretches, iniquitous, fallacious, fanatical" (2:332). The list might be extended almost indefinitely from his own characterizations: cruel, mercenary, indifferent, faithless, negligent, unimaginative. . . . At times, for individuals and some nomadic groups, he gives much warmer depictions at sharp variance with this catalog, but they do not much affect the overall tenor of his generalizations.

Doughty sometimes makes his Arabs seem barren of humanity itself. At Maan they wrangle continually like "rats in a tub" or "fiends in the end of the world" (1:73). On the *Haj,* the cameleers are "wolves" and "hounds" (1:107); there is neither comfort for the sufferer nor respect for the dead. The old *kella*-keeper Mohammed Aly has "bestial insane instincts" (1:131), and so on. Most of these subhuman chords are struck early in the book, but "Arabians" in general are called "bird-witted" (1:448), and the savage and primitive aspects of nomad life are often stressed.

Finally, Doughty shows unmistakably from time to time that he himself conceives of natural barrenness as a metaphor. For the irascible Mohammed Aly, Islam is the only "solace here in the deserts of his corrupt mind" (1:132). Some young men of the Welad Aly sit drowsing in the afternoon "as though they were weary in the wilderness of their own minds" (1:415). Even the narrator confesses late in the book to a "drought of spirit" (2:424). This is where Doughty moves beyond earlier travel books and into the company of poets such as Théophile Gautier, Leconte de Lisle, and Coventry Patmore, who were using the desert symbolically; this is why we can compare him with Hardy and the Hopkins of sonnet #43 ("The mind has mountains") in his own century, with T. S. Eliot and Robert Frost in ours. Doughty too portrays hollow men in a wasteland: he has his own desert places, a point to which we shall return.

One hollowness that he dwells on particularly is the lack of law. Many Europeans who have seen the nomad life have praised or envied its freedom, and Doughty is not oblivious to that virtue, especially when he is trapped in forts or towns. In the *kella* he longs to escape to the "freeborn Aarab" in "the free High Arabia!" (1:419, 566). Delivered from Kheybar, he hails the "blissful free air" of the Harra, and in Aneyza he yearns to "be free again, among the Aarab" (2:237, 483). But balancing and overbalancing the admirable "franchise of the desert" is the crippling, all-pervasive "fear of the desert" (2:248), whose object is not, this time, the

land itself but humans. More than any of his predecessors, Doughty exam-
ines the darker side of nomadic freedom: the "anarchy of the desert"
(1:200). This begins a little later than most of his major themes, but as a
preoccupation it rivals emptiness, to which it is related. As emptiness is a
concomitant of land that is barren of food and water, anarchy is the condition of a people barren of the arts of civilization and one of the ways in
which they are considered "primitive."

Though at first it seems only a state of affairs incidental to the season of
the *Haj,* when roving bands of thieves preying on the pilgrims make the
country "more than commonly insecure" (1:218), we soon learn that anarchy is endemic. Why, Doughty is asked by friends at the *kella* before
setting off with the Beduin, will he hazard himself in a "lawless land . . .
under no rule" (1:244–45) where his letters of protection from government officials will mean little? And basically his friends prove correct: not
only do the sheykhs recognize only such authority as is present in force or
convenient to obey, but they themselves rule only by consent; "the
sheykh's authority cannot compel his free tribesmen" (1:453). In practice
the nomads are "only subject to their own rash wills" (1:440).

The picture Doughty paints of existence lived on these terms is powerful. If his desert is an ocean, it is one that swarms with pirates outside
every anchorage, and the only safety is in numbers. Every night is a time
of alarm; the moon is welcomed for reasons of security. One lives in fear of
old blood-debts being collected—a problem the Greeks had regulated by
the time of *The Oresteia* and the Hebrews by Exodus—and of robbers, who
may skulk singly or ride in bands of camel raiders: a *ghrazzu*. Doughty's
account of one such attack and its aftermath (1:387–93) gives a striking
glimpse of "natural" man; here, not Chaucer, or Spenser, but the Hobbes
of *Leviathan* 1:13 seems his guru, while Locke and Rousseau look on dis-
mayed. "Their ghrazzus and counter-ghrazzus are the destruction of the
Aarab. Reaving and bereaved they may never thrive; in the end . . . it is
but an ill exchange of cattle" (1:391). Doughty suggests sending scouts on
ahead to warn of raids but is told that they would be picked off by lurking
robbers. It is Ishmaelite country, in which every man's hand is against
almost every other man.

Almost: among the few tenuous forms of order, practically the only
enduring allegiance is tribal; as Lawrence found when he tried to unite
them against the Turks, "The Arabs see not beyond their factions"
(2:546). Groups of tribes who go to war as allies may turn on one another

in the fray. The traditions of hospitality—sharing food or drink, claiming protection—offer a precarious refuge from the general insecurity, but today's hosts might yesterday have murdered the guest in the *khala*—or may tomorrow, for there is "no conscience . . . abroad" (1:535). A strong prince such as Ibn Rashid is simply "the hawk among buzzards . . . in a land of ravin" (1:661). Despite such efforts at a social contract, the Arabs emerge as a fearful people, unable to unite for their common good, even fighting their wars as individuals; and Arabia is revealed as a "lawless waste land" (2:182).

Bareness—more precisely than anarchy—is the anthropological counterpart of the land's emptiness, and it comes up even more often. After barrenness itself, *Arabia Deserta* has no more prominent theme; bareness is the nexus between the nomads' primitive simplicity, the hunger and austerity of their lives, the surrounding natural emptiness that conditions them, and Doughty's own deepest impulses.

As we would expect, bareness takes various forms, some of them quite harsh, but none merits a reproach and some have a bright side. Leading his "bare life" in the waste with the "necessitous simplicity" of the beasts and birds, the "light-bodied Arabian" often hungers and thirsts (1:169, 281; 2:534). Often half-starved himself, Doughty renders feelingly the prolonged deprivations of that "country in which he is feasting who is not hungry" (2:74). " 'O my God!' " cries a Beduin matron when he tells of Europe's lushness. " 'Here . . . is nothing, save . . . bare thirst and hunger' " (1:435). Near Seleymy there is a memorable meeting with a "gaunt desert man" who seemed to have "fasted out his life in that place of torment . . . so that nothing remained of him but the terrific voice!" (2:307). By the end of his first summer, Doughty could hardly conceive that once upon a time he had breakfasted daily, and yet he subsisted on their thin fare. A herdsman may live upon nothing but "milk-meat and wild salads . . . : but I have learned by experience that it may well suffice in the desert" (1:222). The sober diet at Ibn Rashid's palace in Hayil is contrasted favorably with the gluttonies of Europe. Still, hunger remains "the desert disease."

The nomads are likewise barely clothed and housed. At the *kella* Doughty sees how the "gate Arabs" in winter "could not sleep past midnight, but lay writhing, with only their poor mantles lapped about them, in the cold sand and groaning for the morning" (1:243). Later, as autumn rain and wind cut through his "worn tent-cloth," Mehsan laments "the everlasting infelicity of the Aarab, whose lack of clothing is a cause to them of many diseases," and prays Allah to "pity the sighing of the poor, the hungry, the naked" (1:612). Besides noting that a "clean heart" under a "bare shirt" is usually sufficient and sometimes admiring the simple appointments of houses and palaces, Doughty does not try to mitigate this evil. Nor does he attempt to hide the rampant poverty amid this "indigence of all things," though he observes, "We see in the Arabs' life that those which need most are of most hospitality" (1:182). More typically he records without editorial comment the various examples of bareness: the merry Fehjies who live as birds, without hope or fear; the empty, idle, but care-free Beduin; the "naked" dewless sunrise, bare of color; the land bare of birdsong; and his own bareness, to go with "no disguise" (1:317).

Only on rare occasions, after chapters of grim catalogs, does he surprise us with an outburst such as "Bare of all things of which there is no need, the days of our mortality are so easy. . . . Such is the nomad life, a long holiday, wedded to a divine simplicity, but with this often long tolerance of hunger in the khála" (1:490). And we had thought they were suffering! Even this hunger, it turns out, has its uses. Enduring "their summer-famine with the nomads," taking the night's freshness as "our daily repast," and lying out amid stones under the stars, "I have found more refreshment than upon beds and pillows in our close chambers." What happens then is straight out of Marvell's "The Garden." As the life of his "wasted flesh" ebbs, that of his spirit flows, quickens, and lifts "her eyas wings unto that divine obscurity" (1:520). Not surprisingly, he then thinks of the early Christian hermits, for Doughty was neither the first nor the last to use hunger as a launching-pad for transcendental meditation. What is startling—and characteristic—here is the way bareness, which causes so much physical suffering, is suddenly made the means of transcending the world and the flesh and leaping back among the quasi-religious emotions associated with the Great that we seemed to have left so far behind.

Arabia Deserta is full of paradoxes. We have seen Doughty balancing anarchy against freedom, barrenness against bareness, misery against ecstasy. We have examined some Great aspects of the book, but this is also a work of minutely observed details: inscriptions, desert herbage, well-tackle, whether Khalil will receive his four-ounce barley cake or his few drops of coffee this morning, how a camel lies down and gets up. Similarly, though many have written of the "Elizabethan richness" of Doughty's prose texture, we have seen that poverty, hunger, bareness of many kinds, including the "austere delicacy of the desert" (2:270), kept attracting his attention and sometimes his approval. He esteemed the Edomites wise to maintain such simple dwellings, admired "the sufficiency of the poorest means in the Arabs' hands to a perfect end" (2:348), and when in villages longed for the free nomad life again. The dominant (though not the only) note of the *Arabia Deserta* music is fascination with what is barren, bare and empty in nature and man. I have suggested whence this came: it is time to ask whither it went, and to consider the implications for Doughty.

If he had not been such an unclubbable man, one could speak of a cult having subsequently formed, not so much around Doughty as around his ideas, though T. E. Lawrence was a genuine disciple. In *Persian Pictures* Gertrude Bell is in the same psychic territory, though she is more diffident than Doughty: "Even the most trivial evidences of the lordship of man afford a certain sense of protection. . . . But here there is nothing—nothing but vast and pathless loneliness, silent and desolate."[9] Closer to our own time, Wilfred Thesiger has written strongly of the desert's appeal, and younger writers such as Peter Iseman continue the tradition. But it was the self-conscious and articulate Lawrence who best understood what Doughty was saying and expressed the lure of Arabia for both of them. "The gospel of bareness in materials is a good one," he wrote to V. W. Richards (15 July 1918), "and it involves apparently a sort of moral bareness too." Ronald Storrs adds, "The Bedu embodied Lawrence's doctrine of bareness in materials,"[10] and cites the scene in *Seven Pillars* where Dahoum draws Lawrence to the east windows of a Roman ruin in Syria, the ones facing the empty desert. In Gwendolyn MacEwen's poetic rendering:

<blockquote>

all
We breathed was pure desert air.
We call
this room the sweetest of them all,
You said.
And I thought: *Because there is nothing here.*[11]

</blockquote>

Lawrence's writings, including his remark that "none of us triumphed over our bodies as Doughty did" (1:18), illuminate certain aspects of *Arabia Deserta*. It is worth noting that sleep, which Doughty terms "our life's only refreshment" (1:536), Lawrence called his greatest pleasure.

The doctrine of "less is more" (or better), which has gained ground after each war of this century, is adumbrated in Doughty's praise of the nomad's life: "Cheerful is the bare Arabic livelihood in the common air, which has sufficiency in few things snatched incuriously as upon a journey! so it is a life little full of superfluous cares" (1:582). He relates their happiness to their frugality, judges the princes of Hayil happier for having fewer books, and assures his friends, "He is not poor who has no need" (2:386). Everywhere we see him trying to reduce his needs and expectations, or admiring those who have reduced theirs. "Sufficiency in few things": was Doughty, despite his voluminousness, one of our first minimalists in life and thought? It would be a paradox in keeping with those noted earlier. Writers on the subject who define minimalism as "a reduction of forms to a primary state, often related to basic structures in geology, physics and chemistry," revealing "serious lacks in the development of our society," or who note that the "puritan simplicity of its forms . . . could be compared with the atmosphere evoked by monuments of archaic culture,"[12] could easily be discussing *Arabia Deserta*. "No longer sure of his position in the universe" either, Doughty would have agreed that "A thing must be shown with the greatest clarity" so long as "the means used are minimal."[13] Richard Wollheim, who coined the term minimal art in 1965, traced the phenomenon back fifty years, but with Doughty the platform is essentially in place, which may help explain his book's continued and increasing appeal.

We are now in a position to understand many of the preferences and puzzles set forth in *Arabia Deserta*, including the question of his motivation. Why did he remain so long immersed in the emptiness, squalor, and barrenness of Arabia, risking health and life itself? The answer is before us in the text, if we can accept it: for the life that could be led there. Four times in the second volume he reiterates his verdict that the nomadic existence is "the best life" (2:252). He startles Zeyd by asking to be "abandoned" (with a camel) in a ravine of Ybba Moghrair that has a spring and greenery (1:349). Why? But where else should a minimalist live? "He is a free man," says Doughty, who can tote all his earthly goods on one shoulder, and he rejoices when he *can* finally carry his (2:303, 360). He repeatedly affirms the goodness of sleeping in the sand under the stars or even in the rain, and often approves of displays of Moslem austerity: a few things suffice. It is difficult to say how much of this penchant Doughty took to Arabia; from the book we know only what he brought away: "And in truth if one live any time with the Aarab, he will have all his life after a feeling of the desert" (2:481). This we can be sure from his later writings he retained, and we can surmise that it had developed before he left Arabia. For unless Doughty was miscast as "Tom Truth," we cannot discount the preference for the bare life in tents he says he expressed during his travels, or the poignant ending when he sees Jidda and knows his journey is over: "I beheld then the white sea indeed gleaming far under the sun, and tall ships riding, and minarets of the town! My company looked that I should make jubilee" (2:573). And did he? Doughty comments only: "In this plain I saw the last worsted booths of the Ishmaelites. . . ."

NOTES

1 Joseph Addison, *The Spectator,* no. 412, 23 June 1712.
2 George Gordon, Lord Byron, *Childe Harold,* Canto 3, LXII.
3 See "The Arctic Sublime," in *Nature and the Victorian Imagination,* ed. U. C. Knoepflmacher and G. B. Tennyson (Berkeley and Los Angeles: University of California, 1977), 95–112.
4 Hardy, *The Return of the Native* (London: Macmillan, 1963), chap. 1, 12–13.
5 See my "Spiritual Geology: C. M. Doughty and the Land of the Arabs," *Victorian Studies* 16, no. 2 (December 1972): 163–81.
6 The theme of desolation persists in Doughty's poems, e.g., *The Titans.* Cf. Samuel C. Chew, "The Poetry of Charles Montagu Doughty," *North American Review* 222 (December–February 1925–26): 287–98.
7 "Charles Doughty," *North American Review* 214 (1921): 258.
8 "*Arabia Deserta,*" *The Adelphi* 3 (1926): 657.
9 Originally published as *Safar Nameh. Persian Pictures,* 1894. Repr. *Persian Pictures* (New York: Boni and Liveright, 1928), 72.
10 "Charles Doughty and T. E. Lawrence," *The Listener,* 25 December 1947, 1093.
11 From "The Absolute Room," in Gwendolyn MacEwen, *The T. E. Lawrence Poems* (Oakville, Ont.: Mosaic Press, 1982).
12 E. Develing, Introduction to *Minimal Art,* exhibition catalog (n.p.: n.p., 1968), 11–14.
13 Alan Leepa, "Minimal Art and Primary Meanings," in *Minimal Art,* ed. Greg Battcock (New York: Dutton, 1968), 205–7.

STEPHEN E. TABACHNICK

Doughty's Menagerie

Charles M. Doughty has often been accused of being a rare species of writer, and *Arabia Deserta* has been called a hybrid beast that unites several different species of humanistic and scientific writing. But few commentators have noticed that the book itself contains a complete menagerie, including real animals rendered in painstaking detail, humans who become magically transformed into beasts, and purely imaginary half-human, half-animal creatures.[1] Like a *Mundel* or wizard, Doughty as writer ranges through this vast zoo at will, mixing species and genres, denotation and connotation, reality and fantasy. He produces a book which reads like a combination of Frederick Zeuner's *History of Domesticated Animals,* James Frazer's *Golden Bough,* medieval bestiaries, a Beduin oral narration, and, in the suddenness of its human-animal and human-monster transformations, a comic book. In its varied use of animal fact and image, Doughty's book achieves something of the interweaving of animal science and art that Herman Melville creates in *Moby Dick,* becoming, however, a Noah's Ark of different species in the process. Doughty's unique use of animal imagery also reveals the influence of the East on him as a writer, despite his overt denials of such influence.

Doughty's credentials as a factual reporter of the habits and uses of desert animals exceed Melville's expertise on whales, judging from the fact that *Arabia Deserta* has been cited in a recent scientific article on animal husbandry and has been termed "the Arabian horseman's Bible."[2] Indeed, in the course of its thousand-plus pages, the book offers a vast number of observations concerning the shepherding customs of the Beduin, the animal populations of the Arabian town and desert, and the types and habits of, among others, camels, horses, sheep, antelope, leopards, rabbits, foxes, hyenas, ostriches, rats, cats, hedgehogs, goats, wild cats, porcupines, donkeys, birds, cattle, wolves, gazelles, and dogs, even to the point of listing many names the Beduin give to canines (1:474). The "Index and Glossary" lists over thirty separate subheadings relating to horses and, as might be expected, more than one hundred for camels. And there are additional entries on reptiles, fishes, and insects as well.

Doughty's devotion to the scientific amassing of facts about desert animal husbandry becomes apparent especially in the scene in which his persona Khalil has been sold a bad camel by his ostensible friend Sheykh Zeyd and his companion. After expressing briefly his displeasure at having been sold the nineteenth-century Arabian equivalent of a broken-down used car, Doughty proceeds to the real point of his paragraph, facts about camels:

> I bought thus upon their trust, a dizzy camel, old, and nearly past labour and, having lost her front teeth, that was of no more value, in the sight of the nomads, than my wounded camel. I was new in their skill; the camels are known and valued after their teeth, and with re- gard to the hump. They are named by the teeth till the coming of the canines in this manner: the calf of one year, *howwar;* of two, *libny;* the third, *hej;* the fourth, *jitha;* the fifth, *thènny;* the sixth, *ròbba;* the sev- enth, *siddes;* and the eighth, *shâgg en-naba, wafîat, mùfter.* (1:401)

The depth of Doughty's knowledge of Arabian horse raising, too, ap- pears informally throughout the book, as when he describes the positive and negative qualities of the Arabian breeds:

> As for the northern or "Gulf" horses, bred in the nomad dîras [areas] upon the river countries—although of good stature and swifter, they are not esteemed by the inner Arabians. Their flesh being only "of greenness and water" they could not endure in the sun-stricken lan- guishing country. Their own daughters-of-the-desert, albe they are less fairly shaped, are, in the same strains, worth five of the other. . . . Hollow-necked, as the camel, are the Arabian horses: the lofty neck of our thick-blooded horses were a deformity in the eyes of all Arabs. The desert horses, nurtured in a droughty wilderness of hot plain lands beset with small mountains, are not leapers, but very sure of foot to climb in rocky ground. They are good weight carriers. (2:419)

Beyond the factual realm, Doughty reveals a genuine aficionado's eye, disparaging ungainly specimens and noting admirable ones:

> Sometimes the Prince Ibn Rashid rides . . . upon a white mare, and undergrown, as are the Nejd horses in their own country, and not very fairly shaped. (1:661)

Abdullah sat upon a beautiful young stallion of noble blood, that sid-
ling proudly under his fair handling: and seeing the stranger's eye fixed
upon his horse, "Ay, quoth my friend, this one is good in all." (2:418)

On at least one occasion, he becomes positively ecstatic about a beautiful
horse, almost personifying her as a woman:

Under the most ragged of these riders was a very perfect young and
startling chestnut mare,—so shapely there are only few among them.
Never combed by her rude master, but all shining beautiful and gentle
of herself, she seemed a darling life upon that savage soil not worthy of
her gracious pasterns: the strutting tail flowed down even to the
ground, and the mane (*orfa*) was shed by the loving nurture of her
mother Nature. (1:69)

Doughty's deep interest in camels and horses extends to all other forms
of plant and animal life he sees, even the most humble and potentially
repulsive:

I remained therefore to labour in the garden: and in those long hours of
silence, I was a worshipper in the temple, and a devout witness of the
still life of Nature. And when I paused great herb-eating rats sallied
from the four ruinous clay walls: every rat cropped a nettle stalk, and
carried back the tall leaf in his mouth to his cave, and returned for more
pasture. (2:138)

Even in the case of these rats, Doughty grants us a feeling of the deep
kinship of all living things in the "temple of Nature" as they, like him,
struggle to survive against the harsh, impersonal forces of their difficult
environment. On 1:371 we read that the spring rat "is a small white aery
creature in the wide waterless deserts, of a pitiful beauty." Geologist
though Doughty may have been by training, and as much attention as he
gives to rock structures in Arabia as "Titanic" presences, we cannot escape
the sense that he values and appreciates all life forms far more.

One of the things he likes most about the Beduin, since he repeats it
more than once, is that "(nor any life, of man or beast, besides the hounds) is
ever mishandled amongst them" (1:353). He even shows sympathy for the
mistreated Beduin dogs when he writes that "The hounds for their jealous
service have never a good word" (1:382). And one of the few times he
criticizes his own people, the British, is when he subtly condemns the
aristocratic habit of fox hunting. Here his description makes the custom

seem absurd, and he pointedly fails to "correct" Amm Mohammed's disapproval:

> I told the good man how, for a fox-brush, sheykhs in my béled [country] use to ride furiously, in red mantles, upon horses—the best of them worth the rent of some village—with an hundred yelling curs scouring before them; and leaping over walls and dykes they put their necks and all in adventure: and who is in at the hosenny's [fox's] death, he is the gallant man. For a moment the subtil Arabian regarded me with his piercing eyes as if he would say, "Makest thou mirth of me!" but soon again relenting to his frolic humour, "Is this, he laughed, the chevying of the fox?"—in which he saw no grace. (2:163)

Doughty's deep fellow-feeling is apparent in practically every passage in which he discusses the treatment of animals, unless the animals themselves become hostile. In the above passage the dogs have become "curs" because they are part of a vicious hunt for sport rather than necessity; we find no similar disapproval of the Beduin or their greyhounds for fox hunting for food (1:372). And when Khalil is attacked by nomad dogs, "I have not spared for stones" (1:383) to protect himself.

The Beduin go farther, hurling the term "dog" at humans as an insult, as Doughty reports. When Khalil fails to guard Hirfa and Zeyd's tent, allowing two men whom he thought relatives to enter while Hirfa is out, she is upset:

> Men who are pilferers of others' provision, are often called "hounds" by the Beduins. . . . When she returned home some hours after, Hirfa came to chide me, "Ha! careless Khalîl, the dogs have been here! why hast thou not kept my beyt [home]? and did I not bid thee?"—"I have watched for thee, Hirfa, every moment, by thy life! Sitting before the booth in the sun, and not a hair of any dog has entered."—"Alas, Khalîl does not understand that 'the dogs' are men." (1:383–84)

Similarly, Khalil himself is called a Christian "dog" on more than one occasion (2:443, 523, 534), and Khalil's friend at Kheybar, Amm Mohammed, condemns his townsmen for their treatment of Khalil by calling them "hounds, apes, oxen" (2:192).

But just as humans can become animals for the Beduin, so animals can become human on occasion:

> Besides the desert hare which is often startled in the ráhlas [camp movings], before other is the thób [lizard]; which they call here pleasantly,

'Master Hamed, sheykh of wild beasts,' and say he is human, *zil-lamy,*—this is their elvish smiling and playing—and in proof they hold up his little five-fingered hands. (1:371)

Proof that a deep totemism reminiscent of that reported in *The Golden Bough* lies behind these various transformations, a wishing that an animal might be allowed to be human or that the person called by the name of an animal will become one, appears when Doughty tells us that

> In all the Arabic countries there is a strange superstition of parents, (and this as well among the Christian sects of Syria,) that if any child seem to be sickly, of infirm understanding, or his brethren have died before, they will put upon him a wild beast's name, (especially, wolf, leopard, wolverine,)—that their human fragility may take on as it were a temper of the kind of those animals. (1:373–74)

Although Doughty writes that the "sun made me an Arab, but never warped me to Orientalism" (1:95), that is, that he never adopted what he regards as the superstitious thought habits of the Middle East, we find on many occasions that he as writer, just like Khalil's Arab hosts, uses animal epithets to transfer to humans certain characteristics. As writer, he would thereby degrade Khalil's opponents at the touch of a wand, as it were, like Circe turning men into pigs, as if in retrospective retribution for all the times he was literally and figuratively oppressed as an alien and pork-eating Christian in Arabia. In so doing, Doughty becomes not merely a spectator of Middle Eastern ways but a participant in them, and a very poetic one, almost despite himself.

In using references to animals he elsewhere praises to denigrate his enemies, Doughty seems to forget these animals' positive qualities completely, perhaps on the principle that when people act like animals they assume the animals' worst, not best, characteristics. In spite of his sympathy for the dogs despised by the Beduin, he like the nomads calls his opponents "dogs" and "wolves" very frequently: "They are wolves to each other and what if some were hounds to me?" (1:107). A Beduin who robs Khalil of his aneroid barometer "ran away with it like a hound with a good bone in his mouth" (2:343). The Arabs are, we are told, full of "canine suspicions" (1:132). Someone who xenophobically attacks Khalil becomes a "dog-face" (1:508). Sherif Salem, Doughty's most dangerous opponent (whose name, ironically, means "peace"), actually becomes a wolf: "The wolvish nomad sherîf was not so, with a word, to be disappointed of his prey" (2:520, 522). And the Beduin, at their most rapacious, become the "human wolves of the desert" (2:494) whom we fear to meet more than beasts.

Cats, the presence or absence of which Doughty usually notes in a benign, neutral manner, come to symbolize evil transcending a dog's open hostility: Mohammed Aly in the *kella*, or caravan way-station, like Sherif Salem, makes "cats'-eyes" (1:205; 2:526) at Khalil before attacking him physically, and the Ibn Rashid ruling family displays a "(feline) prudence" (1:661), amounting to cunning, in its policies. Similarly, the fox, which Doughty defended from British hunters, is used to denigrate Sheykh Zeyd's cunning: "this nomad fox bestowed his sterile colt upon the Moorish wolf Mohammed Aly" (1:142). And the donkey, upon one of which Khalil the "Good Physician," who would cure men's souls as well as their bodies, leaves Damascus (like St. Paul), suddenly proves an apt means of denigrating a fanatic young man whom Doughty detests: the man shows "vast red circles of mule's teeth" (2:352), symbolizing his stupidity in Doughty's view.

Perhaps most contradictory is Doughty's use of birds, which he positively loves, as negative epithets. Signs of his delight in birds and birdsong are everywhere in *Arabia Deserta:* in the desolate lava fields, "I heard again the cheerful voice of the rock partridge" (1:440), and in a remote valley he hears partridges "calling with ripe and merry note, the livelong summer's day" (1:496). In the blinding heat near Aneyza "I heard then a silver descant of some little bird, that flitting over the desert bushes warbled a musical note which ascended on the gamut! and this so sweetly, that I could not have dreamed the like" (2:445). However, in Hayil "my weary hands seemed slow to the bird-witted wretches that had followed me" (2:342). When Khalil rests outside of Aneyza awaiting friends who do not soon appear, Doughty comments bitterly about the Arabs that "Their friendship is like the voice of a bird upon the spray: if a rumour frighten her she will return no more" (2:472). The Beduin are "bird-witted" in battle, "like screaming hawks" (2:36) who cannot organize themselves, and in their need to scavenge for food display "the greediness of unclean birds" and come "clamorously flocking" (1:127) into the *kella.* Ibn Rashid, in a very mixed characterization, "rules as the hawk among buzzards, with eyes and claws in a land of ravin" (1:661), and in an unforgettable but scarcely attractive simile, a dying pilgrim holds "forth his hands like eagles' claws to man's pity" (1:91). Also, Doughty comments with disgust that "of these bird-like Arabians it is the male sex which is bright-feathered and adorned" (1:637).

When Khalil is shunned by an intolerant Moslem divine at the same
time that the man petitions him through an intermediary for medicines,
Doughty finds the occasion for his most complex use of bird imagery as a
means of negative portrayal:

> The peasant divine looked up more mildly, yet would he not hold
> speech with one of the heathen; but leaning over to the negro Aly, who
> brought me hither, he charged him, in a small dying voice, to ask,
> 'Had the Nasrâny a remedy for the emerods [hemorrhoids]?'—the
> negro shouted these words to the company! "It sufficeth," responded
> the morose pedant; and settling his leathern chaps his dunghill spirit
> reverted to her wingless contemplation, at the gates of the Meccàwy's
> paradise. (2:405)

In what amounts to a conceit or extended metaphor, the holy man's spirit
becomes a bird without wings and his voice anything but beautiful and
birdlike, while Doughty has chosen to use the word "Meccàwy" instead of
"Moslem" here because of its resemblance to a hoarse crow's cry. The accent
mark on "càw" points up the pun.

But not only Khalil's enemies become animals in Doughty's recapitulation of his experiences; so does Khalil. We have noted how the Arabs turn
him into a "dog" many times; toward the end of the book, he compares
himself to one: "I had been bitten by their greyhound, in the knee. . . .—
Ah! what horror, to die like a rabid hound in a hostile land" (2:483). Now
we hear Doughty's anguish, clearly indicating his estate as the lowest
"man" on the totem pole in Arabia, as well as his fear of disease. In a more
ironic vein, when Khalil is attacked for being a Christian and learns that a
camel, because irrational, cannot be so attacked, he mutters, "Then account me a camel" (2:443). We feel his bitterness under the irony because a
camel is freer from human enmity than Khalil is at this point. And near
Mecca, when he most fears exposure as a Christian,

> The thelûl [camel] of one who was riding a little before me fell on a
> stone, and put a limb out of joint,—an accident which is without
> remedy! Then the next riders made lots hastily for the meat; and dis-
> mounting, they ran-in to cut the fallen beast's throat: and began with
> their knives to hack the not fully dead carcase. . . . I thought, in few
> minutes, my body might be likewise made a bloody spectacle. (2:517)

Here we have a chilling imaginative displacement of himself into the
camel's skin; and he is almost in fact in the camel's unenviable position as

soon as Salem begins to torment him. But shortly after this incident, Doughty lets us understand that just as he fears the Arabs, so they fear him and view him like "some perilous beast that had been taken in the toils" (2:522). And just as Doughty dislikes polygamy for little reason other than custom, so Sleyman, in Hayil, thinks that "as the horse covers the mare it is said . . . the Nasâra [Christians] be engendered,—wellah like the hounds!" (1:656).

Thus, the transformation from human to animal or, far less frequently, from animal to human (as in the case of the *thob* and the beautiful mare) takes place in *Arabia Deserta* with magical swiftness and completeness and serves to remind us always that Doughty felt that in Arabia he was living in a human zoo, in an unreal fable in which anything was possible. Even Khalil's many comments upon and arguments about Beduin eating habits remind us that we are all ultimately animals, whether we eat pork or porcupines:

> The hedgehog . . . is eaten in these parts by Fejîr tribesmen, but by their neighbours disdained. . . . Selím brought in an urchin which he had knocked on the head, he roasted Prickles in the coals and . . . distributed the morsels. . . . That which fell to me I put away bye and bye to the starveling greyhound; but the dog smelling the meat rejected it. When another day I told this tale in the next tribes, they laughed maliciously, that the Fukara should eat that which the hounds would not of. (1:371)

The Arabs will not, in turn, eat pork, which leads them to call Khalil a Christian "swine" on occasion (1:130).

But Doughty's various uses of animals to describe people (and we must remember that, as writer of the book, he is responsible for the Arabs' dialogue as well as Khalil's), although fearful, imaginative, sarcastic, and witty by turns, do not represent the full extent of his menagerie. In addition to usual animals and animal imagery, he also describes many supernatural creatures, such as genies, monsters (the *ghrol*), witches, Beni Kalb (a dog-people tribe), ghosts, satyrs, werewolves, warlocks, sea-born Christians, and various other bogies. On 1:93 he gives us a picture of a *ghrol*, described as "a monster of the desert," featuring one Cyclops eye and a voice that can be disguised as that of its victim's mother or sister (1:92). On 1:530 Horeysh the guide is worried about whether a sound he hears comes from the ghosts of Christians or Jews. The Beduin swear they have met the Beni Kalb, whose women are human but whose men are "white hounds" (1:171).

Despite Doughty's overt disclaimer of belief in the Arabs' tales and magic, he describes these supernatural beings so well and gives us so many of them that the reader begins to wonder whether Doughty is not of the Arabs' party without knowing it, at least in his role as writer. When he writes, for instance, that "All is horror at Kheybar" (2:97), we can apply this statement to his own literary description of the place, full of Gothic horrors. He packs a full five chapters of volume 2, amounting to perhaps 150 pages, with witch and genie tales; accounts of superstitions; brooding, darkened descriptions of a pestilential physical and mental atmosphere; and his own mental anguish caused by his virtual incarceration by the town's dictator. He recreates this atmosphere so well that the reader lives in it with Khalil, who for three and a half months is kept under threat of execution by the corrupt Turkish commandant Abdullah es-Siruan and under suspicion by the superstitious townspeople, who practice practically every form of magical belief, including dream interpretation, a refusal to eat leeks and chicken meat, and the notion that Christians have the gift of finding treasure. Even Khalil's one seemingly rational friend, Amm Mohammed, who denies the reality of witches, completely believes in evil genies, and Doughty captures his dialogue so convincingly that Amm Mohammed almost persuades us, too, of his belief:

> "The jân are sore afraid of me," quoth Amm Mohammed. An half of the jân or jenûn, inhabiting the seven stages under the earth, are malicious (heathen) spirits . . . and an half are accounted Moslemîn." (2:209)

Amm Mohammed believes that "nearly an half part of all who bear the form of mankind" are such evil genies (2:211), and that they can be differentiated from humans " 'only by a strangeness of the eyes—the opening of their eyelids is sidelong-like with the nose' " (2:214). Furthermore, according to Amm Mohammed, "many an house cat and many a street dog" (2:211) are *jan*.

Witches, it seems, are even more prevalent than genies, and "There were few at Kheybar that could not tell of some night's fearful jeopardy of their precious soul and body" (2:125). Why not, in a setting in which Christians are said to have been born in the sea (2:191) and Khalil is thought a warlock sent to bewitch the village (2:108)? Unfortunately for us as readers, perhaps, Khalil never sees a *jin* or a witch, although he says

"'I would willingly see them'" (2:125). However, Doughty as writer does display a certain affinity with the witches of Kheybar: according to the inhabitants, if the witches meet a man coming home late, "they will compel him to lie with them; and if he should deny them they will change him into the form of some beast—an ox, a horse, or an ass" (2:125). As we have seen, Doughty too proves able to transform humans into animals at a word; but he goes mere witches one better, changing opponents into fabulous creatures upon occasion: "That was but guile of the wild Beduwy, who with his long matted locks seemed less man than satyr or werwolf" (1:636). In the climactic section of the book, Sherif Salem smiles "betwixt friendly and fiendly" (2:534), has a "hardly human visage" (2:536), and becomes at one point "the tormentor" (2:528); that is, an incarnation of the Devil himself.

But the best example of Doughty's own sleight of hand in changing people into beasts, both real and fantastic, occurs not in the Salem or Kheybar episodes of *Arabia Deserta* but in the *kella* with Mohammed Aly, the tower commandant. Here Doughty mixes human, animal, and supernatural metaphors to recapitulate this man's seemingly contradictory, fickle personality:

> "Out!" cried the savage wretch . . . then . . . the Moorish villain suddenly struck me with the flat hand and all his mad force in the face. . . . He shouted also with savage voice, "Dost thou not know me yet?" . . . Mohammed Aly, trembling and frantic, leaping up then in his place, struck me again in the doorway, with all his tiger's force. . . . The sickly captain of ruffian troopers for a short strife had the brawns of a butcher, and I think three peaceable men might not hold him. . . . "—Aha! by Ullah! shouted the demon or ogre, now I will murder thee" . . . but snatching my beard with canine rage, the ruffian plucked me hither and thither, which is a most vile outrage. . . . As we waken sometimes of an horrid dream, I might yet break through this extreme mischief to the desert. (1:206–7)

How can one "know" a constantly changing monster? In the course of this passage, a usually peaceable Mohammed Aly, who suddenly erupts into violence for no reason understood by Khalil at this point, goes from a human "wretch" and "Moorish villain" like Othello to a "tiger" and "demon and ogre," subsiding into a "canine rage" and finally into an ordinary human "ruffian" again at last. Earlier, Doughty has called him a "caterpillar" capable of "creeping" (1:132) into favor, with a "visage much like that of a fiend" (1:131). A short time after the outburst described above, Mohammed Aly is sitting happily, calling Khalil a "beloved." We have witnessed a sudden Middle Eastern outburst of temper and its equally rapid subsidence through the eyes of a Westerner who is at this point in time unfamiliar with this phenomenon. Mohammed Aly's personality remains forever a mystery because of the ability Doughty as author gives him to change constantly. We are indeed in a "horrid" but fascinating dream.

So we have ogres and demons as well as witches and genies in *Arabia Deserta*. But no book on the Middle East would be complete without a mummy, at least since the time of Giovanni Belzoni's excavations in Egypt in the early nineteenth century, and so Doughty gives us one, as if to make the catalog complete. During his explorations in the Borj rocks, he notices that "A loathesome mummy odour, in certain monuments, is heavy in the nostrils. . . . I saw the sand floor full of rotten clouts, shivering in every wind, and taking them up, I found them to be those dry bones' grave-clothes!" (1:149). Like all the other supernatural creatures in *Arabia Deserta,* Doughty's one mummy is at once beguiling and repulsive and fits perfectly the Gothic and fabulous miragelike atmosphere of much of the book, in which nothing is quite what it first appears to be.

On occasion, even complete monsters can become human, reversing the usual transformation and the reader's expectations. We have seen Mohammed Aly lose his rage and become affectionate toward Khalil again. Similarly, the devilish and half-human Salem does, after all, offer Khalil a drink when he is thirsty, because "there remained a human kindness" (2:527) in Salem. The wicked jailer Abdullah es-Siruan desperately wants Khalil to say the forgiving "last word of Peace" (2:235) as he leaves Kheybar. And Mohammed Ibn Rashid, for all his hawklike cruelty, is characterized by Khalil, after all is said and done, as a " 'worthy man' " (2:543), much to the good sherif of Mecca's surprise. The wonder is not, perhaps, that various wicked Arabians should be characterized by Doughty as animals and monsters but rather that Doughty allows us to see some good in all of them and some connection to ourselves. But then, he writes that "there is no land so perilous which by humanity he [the traveller] may not pass, for man is of one mind everywhere, ay, and in their kind, even the brute animals of the same foster earth" (1:305).

In the end, Doughty's menagerie primarily represents the human empire which was, it appears from his report, not much different in nineteenth-century Arabia from what it is here and now, in our variegated world. His book tells us, via its cartoonlike transformations and hidden monsters, that character is fickle and difficult to understand, especially across cultures. Would Mohammed Aly's outburst, completely incomprehensible and unforgivable to Khalil the Englishman and today's Western reader, have seemed equally demonic to a Middle Easterner used to such sudden explosions of temper and sudden repentance? After all, it emerges that Mohammed Aly thought, albeit mistakenly, that Khalil was deliberately trying to shortchange him for his services. Is Khalil himself the martyr that he seems to us (and to himself) to be, or a warlock come to bewitch and threaten Arabian villages with strange new ideas? Perhaps who is being transformed into what depends entirely on the perspective of the person watching. As Doughty comments in his role as narrator, "must I not seem to them, in holding another opinion, to be a perverse and unreasonable person?" (1:216). And in a very forward-looking relativistic passage, he also says, "All things are much as we esteem them" (1:415). Perhaps, as Amm Mohammed claims, half of mankind are really monsters disguised as humans: we ourselves could be perceived by people of other cultures as strange beings and see them as grotesque.

No less than character in *Arabia Deserta,* "fact" proves a subtle quantity, for by gradations it becomes fantasy, whether Doughty consciously wanted this to happen or not. Seen in a sandstorm, a camel can become a *ghrol.* Is the strange bird on the frontispiece at Medain Salih's Nabataean ruins "some kind of sea-fowl" as some people say, or a falcon, as others conjecture (1:155–56)? Are the el-Hejr monuments an exciting "sleeping riddle" (1:147), as Khalil thinks at first, or only "rat holes" set in "ghastly grinning ranges" (1:553), as he feels the third time he visits them? When reading *Arabia Deserta* we can never quite trust our eyes or minds because of the way Doughty mixes fact and fiction. We half-expect unknown creatures to lurk in the forbidding Empty Quarter, which Khalil must reluctantly leave a blank on his map.

Doughty's book, with its record of a massive hunt for facts, helps us know Arabia, but it also teaches us subtly how much we will never know about any place and about life itself. Doughty comments that "Commonly the longer one lives in a fabulous time or country, the weaker will become his judgement" (1:216). The reader emerges from the "fabulous country" of *Arabia Deserta*'s 1,300 pages like Khalil on the beach at Jidda, with his "judgement" of reality weakened and his perspective on life enormously enriched.

NOTES

1   Anne Treneer, however, has an excellent chapter on "The Land and the Creatures" in *Arabia Deserta* (Tr, 56–73).
2   See A. E. Dorman, "The Camel in Health and Disease," *British Veterinary Journal* 140 (1984): 616–33, and George Conn, *The Arabian Horse in Fact, Fantasy and Fiction* (New York: Barnes and Noble, 1959), 5. The intelligence manual by Hugh Scott et al., *Western Arabia and the Red Sea* (London: Naval Intelligence Division, 1946), also quotes Doughty on Arabian flora and fauna at several points.

EDWARD A. LEVENSTON

The Style of Arabia Deserta: A Linguistic Analysis

The style Charles Doughty created for *Travels in Arabia Deserta* is quite without parallel in the history of English prose literature. It is a unique instrument forged for a unique purpose. Doughty himself gives us a hint toward understanding the function of this style when, in the preface to the first edition, he likens the book to "a mirror, wherein is set forth faithfully some part of the soil of Arabia, smelling of *sámn* [butter] and camels" (1:29). The style of a text is the linguistic equivalent of the smell of an environment—inescapable, all-pervasive, and distilled from several elements. What those elements are and how they serve to evoke the "smell" of Arabia is what I shall explore in this essay.

Doughty's preoccupation with the "soil of Arabia," to the exclusion of any topic not related somehow to his experience of Arabian life, is vividly demonstrated by the beginning and end of the book. *Travels in Arabia Deserta* begins with a question from an unnamed friend of Doughty's:

> "Tell me (said he), since thou art here again in the peace and assurance of Ullah, and whilst we walk, as in the former years, toward the new blossoming orchards, full of the sweet spring as the garden of God, what moved thee, or how couldst thou take such journeys into the fanatic Arabia?" (1:39)

Setting aside the content of this inquiry, let us examine closely the form it takes. That the remark was made in Arabic can be inferred, though it is not directly stated. The use of the archaic second person singular forms (thou, art, thee, couldst) reflects the distinction in Arabic between second person singular and plural forms. The spelling "Ullah" represents for Doughty a closer approximation of the Arabic pronunciation of God's

name than the conventional English representation "Allah," with its mis-
leading suggestion of a half-open front vowel in the initial syllable. ("No
Arab could well understand a Frank who pronounced God's name thus"—
from Doughty's glossary [2:688].) And the final phrase "into the fanatic
Arabia" echoes the Arabic use of the definite article—Beled el-Aarab—
when referring to the Arabian peninsula.

The reader has been led into this question with only a very abrupt
introduction:

> A new voice hailed me of an old friend when, first returned from the
> Peninsula, I paced again in that long street of Damascus which is called
> Straight; and suddenly taking me wondering by the hand "Tell me (said
> he) . . ." (1:39)

Thus, from the very outset of the narrative, and without much warning,
the reader is expected to set aside much of his British cast of thought,
interact in Arabic, and become part of the Moslem world, sharing the
"peace and assurance of Ullah."

The book ends, twenty-one months and over twelve hundred pages
later, even more abruptly. Doughty, dressed as an emir-el-Aarab (Arab
prince), has finally reached Jidda after incredible trials and hardships. He
comments only:

> We passed the gates and rode through the street to "the Sherîf's palace":
> but it is of a merchant (one called his agent), who has lately built this
> stately house,—the highest in Jidda. (2:574)

And then—I quote the final paragraph in its entirety:

> On the morrow I was called to the open hospitality of the British consu-
> late. (2:574).

Not a word about the details of the reception Doughty received or the
personality of the consul, for these are totally irrelevant to the themes and
purpose of the book. To read *Travels in Arabia Deserta* is to share Doughty's
sojourn in an alien society, to become with him a desert nomad, to put
aside one's native language and one's native habits, yet never to lose one's
own inner integrity and non-Mohammedan faith.

Doughty lived through these experiences in Arabic; though he teaches
his Beduin hosts a few words in English ("Girl, bring milk," "tobacco,"
and "werigud"), there is no record anywhere in the book of his having

conversed in English at any time during his nearly two years of wanderings. But the reader who knows no Arabic must relive this experience *in
English*. And therein lies the miracle of *Travels in Arabia Deserta* and the
fascination of the style created by Doughty to serve this extraordinary
purpose.

It is important to stress that Doughty is not writing for readers who
know any Arabic when they begin reading the book, though certainly
they will have picked up a considerable amount by the time they reach the
end. For such an Arabic-ignorant reader, those few features of the book's
opening question noted earlier serve essentially to suggest that it was not
said in English rather than specifically to indicate that it was said in
Arabic. (Hemingway in *For Whom the Bell Tolls* makes exactly the same use
of "thou" whenever he wishes to suggest that his characters are speaking
Spanish [cf. Ta, 60].) In this case we can infer that Arabic is the friend's
language of utterance from the sentence's mention of Damascus, the site of
the encounter, rather than from any specifically Arabic borrowings.
Though Issam Safady, a native speaker of Arabic from Hebron, feels that
"Arabic syntax and phrasing . . . are the source of the additional enjoyment I find as an Arab in reading *Travels in Arabia Deserta*,"[1] the point is
that this is an *additional* enjoyment. The main delight of the style, equally
available to all readers, is the impression it gives us of another way of
looking at the world. And we often assume that this is an Arabic way,
even when we know no Arabic. As Lascelles Abercrombie wrote to Walt
Taylor, expressing the insight of the kind of reader Doughty hoped for:

> What you say about the Arabic structure of his style is startling to me;
> for I have for years been telling people that C.M.D. thought in Arabic
> and then put it into English. This was pure guesswork, founded on
> nothing at all as far as *knowledge* goes; but it is most gratifying to find I
> was right.[2]

Though Walt Taylor (one of the first scholars to examine the language
of *Arabia Deserta* in detail) grants the appropriateness of the style to the
subject-matter, he denies any causal connection between the two:

> I do not suggest that Doughty wrote in an Arabicized style merely
> because he was writing about Arabs and Arabia. He was too great a
> master to play such a trick with the English language. His justification
> is much more important and much more subtle; it was precisely in
> Arabic that Doughty found his model for pure English.[3]

It is certainly true that Doughty himself had greater ambitions than the mere creation of a style appropriate to a tale of wanderings in the deserts of Arabia. As he wrote to his biographer, "A principal cause of writing [*Arabia Deserta*] was besides the interest of the Semitic life in tents, my dislike of the Victorian English; and I wished to show, and thought I might be able to show, that there was something else" (H, 114–15). However, if his aim was by example to reform English prose, he failed in that purpose. He succeeded in creating something else—but no one else could use it. The circumstances that produced the style of *Travels in Arabia Deserta* could no more be repeated than Doughty's own wanderings could be relived by later generations. When T. E. Lawrence came to record his desert exploits in *Seven Pillars of Wisdom,* he too sought and found an appropriate style. But it is not the style of *Travels in Arabia Deserta.* That was and remains uniquely matched to Doughty's own experience.

What are the techniques used with such skill by Doughty that he can almost persuade a reader who knows no Arabic that he is reading Arabic? They are, with one exception, of two kinds, and they complement each other:

1. Distancing: the use of linguistic features, at all levels—graphic, phonological, grammatical, lexical—which are archaic, unusual, not contemporary in idiom, and serve to *distance* the reader from all familiar responses to English.

2. Arabizing: the use of linguistic features at two levels—phonological and lexical—which are specifically and patently Arabic in origin and serve to bring the reader *closer* to an Arabian view of life. By "patently Arabic," I mean those features which are obviously Arabic even to readers who know no Arabic: lexical items, paralinguistic noises and gestures, and of course the occasional transliteration of whole utterances in Arabic.

Doughty's use of Arabic *syntax and idiom,* however, constitutes a special third category which straddles the first two in its effects. For the reader who knows no Arabic, the effect of Arabic syntax or literally translated idiom in English is usually to move him away from English norms without bringing him closer to an Arabian view of life—the expression simply seems strange and he does not know why; for him, it is a distancing feature. For the reader who knows Arabic, such a deviant English utterance is immediately recognizable as Arabic-based—indeed, he can literally translate the Arabic-based syntax or idiom back into Arabic, thus reconstructing its original Arabic form; for him, it is an Arabizing feature. For the reader like Lascelles Abercrombie, however, who strongly suspects that the structure of a given sentence is Arabic-based but who knows little or no Arabic and is therefore unable to be sure of the correctness of his suspicions, the effect is both to distance him from familiar responses to English *and* to bring him closer to an Arabian view of life.

I shall therefore discuss the linguistic features of the text under *three* headings: distancing features, Arabizing features, and Arabic syntax, whose function depends on the knowledge and acumen of the individual reader. Doughty's own attitude toward the reader is, as we shall see, ambivalent. On the one hand, he assumes the reader knows no Arabic and provides a detailed glossary. Yet occasionally he will quote an entire utterance without translation, either in the text or in the glossary (see below).

All the linguistic features to be discussed occur both in the narrative and descriptive passages and in the many conversations quoted directly in the course of the narrative. Detailed statistical analysis would no doubt confirm Walt Taylor's guess that archaisms occur proportionately more frequently in the conversations. And such Arabic expletives as *wellah* (verily, indeed) and *billah* (by Ullah) obviously occur only in the reported speech. However, the bulk of this essay will survey the linguistic features of the style without making a distinction between narrative and conversation, though in most cases it will be clear from the nature of the example which is being quoted. Let us look first at the features which explicitly bring the reader closer to an Arabian view of life.

I.I. ARABIZING FEATURES: ARABIC VOCABULARY

Doughty's use of Arabic vocabulary, like most of his lexical revivals and innovations, has been well studied by Walt Taylor, who accurately describes Doughty's practice when introducing Arabic words:

> When Doughty uses an Arabic word for the first time, whether it is already anglicized or not, he normally writes it in italics and adds an explanation or translation of the word: he presents it, that is, as an Arabic word written in transliteration, and not as an English word. Having once defined the word he is free to use it later in the roman alphabet (with or without inverted commas), without further explanation to the reader. . . . Thus *wasm* (a tribal mark) becomes 'wasm' or simply wasm, used as an English word without apology. Soon, there

may be a possessive form wasm's, and the word forms an English plural
wasms. [1:166][4]

This gradual integration of a strange word into everyday vocabulary parallels Doughty's own experience of learning the language and the culture.
And by participating in this learning experience the reader also gradually
acquires almost all the words needed to describe daily life in the Arabian
desert or desert township. At first camels are simply camels; as we read on
we learn to distinguish a handsome *thelul* from a slower *naga:* "I found a
likely young man of the Khamâla, who had a good thelûl; for ten reals he
would mount me upon another, and for the price I might leave him my
nâga" (1:553). The vast majority of words used in this way are of course
nouns and required to describe features of Beduin life for which no equivalent exists in English: *radif* (the back rider on a dromedary), *samn* (clar-
ified butter), *khanjar* (crooked girdle-knife). Even when equivalents do
exist, Doughty frequently uses the Arabic word, since the apparent equiv-
alence is illusory: coffee is not the same as *kahwa,* neither in quality nor
quantity; a housewife has neither the same duties nor the same respon-
sibilities as a *jarra.* In such cases we do not find or expect consistency.
Doughty is not writing in Arabic. But the occasional use of the Arabic
word for a familiar concept—*hareem* for women, *rafik* for travelling companion—is a necessary and constant reminder of the vast difference between the conventions of the English town and countryside and those of
Arabia Deserta.

There are interesting differences, not noted by Walt Taylor, between
the use of Arabic made by Doughty in the descriptive and expository
sections of the narrative and his rendering of Arabic conversation. Whereas in the narrative the Arabic words are almost entirely nouns, within the
conversations Doughty introduces other parts of speech. There are many
adjectives, particularly those used to affirm or deny personal qualities:

". . . and see, I said, that thou art not false, Sâlem."—"Nay, wellah, I
am not *khayin* [treacherous]. . . ." (2:527)

"Wellah, sheykh Khalîl, we are *ghrashemîn,* rude (he said) and ignorant." (2:125)

Both these utterances contain *wellah*—by God!—which, as Doughty
points out in his glossary, is not really an oath but "is come to signify
verily, indeed" (2:692). In modern linguistic terms it is a sentence adverb,

an *attitudinal disjunct,* and, though most frequently utterance-initial, can (like *billah*) occupy just about any position in sentence structure:

". . . we found it all wellah in the sand . . ." (1:565)

"The head [of a lance] is large as an hand-breadth and waggleth billah as a tongue, athirst to lap up his enemies' blood." (1:610)

"It is thus amongst us Beduw, *ayb,* a shame, wellah." (1:273)

Verbs also occur, in both inflected and uninflected forms, though only infrequently:

"Give us tobacco (cried he), and come down and drink kahwa with us, and if no we will *nô'kh* (make kneel) thy camel, and take it perforce." (2:78)

No'kh here is the imperative form, the actual command given to the camel, not the inflected form appropriate to the sentence. Contrast " 'The Engleys also *yuháshimûn* (favour) the Sûltàn el-Islam' " (1:595), where the verb is quoted in the third person plural form, as befits the context. This particular structure also occurs several times in the narrative when Doughty feels the need to describe an action for which English lacks a word:

Villager passengers in the summer heat *yugáillûn* [they take rest at noon]. (1:594)

The sun risen, they [the camels] are driven again to the watering . . . and then turning away of themselves *yusuddirûn,* they "breast" upward. (1:507)

So far I have quoted single Arabic words that become integrated within the structure of an English sentence. There are also plenty of sentences that are entirely Arabic. These range from short, one-word utterances (*bess*/enough; *arakh*/I depart; *khalas*/he is ended) to simple questions and answers (*min eyn*/from whence; *la tanshud*/ask not of it), with occasionally even longer utterances, particularly when these are phatic formulae rather than creative uses of language:

she murmured a sweet proverb of their dîra, *widd el ghrarîb ahlhu,* "the desire of the stranger is to his own people; speed the stranger home." (2:298)

Issherub wa keyyif râs-ak. Drink! and make thy head dream with pleasance. (1:587)

Doughty's translations are of course invariably into archaic English: "from whence" rather than "where from"; "pleasance" and not "pleasure."

Both features of Doughty's style I have been discussing—the use of non-English words and the interpolation of non-English sentences—occur also in the speech of bilinguals whenever they converse with other bilinguals. This is known to sociolinguists as code-switching and has a large and growing literature.[5] The two main questions this literature tries to answer are (1) what grammatical constraints govern the *position* of code-switching in sentence structure? and (2) what *motivation* is there—linguistic, psychological, or sociological—for code-switching? It would be interesting to see how far Doughty's practice in writing confirms the findings of linguists who have analyzed bilingual conversation. My impression is that the parallel is very close; Hebrew-English bilinguals, for instance, in a conversation whose base language is English, will use the Hebrew attitudinal disjunct *davke* in almost any position in English sentence structure, much as Doughty varies the position of *wellah* and *billah*.

What emerges clearly from the study of bilingual code-switching is that it is not to be regarded as a deficiency, an inability to express oneself adequately in a single language, but rather a skill, an ingenious exploitation of a twofold repertoire of linguistic resources. Bilinguals enjoy code-switching; it creates an intimacy of shared knowledge. The relevance of these findings to the study of Doughty's style in *Arabia Deserta* is clear: he treats his reader as a fellow-bilingual even though he knows that this is normally not the case. Translations and glossary entries are provided for those unfortunate readers who do not meet his ideal. And sometimes even these are missing. It is impossible to work out precisely the literal meaning of the "scoffing Syrian epigraph" quoted as "deriding the folly of any pilgrim who will bring his querulous hareem upon this voyage": "*Ibn el-karra, ellathi behájiz el-marra*" (1:121).

I.2. ARABIZING FEATURES: ARABIC PARALINGUISTIC NOISE AND GESTURES

Besides the direct lexical borrowings from Arabic I have been discussing so far, there are two other linguistic techniques used by Doughty which explicitly function to persuade the reader he is experiencing Beduin speech at first hand. Both are features of speech behavior not normally found in dictionaries or grammar books and consequently little studied by orthodox stylisticians—I find no mention of them in existing studies of

Doughty. They are the transcription of paralinguistic noise and the description of gesture.

The term paralinguistic noise covers primarily the range of sounds produced by members of a particular speech community to express emotion: joy, pain, disgust, anger, amazement, and so on.[6] It may also be extended to include the sounds made to communicate with animals[7] and perhaps the way natural noises are imitated. All these noises seem "natural" to those who produce them—doesn't everybody respond "ouch!" to sudden pain? Actually they are as arbitrary as any other lexical features of language—speakers of Mende in Sierra Leone react to pain with a high-pitched glottalized "ee!"

To express surprise, Doughty's desert companions do not go "ooh" or "ah." They utter with falling intonation a diphthong, of which both elements may be stressed, preceded by a glottal stop. It could be transcribed [ʔæI] and is written by Doughty as "eigh." Thus Amm Mohammed, trying—with no great success—to teach Khalil the wisdom of lying about one's origins when travelling in foreign parts, tells of a visit he once paid to some Persian pilgrims:

> "When I went to their tents, they said to me, 'O Haj Mohammed, be'st thou shîiy or sunni?' 'Eigh! Sirs, I answered, I am a shîiy.'—'Ah! forgive our asking, dear brother Mohammed; and dine with us today.'"
> (2:224)

Disgust often coupled with anger is clearly the effect of "akhs" [aχs], not a "word" listed by Doughty in his glossary:

> but when the smooth Mecca merchant heard that the stranger riding with the camel-men was a Nasrâny, he cried, "Akhs! A Nasrâny in these parts!" and with the horrid inurbanity of their (jealous) religion, he added, "Ullah curse his father!" and stared on me with a face worthy of the koran! (2:527; see also 2:280–81 for a very similar example)

And "ouf," the noise which for English speakers signifies effort, is used by Doughty's companions to underline wonder or amazement:

> "His tent is large, so large! and he is rich, so rich,—ouf! all is there liberality." (2:300; see also 2:571)

Though readers of *Travels in Arabia Deserta* will hardly emerge with enough Arabic to converse with a Beduin, they should be able to cope with a Beduin camel:

the householders, going forth from the booths, lure to them as they run lurching by, with loud *Wolloo-wolloo-wolloo,* and to stay them *Wòh-ho, wòh-ho, wòh-ho!* they chide any that strikes a tent-cord with *hutch!* (1:261)

Every man drives up his beasts, with *weeaho! weeaho! weeaho!* encouraging them to drink. (1:428)

The bearing camels they make to kneel under their burdens with the guttural voice, *ikh-kh-kh!* (1:262; see also 2:290, where the same command is described as "hissing")

Finally, somewhere between the paralinguistic noises discussed so far and conventional lexical items are the onomatopoeic words used to represent specific sounds. Like the commands given to camels, these are included by Doughty in his glossary. Beduin bullets go "trang!" when you fire them (2:169) but "deh!" when they hit you (1:393). And as for the sound of a comet passing through the desert sky:

They remembered another in the last ten years, which shot over the earth in the night-time, casting a noon-day gleam upon the dark wilderness. "The sound of it was *ker-ker-ker-ker;*"—but thus say the Aarab in their talk of all travelling noises. (1:510)

Like paralinguistic noises, gestures are also arbitrary and restricted to specific speech communities. English speakers may find it natural to point with their forefingers, but speakers of other languages use their thumbs— or even their chins. Doughty is alive to the importance of gesture as an inseparable feature of face-to-face communication[8] and gives us several insights into the gestural conventions of Beduin Arabs:

The men rose after their breakfast and loaded upon the camels,—but not my bags!—and drove forth. I spoke to the elder Heteymy . . . but knitting the shoulders and turning up his palms he answered gravely, "What can I do? it is Sâlih's matter, wellah, I may not meddle in it." (2:82)

Later the same day it begins to rain:

I said to Thaifullah, "God sends his blessing again upon the earth."— "Ay verily," he answered devoutly, and kissed his pious hand towards the flashing tempest, and murmured the praises of Ullah. (2:83)

Though this second example may seem self-explanatory it is, like nearly all gestures and paralinguistic noise, complementary to the spoken word and not fully comprehensible without its verbal context. I conclude this section by quoting three gestures without the speech that accompanied them. See if you can guess what they mean before you look them up:

". . . he stroked down his visage to the beard . . ." (2:29)

". . . he clapped the left palm to the side of his neck . . ." (2:31)

". . . with an Arabian gesture, balancing his outstretched hand down to the ground . . ." (2:50)

2.1. DISTANCING FEATURES: LEXICAL

Turning now to those features of language which Doughty uses to distance his text from the prose norms of his times, let us look first at his choice of words. Of the forty-one pages of Walt Taylor's study, *Doughty's English,* twenty-five (1939:11–35) are devoted to an elaborate classification and listing of the different elements of Doughty's vocabulary: extensions of meaning of existing words, innovation, compound words, compound adjectives, Arabic words, dialect, Chaucerian and Spenserian words, other obsolete words, learned words, colloquialisms, Arab measurement, and homonyms. It is easy to find fault with his classification, both in principle and in detail. He does not clearly distinguish between obsolete words and obsolete meanings of words in common use. Many of the words he classifies as "dialect" have been shown to occur in works of literature Doughty is known to have studied.[9] And his lists of items under each category, though impressive, are by no means exhaustive.[10] Even from the few quotations I have given so far—all chosen for reasons quite unconnected with Doughty's non-Arabic vocabulary—it is possible to supplement Taylor's list of obsolete "words" with usages that, as he says, "for the most part fell out of use in the seventeenth century, some of them in the sixteenth" (1939:29):

lure v.i. "to call loudly." (Last recorded as an intransitive verb in 1626. Current uses are all transitive.)

perforce adverb "by violence, forcibly." (Last recorded in 1670, though the current meaning "by necessity, unavoidably" could also apply in this context.)

Similarly, for each of his categories it would not be difficult to cite further examples. Among the compound nouns he does not cite "boy-fool" (1:418). To the compound adjectives add "wooden-weary" (1:473).

Nevertheless, it is an impressive piece of scholarship, essential reading for anyone interested in Doughty's style, and this study is intended to supplement, not supersede it. Taylor sums up his feelings about Doughty's vocabulary in the following words:

> Doughty gave himself freedom to use any word which served his purpose, whether that word were current or obsolete, or a dialect word or a colloquialism; and where existing words failed he made new ones from English roots, or Latin, or French, or Arabic; or he gave a new meaning, where that was convenient, to an existing English word.[11]

To which one should add that Doughty's immediate purpose—the creation of a style appropriate to the description of his desert wanderings—was well served by the *juxtaposition* of words from so many diverse sources, all together creating the effect of strangeness that I have tried to define. Doughty, for example, calls the mid-afternoon call to prayer "the half-afternoon íthin" (2:380), juxtaposing a compound neologism (not listed in Taylor) with an Arabic word no longer italicized.

There are, however, several disadvantages to studying Doughty's vocabulary exclusively in terms of individual words or meanings and their provenance. First, it distracts attention from the solid core of familiar, everyday words. Doughty describes the Solubba, the tinkers of the desert, as follows:

> In summer, when the Beduw have no more milk, loading their light tents and household stuff, with what they have gained, upon asses, which are their only cattle, they forsake the Aarab encampment, and hold on their journey through the wide khála. The Solubby household go then to settle themselves remotely, upon some good well of water, in an unfrequented wilderness, where there is game. They only (of all men) are free of the Arabian deserts to travel whithersoever they would; paying to all men a petty tribute, they are molested by none of them. Home-born, yet have they no citizenship in the Peninsula. No Beduwy, they say, will rob a Solubby, although he met him alone, in the deep of the wilderness, and with the skin of an ostrich in his hand, that is worth a thelûl. (1:324–25)

There is scarcely a word here worthy of philological comment, apart from the Arabisms *khala* (desert waste) and *thelul,* the use of "remotely" as an adverb of place for "in a remote place," and the archaic "whithersoever." Everywhere else the vocabulary is totally familiar, if occasionally with a slightly unusual flavor (free *of* the deserts, in the *deep* of the wilderness). Doughty is never wantonly obscure. When familiar words express his meaning fully, he is content to use them. He just does not see himself as confined to the vocabulary of his time. The total vocabulary of English, from all times and all dialects (within the British Isles), existing and potential, is equally available for use. However, though his work is consequently "not intended for the present common English sense" (H, 176–77), it does not everywhere call for the same high level of philological alertness.

Second, a simple list of the different categories of unusual words obscures the relative frequency of each type. Though Taylor is able to quote a few colloquialisms, including the remarkable fact that Doughty is the first English writer to use the Americanism "fresh," meaning "forward, impertinent," they are almost entirely absent. Doughty is never deliberately informal and avoids all slang. Even the few utterances to which he attempts to give an informal flavor sound curiously stilted: " 'How may your lubbers slug out these long days till evening?' " (1:265). The overwhelming impression created by Doughty's lexical choices is of a distinct preference for archaisms. These range from idiosyncratic revivals of obsolete words (chough, rundle), through conventional archaisms (lief, ofttimes), to words normally regarded as "literary" (limn, mischance). What they have in common with the occasional dialect word or neologism is, in varying degree, their unfamiliarity.

Third, concentration on the individual words ignores Doughty's patterns of collocation, his preferences in bringing words into direct association within the same structure, adjective with noun, verb with subject or object. In this area of language use such associations of words are not right or wrong, but more likely or less likely. Whereas most of us (by definition) choose the more likely combinations, poets and artists in prose— and Doughty was both—can couple what words they please. "Idle" normally collocates with "chatter," "hands," "fellow," and their synonyms; Doughty writes of Beduin "for pastime limning with their driving-sticks in the idle sand" (1:265), with perhaps a suggestion of the obsolete sense: "empty, void." He also has a liking, particularly when describing character and behavior, for bringing together adjectives and nouns of Latin origin: "protesting with nefarious solemnity" (2:530), "their (feline) prudence," "the sordid inhospitality of the towns." Such collocations are characteristic of Doughty in his role of commentator and narrator. When directly quoting Arabic speech his style is different; he tends to avoid Latinate diction and use simple but unusual verbal collocations translated literally from the Arabic:

> I have heard one, in other things a very worthy man, in such form chide his unruly young son: "Ullah rip up that belly in thee! Curse the father (thy body) of that head and belly! Punish that hateful face!" (1:309)

Or, to quote a blessing instead of a curse, though with the same synecdoche of "face" for "thee": " 'God give peace to that head, the Lord suffer not thy face to see the evil' " (2:69). Here Doughty adds an explicit comment on the underlying Arabic idiom; in such a case Doughty, by pointing out the Arabic origin of the English phrases, moves the reader toward an Arabic view of life as well as distances him from English: "And such are phrases which, like their brand-marks, declare the tribes of nomads: these were, I believe, northern men" (2:69).

2.2. DISTANCING FEATURES: ARCHAIC SYNTAX

Taylor's comment quoted above on the vocabulary of *Travels in Arabia Deserta* (suitably rewritten with "structure" substituted for "word") applies almost as well to Doughty's syntax: "Doughty gave himself freedom to use any structure which served his purpose, whether that structure were current or obsolete, or a dialect structure or a colloquial one: and where existing structures failed he made new ones from Arabic." Consider the conversation between Khalil and his travelling companions to Aneyza, when they see he has not said the "dawning" prayers:

> 'Thou didst not say the prayer!'—"Friends, I prayed."—"Where washed you then?" (2:362; see also 2:240)

The first utterance contains the archaic second person singular form but uses the auxiliary "do"; the last utterance contains the modern second person form but avoids the auxiliary "do." Both sentences have an archaic ring. But though the effect is consistent, the means clash.

There are of course many archaic syntactic features for which Doughty shows a distinct preference. He normally avoids negative declarative sentences with "do": "the virgins smile not" (1:386), "we found not any inscription" (1:581), "he knew not" (2:482). Similarly, he prefers negative imperatives without "do": "'speak not'" (2:125), "'walk not'" (2:365), and interrogative structures without "do": "'what think ye'" (2:441), "'and how seest thou Horeysh?'" (1:532). Yet to each of these preferences exceptions can be found: "'You did not see him!'" (2:72), "'do the Nasâra hold thus and thus?'" (2:397).

It is in the light of such inconsistency that the following list of archaic syntactic features should be read. They certainly predominate in the text. But though Doughty prefers the older forms of the language, he is not bound to them and wherever possible I shall note his use of less archaic alternative structures.

i. "There" in existential sentences. In Modern English, the use of existential "there" is limited to "be" and a few copulative verbs ("there seems no reason," "there remain a few problems"). Doughty follows older patterns of the language. He frequently uses "there" to introduce intransitive verbs of motion: "There came in some of the poor nomads among us. . . . There were come in some of their women" (1:126). (Note also the archaic use of "be" as auxiliary with "come.")

He introduces passive verbs with "there," particularly when the subject is complex and, if initial, would yield a top-heavy sentence: "There were daily served in the Mothîf to the guests, and the rajajîl, 180 messes of barley-bread and temmn of second quality, each might be three and a quarter pints" (1:663); "There were brought to me cases of a sudden kind of leprosy" (2:18).

And occasionally he will even use "there" before an active transitive verb: "There met us a slender Beduin lad coming up after the cattle" (2:508).[12] To all these structures there are numerous exceptions: "Some of the villagers came up to me" (2:96); "A nomad family met us (of Hatheyl or Koreysh) removing upward" (2:562).

ii. "Be" and other subjunctive forms in open conditions.[13] "If the ráhla be short the Beduw march at leisure. . . . if aught be amiss the herdsmen are nigh to help them [the *hareem*]" (1:261); "But if a poor man in an expedition bestow some small thing in his saddle-bag, it is indulged, so that it do not appear openly" (2:396). (Note also the use of "do" after "so that," here used in the sense of "provided that," "so long as.")

iii. Other uses of the subjunctive. Doughty frequently uses "were" with a singular subject in sentences where contemporary writers—his contemporaries as well as ours—would prefer the use of a modal auxiliary:[14] "—a word half-uttered were [= would be] enough for the wise, but twenty cannot admonish the imprudent" (1:418); "Might not his treacherous sword-stroke, whilst I slept, have ended my days in the world? but this were [= would be considered] fratricide in the faith of the Arabian desert" (1:406).

Yet contrast in the very next sentence Doughty's amplification of the same thought: "The murderer of his rafîk would be infamous whilst he lived, no faithful man in the Beduin menzils ought to suffer him to sit in his beyt" (1:406). Here "were infamous" is equally appropriate.

Doughty is also fond of the past perfect in the apodosis, the main clause of an unfulfilled conditional sentence, especially when the protasis, the subordinate clause, is merely implied or is expressed by some other means than the conjunction "if":[15] "the pleasant contagion of the Arabs' religion has spread nearly as far as the pestilence: a battle gained and it had overflowed into Europe" (1:142); "A powder blast, the running brunt of a palm beam, had [= could have] broken up this clay resistance" (1:329) (the reference is to the inadequate clay turrets built to defend the palm orchards of Teyma); " 'Abdullah is a melaun indeed, and, but we had been there, thou hadst not [= wouldst not have] escaped him today' " (2:182).

A counter-example is Doughty's description of the torments of prolonged camel riding: "They [the Aarab] scoured before me all the hours of the day, in their light riding, so that with less than keeping a good will, death at length would have been a welcome deliverance out of present miseries" (1:627). "Had been" would be more in line with the preceding examples.

It is the use of syntactic archaisms, perhaps more than any other feature of Doughty's style that, in the words of T. E. Lawrence, "demands a hard reader" (1:27). And Doughty himself may have had the style partly in mind when he wrote "the book is not milk for babes" (1:29). A consistent archaism, coupled with such a range of alien and recondite vocabulary, could well have made the book unreadable, even to the "philologically educated." Doughty was wise to "use archaic grammatical forms side by side with current grammatical forms which serve the same purpose."[16] And the main purpose of this section of the essay has been to document this remarkable inconsistency, described by Taylor but not demonstrated in detail.

3. ARABIC SYNTAX AND IDIOM

The pervasive influence of Arabic syntax on the sentences of *Travels in Arabia Deserta* can be illustrated by two typical sentences, one direct speech and one narrative comment. Doughty tells of a belief prevalent among the Beduin that "no kafir [heathen, non-Moslem] may endure to look upon the *séma* [sky]":

> I came almost nowhither where some children and women have not said to me, 'Lift up thy eyes thou to the séma.' (1:522)

It could perhaps be maintained that this is an acceptable English imperative sentence, since second person pronouns can be inserted for emphasis—you look up; look up, you! But the precise placing of "thou" between object and adjunct is rare to the point of deviance in English; in Arabic it would be the normal structure: *irfa einak (ya) inte lasema*. The same kind of relationship, between a somewhat deviant English sentence and a perfectly normal Arabic sentence obtained by literal translation, exists in the following comment made by Doughty on the problem of ruling over the Beduin: "Bitter is the heart and the sword is sharp, of him who rules over the wandering tribes of the khala" (1:611). Here the two coordinated clauses with which the sentence begins—the first with an unusual order of words, "marked" in sequence, and the second with the more usual order, "unmarked"—give the utterance a distinctly poetic ring. In the corresponding or underlying Arabic sentence the syntax is unremarkable. It is the first clause which has the usual order, that is, which is unmarked in sequence, and the second which is reversed to avoid ambiguity (bitter is the heart and sharp). Interestingly, this sentence is quoted by Annette McCormick in that chapter of her thesis where she discusses the influence of the Bible on Doughty's style. She cites a wealth of examples of sentences whose parallelism is reminiscent of Hebrew poetry: "Great are their flocks in this dîra, all of sheep, and their camels are a multitude trooping over the plain" (2:78). But this could just as well be reminiscent of the Beduin poetry Doughty heard as he sat in the nomad tents. McCormick herself is careful to comment on "the Semitic languages," where "relationships are expressed through the juxtaposition of ideas without connectives (or with very slight connectives and those usually coordinating)." She goes on: "This peculiarity of the Semitic languages may have been borne in upon Doughty as he heard the Arabs talk: certainly the same lack of subordination and of transition is observable in their conversations recorded in his book. But he himself, in the parts of his book that do not reproduce Arabian speech, but convey his own observations, used it widely, page after page."[17] The accuracy of this assessment is borne out by the description of the Solubby quoted above, chosen for lexical rather than syntactic reasons. Note, for example, the parallelism in the third sentence: "they only . . . are free to travel / molested by none," and the almost unexplained juxtaposition of facts in the fourth: "Home born, yet have they no citizenship."

None of the sentences quoted so far to demonstrate the influence of Arabic sentence structure have been totally unacceptable English sentences though such do occasionally occur, notably in passages of direct speech. An obvious example is the reply of one Beduin to Khalil's question "What is thy tribe?": "I Harby" (*ana Harby*, with normal Semitic lack of copula in a nominal sentence). A less obvious example is the following, also from a story quoted directly: " 'There was a poor man who dying by the way, his friends, digging piously with their hands, laid him in a shallow grave' " (1:120). The resumptive pronoun "him" would be deleted in normative English[18] since its function is realized by the relative pronoun "who." In Arabic such a pronoun is obligatory since the relative clause is introduced by a subordinating conjunction.

Difficult to classify in terms of acceptability is Doughty's practice of using "the" followed by an adjective to represent a *single* person: "the sick staggered forth" (i.e., the sick man), "but the deaf would sit no longer" (i.e., the deaf man). Neither of these sentences would be problematic in Arabic, where the adjective is marked for number and gender.

Finally, combining both lexical and grammatical features from Arabic, are the many idiomatic expressions which Doughty renders literally into English, both in dialogue and in narrative comment, sometimes with an explanation but just as often without. After describing the hostility of some of the inhabitants of Teyma, Doughty adds the comment: "Yet they durst not insult the Nasrâny in the village because I was with the Beduw, and in the countenance of their own sheykhs" (1:599). The meaning—under the protection of the sheykhs—is clear from the context. It is only in the following chapter, when the phrase is accompanied by gesture, that we learn the Arabic idiom underlying the remark:

said Bunder, "Mohammed, what Beduw hast thou brought to Hâyil?—the Thuffîr! and yet thou knowest them to be gôm [enemies] with us!"
Mohammed: Wellah, yâ el-Mohafûth, I have brought them *bî wéjhy,*

under my countenance! (And in the Arabian guise he stroked down his visage to the beard)—because I found none other for the carriage of your temmn." (2:29–30; see also examples on page 103 for further instances of literally translated idiom)

CONCLUSION

It has not been possible within the limits of this essay to do much more than survey the range of linguistic techniques used by Doughty in creating the unique style of *Travels in Arabia Deserta*. In particular, the extent to which he was influenced by Arabic has only been hinted at. And no attempt has been made to identify sub-varieties within the overall variety that the book embodies. In this respect, Tabachnick's use of the term "register" (Ta, 57) to describe the range of tonal effects achieved by Doughty is eccentric. Linguists use the term "register" to describe a "variety of language distinguished according to use"[19] and in this sense there are no "registers" in *Arabia Deserta,* only (as Tabachnick in fact points out [Ta, 57]) a constantly shifting variation of the density and frequency with which the various techniques are employed. All critics are in fundamental agreement in insisting that *all* features of his style are to be found in *all* sections of the narrative, even if the proportion of archaisms or Arabisms may vary slightly between narrative and conversation. In the final analysis, what is remarkable about the style of *Travels in Arabia Deserta* is the extraordinary homogeneity it seems to have, for all its diverse origins. It may be true that, in McCormick's words, "one of the reasons that it is difficult to read is that so many different styles of writing, come together in its pages; it is, in fact, a palimpsest of English prose."[20] Or as Barker Fairley puts it, "He sees our prose, primitive and cultured alike, as part of a common and unbroken heritage. The sense of continuity is very powerful in him and in obedience to it he blends ancient and modern in a way that is altogether his own and sometimes disconcerting" (F, 239). The point is that the different elements do "come together"; he does succeed in "blending" them. Though occasionally disconcerted, those readers who acquire a taste for Doughty read him mainly with awestruck delight: awe at his versatility and delight in his mastery of his resources.

NOTES

1   Issam Safady, "Attempt and Attainment: A Study of Some Literary Aspects of Charles Doughty's *Travels in Arabia Deserta* as the Culmination of Late-Victorian Anglo-Arabian Travel Books to the Levant," Ph.D. dissertation, University of Kentucky, 1968, 169–71.

2   Lascelles Abercrombie, in a letter of 9 March 1937 to Walt Taylor, quoted in Walt Taylor, *Doughty's English*, S.P.E. Tract, no. 51 (Oxford: Clarendon Press, 1939), 40.

3   Ibid., 4.

4   Ibid., 21.

5   See Joshua A. Fishman, "The Sociology of Language," in *Current Trends in Linguistics*, vol. 12, ed. Thomas A. Sebeok (The Hague: Mouton, 1974), 1646–57.

6   For a fuller description and discussion of the range of paralinguistic phenomena, see Fernando Poyatos, *New Perspectives in Non-Verbal Communication* (Oxford: Pergamon, 1983), 187–91. The sounds discussed here are mainly what Poyatos calls "alternants," of which he says that "they differ radically from other paralinguistic phenomena because of their lexical value, that is, their segmentality."

7   See James Bynon, "Domestic Animal Calling in a Berber Tribe," in W. C. McCormack and S. A. Worms, eds., *Language and Man: Anthropological Issues* (The Hague: Mouton, 1976), 39–65; quoted in Poyatos, *New Perspectives*.

8   Poyatos, *New Perspectives*, 196, defines gestures as "conscious or unconscious body movements made mainly with the head, the face alone or the limbs, learned or somatogenic, and serving as a primary communicative tool, dependent or independent from verbal language, either simultaneous or alternating with it." Those I have listed are mainly conscious, learned, and dependent, some simultaneous and some alternating.

9   "Of the 68 words in the dialect list, 30 occur in the reading Doughty is known to have done. . . . Surely it is more in accordance with what we know of Doughty to take these words as obsolete, borrowed from some literary source rather than as dialect." Annette Marie McCormick, "The Origin and Development of the Style of Charles M. Doughty's *Travels in Arabia Deserta*," Ph.D. dissertation, University of London, 1951, 245–46. She gives Gavin Douglas's sixteenth-century translation of the *Aeneid*, for instance, as the source of "scrog," and Sir Thomas Elyot's Latin-English dictionary, *Bibliotheca Eliotae* (1548), as the source of "spence," "whister," and "withwind."

10 See ibid. for a much fuller list.

11 Taylor, *Doughty's English*, 11.

12 *O.E.D.* gives no quotations later than 1548, and Frederick Visser comments: "its use with transitive verbs in the active voice seems to have died out in the course of the sixteenth century." *An Historical Syntax of the English Language*, 3 vols. (Leiden: Brill, 1963–73), 1:52.

13 Visser comments: "the use of the modally marked form gives the utterances a slightly archaic flavour" (ibid., 2:886).

14 H. W. Fowler's comment on such structures is that they "diffuse an atmosphere of formalism over the writing in which they occur." See his *Dictionary of Modern Usage,* rev. Ernest Gowers (New York and Oxford: Oxford University Press, 1965), 596.

15 See Visser, *An Historical Syntax,* 3: part 2 (1973), 2216.

16 Taylor, *Doughty's English,* 36.

17 McCormick, "Origin and Development," 108–9.

18 Its retention could also be regarded as an archaism, since it occurred in earlier stages of the language, but according to Visser "it passed into obsolescence after the first half of the eighteenth century" (*An Historical Syntax,* 1:522).

19 See M. A. K. Halliday, A. McIntosh, and P. D. Strevens, *The Linguistic Sciences and Language Teaching* (London: Longmans, 1964), 87.

20 McCormick, "Origin and Development," 249.

JANICE DELEDALLE-RHODES

The True Nature of Doughty's Relationship with the Arabs

The opinions concerning the Arabs expressed by Doughty in *Arabia Deserta* have been the object of much discussion, not to say controversy. The aim of this article is to show that these opinions are better understood not at their face value but at another level: as an indication of Doughty's attitude toward the Arabs and of the true nature of his relationship with them. In order to grasp this fundamental significance of Doughty's remarks, it is first of all indispensable, I think, to reinsert them in a wider context of travel literature.

When speaking of the Middle East and of its inhabitants, usually referred to by travellers as "Orientals,"[1] most pre-modern travel writers (and this includes many nineteenth-century ones) use stereotypes; their personal experiences, which they are recounting with the avowed aim of "informing" the reader, are either filtered through these stereotypes or crystallize around them. Henry Maundrell, in his *Journey from Aleppo to Jerusalem in 1697,* confronted by the necessity of paying a toll to the local authorities, concludes rather rapidly that the Turks are "rogues and robbers."[2] "A Turk will always cheat when he can find the opportunity," he observes in his "Account of the Turks" at the end of his book: "lust, arrogance, covetousness and the most exquisite hypocrisy compleat their character," he adds.[3] Small wonder that the Europeans frequent them as little as possible, as Maundrell confesses, and small wonder, in that case, that these Europeans never acquire the experience enabling them to modify their opinions. C. R. Cockerell relates, in *Travels in Southern Europe and the Levant,* an incident in which a Turkish notability presents him with an intaglio; wishing to return the politeness the traveller immediately offers his host a little of his best Dartford powder "which after some pressing he accepted; but at the same time added that he hoped I did not mean to pay him for the intaglio." Cockerell's initial reaction is one of extreme embarrassment at having made too obvious and hasty a gesture. But, he will conclude, "my embarrassment was perfectly needless. A little experience taught me that this was only the shallow ruse of the Oriental." The incident is significant and worth analyzing. The traveller has been caught off balance in an unexpected situation. He records his first, spontaneous reaction, which was certainly the correct one in the circumstances, for he had in fact been guilty of a breach of politeness; but he will quickly adopt the old stereotype of the "cunning Oriental," which consoles him and convinces him that what he had felt to be a mistake was not one at all: "looking back, I have often laughed to think of my greenness at the time," he concludes.[4]

Such is the power of stereotypes that travellers are usually invested by them unawares, especially in cases where they have to justify their acts or to defend themselves physically or morally: stereotypes then appear magically to hand as a useful weapon, sovereign remedies against the innumerable blunders that travellers commit in the course of their often devastating incursions into unfamiliar civilizations.

These stereotypes are more numerous and much more varied than is commonly supposed. I have analyzed most of them extensively elsewhere[5] and will do no more here than mention a few of the most common ones. They are often unfavorable. For instance: Orientals are comic figures. This is, admittedly, an old stereotype which is not often used by nineteenth-century travellers who, in the main, tend to consider things Oriental more seriously, but it still appears in W. M. Thackeray's account,[6] is a leitmotif in E. C. G. Murray's *Turkey: Being Sketches from Life,*[7] and will even reemerge surprisingly and anachronistically at the end of the century in the work of W. B. Harris.[8] The Oriental is also reputed to be "a child": Sir Richard Burton alludes to "the childish East."[9] Harriet Martineau, worrying how to "manage" Orientals, eventually finds the solution: "we treated them as children; and this answered perfectly well";[10] and for once her cousin, that liberal spirit, Lady Duff Gordon, is in agreement with her. The Arabs, she declares, "are extremely clever and nice children."[11] Many travellers also consider Orientals "liars" or "hypocrites,"[12] and those who are preoccupied by religious issues often dub them "fanatics," although in actual fact few travellers in the Middle East experienced any difficulties on account of their religious opinions.[13]

The stereotype is not always unfavorable. Most travellers find Orientals "hospitable," and nomads are generally accounted to be "free." But stereotypes, favorable or unfavorable, do not stand up to analysis, and, as I have pointed out in a study of the subject, the "legendary hospitality of the East" must be replaced in its own socioreligious context for its functioning to be understood correctly, while the theory of the "freedom" of the often destitute nomad, bound to his itinerary by economic and alimentary imperatives, is perfectly illusory and reflects nothing more than the delight of travellers themselves, "freed" from the confined nineteenth-century middle-class English context, to whose benefits and advantages they are equally free to return when they so desire.[14]

The experience of these writers and of most of their predecessors and contemporaries does not inform readers of any truth about Eastern peoples. The analysis of each stereotype found in their writings can inform them, on the contrary, about the cultural and ideological situation of the writers themselves. In other words, the stereotype is a construct, or, in terms of Peircean semiotic, an "object," created by the "interpretants" of the traveller.[15] This provides the answer to a question which must occur to every student of travel literature: How is it that different travel writers apply identical stereotypes, as we have seen above, to widely differing populations? and its converse: How is it that different writers apply different stereotypes to the same population? How does it happen, for instance, that for Wilfrid Scawen Blunt and many other travellers the Beduin are honest, upright, civilized human beings,[16] whereas William Gifford Palgrave, writing at about the same period, presents them as "savages" and expresses the wish that

> those who indulge their imagination in ideal portraits of desert life, and conceive the Bedouins and their condition to be worthy of admiration and envy, would pass but three days in a Sherarat encampment, and see, not through the medium of romancing narratives . . . , but with their own eyes, to what depth of degradation one of the noblest races earth affords can descend under the secular influence of nomad life.[17]

How is it possible, again, that E. G. Browne should consider the Persians exquisite and refined philosophers and idealists,[18] when for Doughty, Morier, and others they are debauched and decadent liars?[19] It is obvious that none of these statements is true as regards the whole of the population concerned. What is true in the first example is that the primitive living conditions of the inhabitants of the desert appear as a highly desirable state to the traveller who harbors the idea of a retrospective Utopia or is simply sick and tired of a Europe gone stale and corrupt and already on the way to industrialization. In Blunt's case it must be added of course that his horror of imperialism and his ideas on self-government led him quite naturally to insist on the numerous positive aspects of the indigenous social and political organization of Arabia.

As for the second example, that concerning the Persians, the same main interpretants are involved as well as others based upon more immediate personal experience: for instance, Browne had no knowledge of illiterate Persian peasants because he confined himself to the company of poets and philosophers of whom Doughty, in his turn, had no knowledge, basing his remarks on a group of Persian pilgrims encountered in the *Haj*.

Concerning the statements made about the Persians (or any other Eastern population) being "liars," these are based on assumptions concerning the nature of truth which are not and cannot be universal and are thus in fact not applicable. Palgrave goes a great way toward explaining the latter point when he affirms that excessive politeness on the part of the Arabs is "a frequent source of innocent deceptions, if deceptions indeed they can be called,"[20] but comes to grief in a final remark when he declares that one of the reasons for which Europeans accuse Arabs of lying is the latter's "vagueness of ideas" and "corresponding vagueness in the language": an Arab does not attach as much importance to "accuracy" as a European does; however, the nature of this accuracy not being made explicit, the explanation remains unsatisfying.[21] Lord Cromer falls into the same trap when he accuses "the Oriental mind" of "want of accuracy, which easily degenerates into untruthfulness."[22] The difference between these practically identical statements is of course only one of intention: Palgrave was trying to show that he understood Orientals better than did his archenemy Burton, who had said that "Lying to the Oriental is meat, drink, and the roof that shelters him,"[23] while Lord Cromer simply wanted to prove that the Egyptians were incapable of governing themselves. The "want of accuracy" stereotype appears with the Industrial Revolution; it is often resorted to by nineteenth-century travellers exasperated by the "unpunctuality" or "unreliability" of Easterners, but we could show that it has a varying range of applications.

From the few examples I have given it will be quite obvious that any opinions or statements of an author-traveller from A-context about an individual from B-context are based on intellectual, moral, or cultural assumptions which are never stated clearly, and that this considerably obfuscates the issue. Apparently responsible authors can and do contradict one another when their interpretants are totally different. The hostility between W. S. Blunt and Lord Cromer on the Egyptian question is too well known to expatiate upon here, but a comparison between their blatantly contradictory statements about the Arabs renders visible the tip of the iceberg. If it is obvious to the point of caricature that in their case political options predominate, it must not be forgotten that the principle set forth at the beginning of this paragraph remains true even if the effects are less apparent—and consequently more insidious.

We may take the example of the favorable image of Islam propagated by English missionaries in the nineteenth century which often makes its appearance in their travel accounts. I have demonstrated at some length[24] that consciously or unconsciously the statements of the missionaries about Islam are actually destined to bring back lost sheep to the English church, which was losing many of its members to Catholicism, agnosticism, or atheism at the time of the science-religion conflict. Their insistence on the similarities of Islam and English Protestantism, with special emphasis upon the Moslems' strict monotheism, and their horror of anything approaching the worship of saints or "idols" (a jibe at Catholicism via the Eastern church) and the instances the missionaries were able to offer their readers of everyday life in the Moslem East which confirmed the literal truth of parts of the Bible,[25] all this had an ulterior motive which had nothing to do with Islam as such. Christine Bolt judiciously points out that Islam was also favorably publicized by missionaries in Africa in order to wean the Africans from their animistic faiths; it was supposed to be a less complex religion and better suited to "the African temperament." But when conversions to Islam increased to an alarming extent, the missionaries, showing their true colors, were obliged to denigrate what they had previously extolled.[26] This is not to deny of course that many travellers to the Middle East, like Burton or Edward Lane, felt strongly attracted to Islam; but this attraction was a quite personal one and the result of their experiences in Moslem countries.

To sum up, any statement about Eastern populations uttered by an English traveller is to be considered with caution, and it must always be borne in mind that most stereotypes and general appreciations imply, even though this is not always apparent, an unshakable conviction of the superiority of the West.

In this context, how shall we approach Charles Montagu Doughty's *Arabia Deserta,* which is much concerned with Eastern populations; namely, with the inhabitants of Arabia? The author makes a great number of statements about the Arabs.[27] These statements are usually perceived as "favorable" or "unfavorable" and they have been diversely commented on. The form taken by the discussion of these statements is usually a kind of summing-up with a view to answering the question: Did Doughty like the Arabs or not? The critic puts on one side of the balance Doughty's favorable remarks and on the other side his unfavorable ones and decides which weigh the heavier. This may appear to be, on my part, a somewhat simplistic view of the case, but it is a fact that the subject of Doughty's relationship with the Arabs has often been treated in this way. Readers who admire Doughty are embarrassed by his harsh remarks and fall over backwards in their attempts to prove that he also pays the Arabs compliments; other readers confine themselves to discussion about Doughty's style or the dramatic qualities of his presentation of the Arabs,[28] thus avoiding what is, to my mind, the fundamental human issue. Still others have insisted on what they believe (wrongly, in my view) to be the "negative" aspect of Doughty's journey and blame the Arabs for it: "Doughty," declares Martin Armstrong, "is a devout and uncompromising Christian, and was continually coming into contact with Arab fanaticism."[29]

Thomas J. Assad comes much nearer the truth when he points out that Doughty's violent reactions and his clashes with the Arabs are "rather the manifestation of a thwarted inclination to sympathise with [them], the inclination to see in them the strains of his own deep-rooted feelings of the brotherhood of mankind" (A, 124–25). But he also attempts to establish a positive-negative account (A, 124–25, 130–31), arriving at the conclusion that "The significance of the book lies rather in its recording of a human struggle against forces which were physically and temperamentally antipathetic" (A, 131).

As a preliminary conclusion I find this satisfactory and do not deny that this record of a human struggle is interesting; its description, as many critics would say, does possess dramatic qualities. But *Arabia Deserta* is not a novel or a play (although it may, of course, be treated as such), and I contend that in the context of nineteenth-century travel literature on the Middle East the recording of this struggle is not so significant as the fact that it exists and the reasons for its existence. The analysis of some of Doughty's statements about the Arabs and of the context in which they were uttered will help us to understand the nature and the causes of this struggle.

When T. E. Lawrence admitted that it was "not comfortable to have to write about *Arabia Deserta*,"[30] he was obviously not only referring to his too-great familiarity with the book, but to a feeling which many critics appear to share about the ambiguity of Doughty's opinions concerning the Arabs and which Lawrence tries not very successfully to account for a few pages later.[31] This ambiguity is evident throughout the book in reactions and judgments, sometimes in recorded actions, which may seem—especially when quoted out of context, which is often the case—at the best paradoxical, at the worst flatly contradictory. For, unlike other travellers, Doughty does not adopt a systematic, ideologically or culturally identifiable attitude toward Arabs as such. *Arabia Deserta* does not present a clear image of the Arabs. Whereas other travellers write entire chapters on "the character of the Arabs" (or of the Turks or the Persians) which leave readers in no doubt as to what they are supposed to think, readers of *Arabia Deserta*, overwhelmed by the mass of apparently incoherent remarks proffered by the author, are completely incapable, once they have reached the end of the book, of conjuring up in their minds a "portrait" of "the Arab" as presented by Doughty.

The reader cannot decide, for instance, on the strength of the text whether the Beduins are brave or not: on the one hand the author talks of their "constant fortitude" (1:359) and praises their endurance in the desert (1:101); on the other he declares that they are "easily discouraged" and that their "most strength is ever in their tongues" (1:54). "An Arab overpowered will [his feline and chameleon nature] make no resistance, for that should endanger him" (2:394), he will remark later. Likewise the life of the Beduin appears at one moment as a pleasant, pastoral, almost ideal one (1:304–5), while at another certain Beduins are qualified as "wild men" by reason of "their squalid ignorance and extreme living" (1:302).

The Arabs, the author declares, are honest: the nomads can leave their date harvest either unguarded in the wilderness or in the care of the oasis-dwellers: "the householder shall be sure to find his own again where he buried it" (1:323). The traveller notices a "new Beduin mantle, hanging on a thorn" till its owner should return: "such goods of tribesmen are, as it were, committed to God" (1:323). Yet the Arabs' "promises are but words in the air" (2:434) and "all their life is passed in fraud and deceit" (2:354).

On religious topics, Doughty, well known for his intransigence, might

give, one would think, a clearer picture. Are not all Moslem Arabs "fanatics" as he so often exclaims (1:290, 343, 449, 542)? But here again the
traveller recounts so many instances of religious tolerance on their part,
often repeating the dictum taught him by his hosts, *"kul wàhed aly dîn-hu*,
'every one in his own religion'" (1:191; 2:103, 467, passim), and even
relating incidents for which, as he realized and admitted himself, he was
to blame and from the consequences of which he was saved only by the
tolerance and comprehension of his Moslem companions, as in the discussion with the "village pedant" (2:443–44), that the reader cannot discover
if Doughty had any particular idea about what a Moslem *person* could be
like. His harsh strictures on Islam as a religion need not be commented on
here, for *in practice* does Doughty not make distinctions between "bad"
and "good" Moslems, and are not the latter the kindly, charitable, liberal
"friends" who appear at so many stages of his book?

We could thus cite, for every aspect of the character or behavior of the
Arabs mentioned by Doughty, two apparently contradictory reactions or
opinions. A glance at the index, compiled by the author himself, is particularly enlightening. Under the entry "Beduins" we learn for instance that
the latter are at once gay and melancholy, of a quarrelsome yet peace-
loving temperament, patient but unpersevering, and so on. Even their
skin, blackened by the sun and dirt, is, in reality, white (2:590–91).

Moreover, when Doughty's judgments are not mutually contradictory
they are often accompanied by restrictions. The latter may be general, as
when he declares that the sheykh Ibn Jad is a "generous old lion (but as
they be all, an ungenerous enemy)" (1:85) or that "Mûsa's was a candid
just soul, not common amongst Arabs" (1:187), or particular, as when
talking of a tribe of "fanatical Beduins, with whom no keeping touch nor
truth of honourable life, no performance of good offices, might win the
least favour from the dreary, inhuman, and for our sins, inveterate dotage
of their blood-guilty religion," to which Doughty adds immediately, "But
I had eaten of their cheer, and might sleep among wolves" (1:551). Sometimes the first restriction will be accompanied by a second one: "Friendly
is their hospitality at home; but in the way with them you may find
among the same Arabs the behaviour of enemies: yet ever there are some
honourable men, who will at all times be as good as themselves" (1:423).

Again, the reader may sometimes be bewildered by Doughty's habit of
drawing unexpected conclusions from the incidents he relates: thus, abandoned by the Ageyl and his *rafik* (guide), Maatuk, who has betrayed him

for a pipeful of tobacco, Doughty declares himself too exhausted to continue the journey and appeals to Maatuk's sense of honor. Upbraided by
the "good woman" his wife, Maatuk returns to better sentiments and
decides to bring back the Ageyl: "Great is their natural humanity," remarks the traveller, "this Heteymy [Maatuk], who was himself infirm,
bade me rest; and he limped as fast as he might go and shouted after
them" (2:297–98). Thus in one of the most dangerous situations in which
Doughty was to find himself, the "natural humanity" of one who had just
betrayed him is brought to the fore.

Lawrence explains this apparent incoherence by postulating that if
Doughty remains typically English in outlook he expresses himself in a
typically Beduin manner.[32] Lawrence's famous passage may be a good
piece of writing, but his "climatic" explanation is hardly convincing. Recently, S. E. Tabachnick, in an illuminating study, has addressed the
problem by using the techniques of narrative analysis, showing how distinctions can be made between narrative voice, protagonist, and artist (Ta,
48–51). He concludes:

> Because Doughty the artist is far greater than Doughty the man of his
> times (whom we see in the narrator's voice), his book becomes capable
> of continual self-renewal in all circumstances and periods, like any mas-
> terpiece. We perceive clearly the narrator's and Khalil's prejudices but
> can read through these to a greater sympathy with the Arabs and a more
> complex enjoyment of the book that Doughty the artist has made possi-
> ble. (Ta, 51)

This is an attractive and satisfying description of "what happens in
Arabia Deserta." One would be tempted to go no further. But while such
narrative techniques are useful in unravelling the kind of complications
presented by the text and in distinguishing the different points of view,
these techniques remain descriptive and not explanatory, as their exponents are the first to admit. My purpose here is to treat Doughty as a
single human unit responsible for the writing of *Arabia Deserta* and to ask:
What is the significance of the fact that he functions from different
viewpoints?

I shall try to consider the problem, then, from this angle. The contradictory or incoherent nature of many of Doughty's statements or groups of
statements appears to me to be the guarantee of great credibility and
sincerity. It is obvious that these statements do not concern stereotypes

but living individuals and precise situations. The innumerable incidents recounted in the book occur in widely differing situations. It has been remarked that Doughty insists on his own changes of mood and situation when reporting his personal reactions: it is inevitable that the "hungry . . . weary man" (1:95) should be exasperated by the traditional three-day limitation of hospitality in the desert to the point of uttering some extremely harsh remarks about Beduin niggardliness, whereas in less desperate circumstances he will explain this limitation, of which he cannot but approve, by the often dramatic state of deprivation which he is forced to share with his hosts. In the same way, although he is personally revolted by a lie, he will explain that lying is sometimes necessary in the often belligerent state of affairs in the desert and that it is admitted by the Beduin in order to deceive their enemies (1:283, passim). It may be argued that he was no longer a tired hungry man when he wrote the book, that this enterprise took him almost ten years, and that he could have introduced a little more coherence into his statements about the Arabs.

But Doughty's aim is to tell the truth: "PROSIT VERITATI" (1:29) refers not to the truth as such but to the traveller's truth, the history of his personal involvement with the Arabs. *Arabia Deserta* purports less to tell the truth about the Arabs than to report faithfully Doughty's experience of them, and it should not be treated as a textbook. What appears to us to be more significant than Doughty's actual remarks is the reason for which he proffers them; in other words, his attitude toward the Arabs, and this attitude has nothing contradictory or incoherent about it.

The lack of aggressivity of which Sir Richard Burton, in a famous passage, accuses Doughty (to the surprise, perhaps, of some modern readers who consider him too aggressive) is not the indication of a negative and passive attitude, but on the contrary that of an attitude founded on a certain amount of knowledge, great powers of observation, and a fundamental desire for friendship.[33] Burton's criticisms are completely off-target; Doughty was not, like Burton himself, playing the role of a pilgrim, was not disguised or seeking to violate any laws of the Moslem religion, which he so heartily criticizes but respects *de facto*. Doughty's conscience was clear and he had no need to be continually on his guard. In fact, the confidence he displays toward his Arab hosts never ceases to astonish the reader. Neither is this nonaggressivity the result, as Wilfrid Scawen Blunt appears to think, of a conscious policy toward the Arabs, a useful attitude systematically adopted when and if necessary.[34] Blunt's remark appears in fact quite irrelevant if one remembers the number of incidents that

Doughty's spontaneous reactions provoke. But once again, to calculate the number of quarrels recorded in *Arabia Deserta* appears to be a futile project; what is essential is to find out whether Doughty always desired friendly relationships with the Arabs and if one can detect this desire for friendship even in his frequent clashes with them. Assad believes one can, but points out that Doughty was frequently disappointed by the Arabs and that it was this disappointment which was in great part responsible for many misunderstandings (A, 125).

I would like to go further and insist on the fact that Doughty is one of the few travellers to have expressed his disappointment with the Arabs. I am not referring here to the kind of disappointment felt by Blunt, for reasons which were at once personal and political and who wrote off the Arabs definitely as a bad job,[35] or to the more superficial and literary disappointment expressed by Thackeray, who was annoyed with the East for being dirty and noisy and not at all like the *Arabian Nights*.[36] I am concerned here with a deeper, more human feeling which overcame Doughty sporadically but is certainly not constant. For this disappointment is the proof of two things: one is the high esteem in which at other times Doughty holds the Arabs, the other is the extent of his personal involvement with them. The absence of the expression of disappointment in travellers' accounts does not necessarily signify their satisfaction or approval; on the contrary it is often the manifestation of a deeply rooted conviction of Western superiority, or even tacit contempt for Easterners, or at the very least the traveller's lack of commitment in a journey which remains no more than a parenthesis.

It must be pointed out that apart from Doughty, Sir Henry Layard in his relations with the family of Mehemet Taki Khan, the Bakhtiari chief,[37] and E. G. Browne, who made many friends among Persian intellectuals, few nineteenth-century travellers seem to have had any feeling of friendship for the inhabitants of the East. And for a good reason: feelings of friendship can be established only on a basis of equality, which is a notably absent element in most relationships between the traveller and his Eastern counterpart. Does not Lady Isabel Burton express a generally felt but rarely admitted nineteenth-century "truth" when she boldly and baldly declares: "In the East, it is safer to treat everyone as if he might one day be your enemy"?[38] Doughty's relationship with the Arabs and the opinions he expressed about the latter should be considered in the light of the feelings of friendship and fellowship he so often refers to himself.

Friendship is, in fact, a fundamental theme of *Arabia Deserta*. In the

"Preface to the Second Edition" the author talks nostalgically of the "human fellowship amongst the Arabians" and "some very true and helpful friendships; which, from this long distance of years, I vividly recall and shall, while life lasts, continue to esteem with grateful mind" (1:33). The book begins under the sign of friendship when "a new voice . . . of an old friend" (1:39) hails the author on his return to Damascus from the desert, probably one of the "Moslem friends" who, we learn on the following page, tried to dissuade Doughty from undertaking his perilous journey. The friends Doughty makes in the desert and in the oases (despite his sporadic restrictions on oasis-dwellers) emerge on the whole as more important figures than the enemies. Zeyd dominates a great part of the first volume. In spite of his misunderstanding with Doughty which the latter eventually clears up and for which he is later forgiven, Zeyd will always remain "my sheykhly friend" (2:118), "my old Fejîry friend Zeyd es-Sbeykàn . . . ; whose was one of the best and least fanatical heads!" (2:557). A great portion of the second volume is devoted to Doughty's friendship with Mohammed en-Nejumy, his "father" at Kheybar, who entreats him to stay and become one of his family. The fact that Kheybar frowned on Doughty because of his publicly displayed religious convictions attests to the strength of Mohammed's feeling for the traveller. The stay in Aneyza, toward the end of Doughty's journey, is rendered possible thanks to the efforts of the emir Zamil and his "entire friends," the "good Bessam" and Abdullah el-Kenneyny, who protect him in times of trouble (2:chaps. 12, 13). Doughty is also on good terms with the more distant and redoubtable Motlog el-Hameydy and old Tollog of the Moahib. In fact, it would be difficult to enumerate all the friends to whom Doughty alludes.

Even at the most difficult moments of his journey Doughty can count on friendly gestures. As he often points out, the Arabs' "natural humanity" is great and their sense of compassion for the weary traveller was responsible for getting him out of many scrapes. When he tries to return to Kheybar his guide deceives him and spreads false rumors concerning the *Nasrany* (Christian). The Beduin are undecided: if Wayil defends him, Mishwat, who had appeared to be friendly, suddenly attacks him. However, Doughty is not blinded by fear and resentment; Mishwat will return to better sentiments and will take his part when Seydan, another sheykh, attacks the traveller. Thus, Mishwat, for Doughty, remains a "friend . . . in his sober mind, he hated in his doting humour 'the God's adversary' "

(1:531–33). Here the author makes an important distinction between the religious convictions of the Moslem and the feelings of the man toward a fellow-traveller. It is because Doughty is capable of making such distinctions that he does not need to behave in the aggressive manner recommended by Burton. His natural "weapons" were not firearms but persuasion and appeals to honor and to the principles common to the "twin bodies of religious faith" (1:579). Doughty also sometimes dedramatized a situation by making a joke. On the extremely rare occasions when he was obliged to use or rather simply to threaten physical violence, he regretted it immediately afterward (2:528).

The quarrel with Mishwat brings us to another important aspect of Doughty's relationship with the Arabs: in nearly every case when the latter manifest feelings of hostility toward Doughty, the traveller's public display of his own religious convictions and his criticism, overt or implied, of Islam are responsible. This is an incontestable fact admitted by the author himself in his more lucid moments and evident to any reader. In fact, we might say that it was the only constant bone of contention, albeit a serious one, between Doughty and the Arabs as a group. But the kind of behavior just referred to, although it sometimes exasperates Doughty's readers as much as it must have exasperated his hearers, is not without a positive aspect, which reveals another facet of the relationship existing between the traveller and his hosts. Doughty was not playing a part in order to defend himself or to please the Arabs, and he had no intention of doing so. He was being honest with them because he thought they were intelligent enough to understand his point of view. That this was indeed so is proved in a large number of cases, where the indulgence of his companions and *their* respect for *his* religious convictions are amply illustrated. But it was an attitude which inevitably led to clashes. It was not a typical attitude of the nineteenth-century traveller who, out of prudence, preferred not to broach such subjects or for whom the idea of a discussion about the comparative merits of Christianity and Islam simply could not arise.

In spite of such clashes, or even by reason of them, the reader of *Arabia Deserta* can be in no doubt that Doughty made many friends among the Arabs and that these friendships were based on feelings of equality and mutual confidence. That these were not merely passing, casual friendships is proved by the account of D. G. Hogarth, who reports the infinite pains taken by Doughty, long after his journey, to attempt to contact these

friends, most of them alas now dead, or their families in order to thank
them and show his appreciation of what they had done for him during his
journey (H, 59, 85–86). Among other details, the story of the Bessam
family, who, having in their possession the notes confiscated from Doughty
at Kheybar, contrived to return them to the traveller at Jidda (H, 91), shows
that the esteem and friendship were reciprocal.

This personal involvement of Doughty with the Arabs, the fact that his
relationship with them was an "emotional experience" (A, 105), precludes
the use of stereotypes. An Arab described by Doughty is never the caricature one finds in so many contemporary travel-accounts but an individual whom the reader cannot possibly confuse with any other character
in the book. Doughty paints no "portrait of the Oriental" as such. As I
have made clear, the generalizations made by Doughty about "the Arabs"
refer to precise contexts and differ from one another as the context differs.

It is only now that we may ask the question: What was Doughty's view
of the Arabs? One of the most relevant comments on this subject was
made by R. E. Roberts in his obituary article in which he insists on
Doughty's recognition of the "fact of our common humanity" and "that
his contact is direct, sincere, instinctive." He is not painting a picture "of
a different creature . . . but of people like himself who happen to have
different habits and a different creed."[39] This last sentence might appear to
minimize unduly the religious tensions apparent in *Arabia Deserta,* as I
will probably appear to some readers as having unduly minimized them
myself. But this is an aspect of the book which has already been over-
emphasized and often masks the capital fact that Doughty treated the
Arabs as fellowmen. That he had an irascible nature and was intransigent
in his opinions has no significance except inasmuch as it brings out all the
more clearly that even hostile encounters in *Arabia Deserta* are *encounters
between equals.* Doughty's views of the Arabs are as numerous and varied as
the individuals and situations concerned.

In English travel literature concerning the Middle East one can distinguish, by and large, five fundamental attitudes toward Orientals.

In a first stage the inhabitants of the East are accounted totally insig-
nificant; they are entirely absent from a work which may be an itinerary
across an apparently unpopulated landscape or a treatise on local geography or archaeology.

In a second stage they make their appearance but are considered only as instruments: they may help to further the journey or may hinder its accomplishment; the appreciation of travellers will be based solely on this consideration and is usually sharply positive or negative.

At another stage travellers will become aware of the *difference* of their Eastern counterpart, whom they take for a curious specimen of another species: travellers confine themselves to the description of the manners and customs of this phenomenon, and any opinions they may express about it will be more stereotyped than personal.

At still another stage, and this is often the case from the beginning of the nineteenth century onward, travellers start to become aware of the human reality of Easterners, sometimes attempting to "understand" them or to "explain" them to readers; at this stage they record opinions which are more personal although still strongly influenced by the existing stereotypes.

Finally, in a few rare cases, travellers identify themselves totally with Easterners, to the point at which the existence of differences which they are obliged to admit in spite of themselves may appear to them illogical, abnormal, or even scandalous.

This is a theoretical statement of the stages in the evolution of relations between travellers and Easterners and of course no strict chronology, either in history or in individual travellers, can be established. Few travellers before the nineteenth century can be said, however, to have gone beyond the first two or three stages. But even in the nineteenth century examples can be found of travel accounts that ignore the local inhabitant completely. In addition, an individual traveller may evolve during his journey and may adopt different attitudes at different stages of his account. But again, one attitude does not replace another immediately and totally and not necessarily in the above order. In *Eothen,* for instance, A. W. Kinglake passes rapidly from the second to the fourth attitude, while Blunt's passionate self-identification with the Arabs will gradually regress. The evolution of Doughty's attitude toward the Negroes in *Arabia Deserta* provides an interesting contrast with his identification with the Arabs, while in Burton's case the last two attitudes can be seen curiously co-existing and overlapping: he justifies himself and his opinions by trying to assimilate himself to the inhabitants of Arabia.

We may safely state, however, that as the nineteenth century progresses the awareness of the human reality of the Easterner increases and leads to the adoption of the attitude based on the feeling (not the abstract idea) of the identity of nature of the local resident and the traveller, with certain differences: if Burton attempts to identify himself with the Arabs (or rather with his idea of the Arabs), Doughty goes further and identifies the Arabs with himself. The adoption of this attitude, although it precludes at once paternalism and stereotyped thinking, cannot fail, paradoxically, to raise all kinds of problems in the concrete relationships of travellers with their hosts. But as I have pointed out, its significance lies in the fact that it is based on the traveller's conviction of the *equality* of Easterner and European. Among nineteenth-century travellers to the Middle East Doughty alone, to my knowledge, made this conviction completely his own and treated the Arabs as men and equals. His views about them as expressed in *Arabia Deserta* reveal the exceptional nature of his relationship with them.

In the context of the history of travel literature the attitude of Doughty constitutes a revolution. The personal involvement of Doughty with the Arabs is at once the fundamental reason for the dramatic qualities of *Arabia Deserta* and also, what is for us more important, the testimony of progress in the transformation of mentalities.

NOTES

1   In pre-modern travel literature the term "Oriental" refers to all inhabitants of the Near or Middle East whatever their ethnic origin or religion. Doughty of course speaks only of "the Arabs" because it was with this population that he was exclusively concerned. However, the aim of this study is to place Doughty in a wider context of nineteenth-century travel literature which concerns a great number of very different populations. I have thus, for the sake of clarity and brevity, sometimes used the term Oriental in the general sense which nineteenth-century travellers give it, as will be apparent from the texts quoted.

2   Henry Maundrell, *A Journey from Aleppo to Jerusalem at Easter in 1673* (Oxford: At the Theatre, 1703; reprint of 1810 edition, Beirut: Khayats, 1963), 5. This is a stereotype which is less common in nineteenth-century accounts. Sir Richard Burton explains this form of "transit-due" which so irritated Maundrell and justifies its existence in *Personal Narrative of a Pilgrimage to Al-Madinah and Meccah,* 2 vols. (London: Longmans, 1855; reprint of 1893 edition, New York: Dover Publications, 1964), 2:114.

3   Maundrell, *A Journey,* 198.

4   Charles Robert Cockerell, *Travels in Southern Europe and the Levant* (London: Longmans, 1909), 10.

5   Janice Deledalle-Rhodes, "*Arabia Deserta* de C. M. Doughty et les récits des voyageurs anglais au Moyen-Orient de 1809 à 1896: Mythes, réalités et transformation

des mentalités," Doctorat d'État dissertation, Université Paul Valéry, 1981, 189–292.

6   William Makepeace Thackeray, *Notes on a Journey from Cornhill to Grand Cairo* (London: 1845; Oxford: Oxford University Press, 17 vols., 1908), vol. 9, passim.

7   Eustace Clare Grenville Murray, *Turkey: Being Sketches from Life* (reprinted in part from "Household Words" under the pseudonym "The Roving Englishman") (London: Routledge, 1854, ed. 1877), 6–8.

8   Walter Burton Harris, *A Journey through the Yemen* (London: Blackwood, 1893), 208, 317.

9   Burton, *Personal Narrative*, 1:129.

10 Harriet Martineau, *Eastern Life, Present and Past*, 3 vols. (London: Moxon, 1848). The edition cited here was published in one volume by Lea and Blanchard (Philadelphia, 1848); quote is on p. 371.

11 Lady Lucie Duff Gordon, *Letters from Egypt* (London: Dent, 1865). The letter quoted here is from Gordon Waterfield, *Lucie Duff Gordon* (London: Murray, 1937), 245.

12 This is a commonplace which can be found in nearly all accounts of the East, as are also the ideas of the hospitality of the Oriental and the freedom of the nomad referred to below.

13 It should be pointed out that we are here speaking of the purely religious aspect of the question. Ill-treatment of travellers for personal, venal, or political motives should not be allowed to confuse the issue, as has so often happened. For instance, the murder of the Orientalist Edward H. Palmer in the Sinai in 1882 which appeared mysterious to his contemporaries was later found to be linked with the political mission he was accomplishing at the time. The French traveller J.-P. Ferrier attributed the murder of Doctor Forbes and the treatment to which his corpse and clothing were subjected to the belief of the Balootch tribesmen that he was an alchemist and that everything that he had touched contained gold. (*Voyages en Perse, dans l'Afghanistan, le Béloutchistan et le Turkestan*, 2 vols. [Paris: E. Dentu, 1859], 2:320–21. This work was first published in London in 1856 under the title *Caravan Journeys and Wanderings in Persia, Afghanistan, Balootchistan and Turkistan*.) It must not be forgotten that European travellers were commonly suspected of being spies or sorcerers owing to their habit of taking notes, making sketches, and asking too many questions. This is attested to by most travel books of the time. Doughty himself incurred suspicion on this account at Kheybar (2:112–15) and at Teyma (1:613). Burton tells the story of a German traveller who barely escaped with his life, so irritated were the Beduin at his habit of sketching all he saw (Burton, *Personal Narrative*, 1:239–41). If the behavior of the traveller happened also to be hostile or arrogant the situation was further aggravated and incidents could hardly fail to arise. The wonder is that there were so few. The fact remains that they rarely originated in religious fanaticism. I have examined this subject in detail and attempted a portrait of the European as seen by the Easterner in a chapter entitled "Le Voyageur vu par l'Oriental" (Deledalle-Rhodes, "*Arabia Deserta* de C. M. Doughty," 424–84).

14 Ibid., 293–308. Cf. in particular the reflections of Alexander William Kinglake on this subject in *Eothen* (London: 1844; ed. Sampson Low, Marston and Co., 1913), 144–45. Burton also talks about the freedom of the desert, as does Doughty, al-

though both recognize, especially the latter, that the desert replaces one set of constraints with another. "A little more of government," says Doughty, "and men such as these traders [the Bishr] would leave the insecure wandering life (which all the Aarab, for the incessant weariness and their very emptiness of heart, have partly in aversion,) to become settlers. Beduins complain in their long hours of the wretchedness of their lives" (1:355).

15 According to Charles S. Peirce's theory of signs, an interpretant is one of the three constitutive elements of a sign, the other two being the representamen and the object. An interpretant is what is determined in the mind of a person by a representamen (writing or image) and what enables this person to refer a representamen to its object. An interpretant is the key element of all communication, on which its quality, contents, and meaning depend. I developed this point in a paper: "La Sémiotique du stéréotype: Une approche peircienne" at the Incontro Internazionale su Applicazioni della Semiotica, University of Palermo, 14–15 February 1984.

16 Wilfrid Scawen Blunt and Lady Anne Blunt, *Bedouin Tribes of the Euphrates*, 2 vols. (London: John Murray, 1879); *A Pilgrimage to Nejd* (London: John Murray, 1881), passim.

17 William Gifford Palgrave, *Narrative of a Year's Journey through Central and Eastern Arabia*, 2 vols. (London: Macmillan, 1865), 1:24.

18 Edward Granville Browne, *A Year amongst the Persians, 1887–1888* (London: Adam and Charles Black, 1893; ed. Cambridge, 1927), 115, 121–22, passim.

19 James Morier insists frequently upon the "hypocrisy," the "insincerity," and the "lying disposition" of the Persians in *A Journey through Persia, Armenia and Asia Minor to Constantinople in the years 1808 and 1809* (London: Longman, Hurst, 1812), 111, 285, passim; *A Second Journey through Persia, Armenia, and Asia Minor, to Constantinople, between the years 1810 and 1816* (London: Longman, Hurst, 1818). "Lying is their great, their national vice," he says in *The Adventures of Hajji Baba of Ispahan* (London: Murray, 1824, ed. 1825), 128. "I could imagine the solemn Persian gentlemen to be the most bad-hearted dunghill souls of all nations," remarks Doughty (1:100), while Burton notes the unflattering reputation of Persians amongst Easterners themselves (*Personal Narrative*, 1:14, 44, 67).

20 Palgrave, *Narrative*, 1:282.

21 Ibid., 1:337.

22 Earl of Cromer, *Modern Egypt* (London: Macmillan, 1908; ed. 1911), 553. Cf. also his remark about "that accurate habit of thought which is the main characteristic of the Western as opposed to the Eastern mind" (ibid., 882).

23 Burton, *Personal Narrative*, 2:211.

24 Deledalle-Rhodes, "*Arabia Deserta* de C. M. Doughty," chap. 1, "Le Voyageur et l'Islam."

25 For instance, in works like those of the Reverend George M. Mackie, *Bible Manners and Customs* (London: A. and C. Black, 1898), and of Canon Henry Baker Tristram, *The Land of Israel* (London: Christian Knowledge Society, 1865), *The Land of Moab* (London: John Murray, 1873), *Eastern Customs in Bible Lands* (New York: Whittaker, 1894), etc.

26 Christine Bolt, *Victorian Attitudes to Race* (Toronto: University of Toronto Press, 1971), 112–13, 116–17.

27 We are here concerned exclusively with Doughty's remarks about the Arab population.

28 Cf. F, chap. 2, and Robin Fedden, *English Travellers in the Near East* (London: Longmans, 1958), who notes Doughty's "sense of drama," 29.

29 Martin Armstrong, "The Works of C. M. Doughty," *The Fortnightly Review* 125 (1926): 24.

30 Thomas Edward Lawrence, Introduction to *Travels in Arabia Deserta*, 1:17.

31 Ibid., 1:20–21.

32 Ibid.

33 Sir R. Burton, "Mr. Doughty's Travels in Arabia," *Academy* 34, 18 July 1888, 47–48.

34 W. S. Blunt, *My Diaries*, 2 vols. (London: Martin Secker, 1919–20), 1:273.

35 "My experience of the Senussia at Siwah has convinced me that there is no hope anywhere to be found in Islam. I had made myself a romance about these reformers, but now I see that it has no substantial basis," wrote Blunt on 24 March 1897 (ibid., 1:276).

36 Thackeray, *Notes on a Journey*, 133, 149–50, 251, passim.

37 Sir Henry Layard, *Early Adventures in Persia, Susiana and Babylonia* (London: Murray, 1887).

38 Lady Isabel Burton, *The Inner Life of Syria, Palestine and the Holy Land*, 2 vols. (London: H. S. King and Co., 1875), 2:280.

39 R. Ellis Roberts, "Mr. C. M. Doughty, Poet and Traveller," *Guardian*, 23 January 1926, 12.

PART TWO

Arabia Deserta *as Science*

J. M. WAGSTAFF

Arabia Deserta *as Geography*

Geography has a variety of meanings in popular and academic usage. It can refer to exploration and the acquisition of "new" information about strange and distant places. Equally, people talk of "the geography" when they mean the physical environment of historical or contemporary events—the stage or setting. Geographers themselves recognize a wide concept of their subject, embracing the recognition and understanding of areal differentiation, spatial distributions, and the investigation of the mutual interplay between man and his environment, both physical and human. *Travels in Arabia Deserta* may be seen as contributing to geography in most of its manifestations and this essay attempts to document the case. It begins by looking at Doughty's contribution to the Western world's knowledge of northwestern Arabia, proceeds to an examination of his understanding of its areal differentiation, considers the view that *Arabia Deserta* is supremely a piece of humanistic and perception geography, and concludes with an evaluation of Doughty's work for reconstructing the historical geography of the peninsula.

EXPLORATION

Most commentators are agreed that one of the principal reasons why Doughty travelled in Arabia was geographical curiosity.[1] This is based upon hints in Doughty's prefaces to *Arabia Deserta* (1:32) and his clear statement that he hoped his "passing life might add somewhat of lasting worth to the European geography" (1:469). It appears to be confirmed by a retrospective justification written to his biographer, David Hogarth (H, 130). Despite its size and proximity to important sea routes, the Arabian peninsula was largely unknown to Europeans in the 1870s. Doughty seems to have hoped that he would be able to remedy this, at least in small

DOUGHTY'S TRAVELS, 1876–78

measure, by contributing historico-geographical and topographical information. In line with the contemporary British understanding of geography, which had a distinctly historical or even archaeological flavor, he probably saw his major contribution as being the location of the mythical rock-cut cities of Medain Salih, about which he had previously heard in Maan, and of other ruined settlements reported to him (H, 25–32). No doubt he was influenced by Alois Sprenger's recently published attempt to clarify the map of Arabia as known to ancient writers, notably Ptolemy.[2] The solution of topographical problems, particularly the course of major *wadis,* perhaps loomed larger after his disappointment with Medain Salih, though it was present in his mind all along. Doughty's diaries show how determined he was to record the landscape, note travel times, and calculate elevations (using an aneroid barometer) (H, 38–40), while *Arabia Deserta* itself reports how he took pains to extract topographical information from any Arab willing to talk about the lay of the land (for example, 1:469; 2:378). Doughty's principal achievement was to resolve a problem in the drainage of northern Arabia by confirming that the Wady er-Rummah system drains a large area, and definitely to the east.[3] This and Doughty's other geographical results were published by the celebrated German geographer, Heinrich Kiepert, in successive issues of his illustrated magazine *Globus.*[4] They were also incorporated into a German map showing the Blunts' travels published in *Petermanns geographische Mitteilungen* in 1881.[5] Doughty's own map was produced by the Royal Geographical Society's draftsmen in 1883, the year he addressed the society on his travels, but he was unhappy with the results (H, 107, 157–59). In fact, Doughty did not contribute a great deal to Europe's scientific knowledge of the topography of Arabia, despite all his pains and efforts. He explored a comparatively small part of the peninsula, within an area of at most 360,000 km^2 out of a total area in excess of 2,700,000 km^2 (see map). He took no astronomical sightings to fix longitude and latitude but relied on compass bearings and deadreckoning based on the day's journey with a self-confessed error of perhaps thirty miles (1:54). His map is decidedly sketchy, particularly in comparison with that published by Musil in 1926 covering part of the area traversed by Doughty.[6]

REGIONS AND REGIONALIZATION

If Doughty's motives for travelling in Arabia were at least partly geographical, then it is appropriate to assess *Arabia Deserta* as a contribution to geography, conceived as something more than the acquisition of topographical information. The attempt requires some criteria. Clearly, these should include the sort of items which contemporaries might have used in the period 1876–87 during which Doughty was travelling in Arabia and writing his great work. But they should also be extended to those which critics might employ today. Geography was little developed in Britain during the 1870s and 1880s; its major exponents worked in Germany.[7] Insofar as there was a consensus of opinion at the time, it was that the subject was concerned with two related endeavors. The first was the investigation of the relationships which were thought to exist between physical conditions, especially topography, and human activities. Physical geography was still seen in Kantian terms as providing a framework for the reasoned study of man, but by the 1880s physical conditions were also generally believed to have causal power with respect to human society.[8] Doughty is likely to have subscribed to these ideas as a result of his interest and training in geology. Richard Bevis has even argued that Doughty was attracted to Arabia precisely because there the teleological issues were presented in a particularly stark form in a terrain where, in Burton's phrase, "Nature scalped, flayed, discovered all her skeleton to the gazer's eye."[9] The second object of geographical endeavor in the last quarter of the nineteenth century arose from the first. It was to recognize and describe regions. These were seen as units of terrestrial space in which distinct ways of life appeared to be not only in harmony with physical conditions but also expressive of them, "caused" by them. Topography was generally thought to provide real as well as convenient boundaries. This meant, of course, that the basis of regionalization lay in geology. Geological investigation was a major interest of the young Doughty and permeates the whole of *Arabia Deserta*.

At first glance, *Arabia Deserta* is not easy to fit into contemporary notions of geography. It is far from being a work of systematic or regional geography; it is arranged as a travel narrative. Moreover, the journey was as much a spiritual and psychological endeavor as a quest for geographical information and that aspect is emphasized in *Arabia Deserta* (Ta, 68–90). Nonetheless, the narrative does suggest that Doughty consciously differentiated major topographical regions and was aware of the nuances of relief within them. In his pages it is possible to distinguish clearly between the limestone uplands of trans-Jordan and the sandstone hills farther to the southeast. In addition, *Arabia Deserta* brings out the relationship of the latter to the great sand desert called the Nefud and contrasts these regions with both the fragmented volcanic massifs to the west and the immense, largely crystalline plateau to the south. These regions have been incorporated into subsequent discussions of the geography of Arabia, though Doughty's contribution is not always specifically acknowledged. Doughty's regionalization is apparent, for example, in Hogarth's summary account of the center of the peninsula in his *Penetration of Arabia* and echoes in his earlier *Nearer East*. [10] It was carried over into the British Naval Intelligence handbook on *Western Arabia and the Red Sea* and finally into such regional textbooks as W. B. Fisher's *Middle East*. [11]

Doughty's descriptions are memorable. He had the ability to conjure up a landscape through the use of heightened language (Ta, 58–59; Tr, 62–63), a skill which many professional geographers have lacked. The limestone hills of ancient Gilead were "fresh to the sight and sweet to every sense . . . , full of the balm-smelling pines and the tree-laurel sounding with the sobbing sweetness and the amorous wings of doves" (1:55–56), but were rather different from the high "limestone downs and coombs" between Shobek and Petra, where there were "hollow park-like grounds with evergreen oak timber" (1:78, 79). Both contrast with the "inhospitable, horrid sandstones" and "cloud-like strange wasted ranges" which lie beyond the "brow of Syria" where Arabia proper begins (1:89–91). Between Maan and Tebuk, Tebuk and Teyma, belts of "deep sand country" bordered the "mountain sandstones" (1:95). In the vicinity of Medain Salih, Doughty's first goal in his Arabian travels, "the mountain sandstone cloven down in cross lines, is here a maze of rhomboid masses, with deep and blind streets, as it were, of some lofty city lying between them" (1:172). The area near Teyma was similar (1:619). Borj Selman, though, was described as full of "sandstone crags," while Jebel Birrd (east of Teyma) was noted as a "high solitary sandstone mountain" (1:255, 346). Elsewhere Doughty saw "wasted sand-rock, spires, needles, pinnacles and battled mountains" (1:284). Along the eastern and northern edges of the sandstone mountains, Doughty saw the "high white borders" of the Great Nefud (1:347). When he crossed part of it, he noted the tendency of at least some of the sand hills to produce a booming sound as the travellers struggled through them, reminiscent of the "giddy loud swelling sound, as when your wetted finger is drawn upon the lip of a glass of water, and like that swooning din after the chime of a great bell, or cup of metal"

(1:352). Later he described the sands in the Kasim district (part of the Nefud as Siri) as "driven-up in long swelling waves, that trend somewhat N. and S." (2:336). To the west of the sandstone uplands lie the volcanic massifs, the *harras* (1:464). They stimulated some of the finest descriptions in *Arabia Deserta* (Tr, 60). The *harras* are immense black platforms, the sharp borders of which Doughty likened to a wall and, on one occasion, to "the ice-brink of a glacier" (1:402, 423; 2:239). In places the surface was shaped into "basalt coombs and crooked folds" (1:475). In one area it looked like "nothing so much as an immeasurable cow-shard" (1:441). In others, it spread out as "a black vulcanic gravel plain . . . in which there rise single black cones, and twin crests," or looked like a "radiant beach of hot lava stones" (1:426–27, 442). "The lava field is now cast into great waves and troughs, and now it is a labyrinth of lava crags and short lava sand-plains" (2:85; cf. 2:254). Below the eastern edges of the *harras* and across the valleys through them were drifts of "lighter pumice, mingled with an infinite cumber of broken-up lava and some basaltic blocks" (1:423) which made travel arduous.

Between Hayil and Boreyda, and then on his journey to et-Tayif, Doughty crossed an immense upland wilderness of "granite grit with many black basalt bergs" (2:321, 492). He appraised its more southerly areas as "the best wild pasture land that I have seen in Arabia: the bushes are few, but it is a 'white country' overgrown with the desert grass, *nussy*" and speculated—correctly—that the quality of grazing might be due to the fact that the area lay just within the border of the monsoon rains, which fall heavily in early autumn (2:493, 500). Much of this granite upland is drained by the Wady er-Rummah and its tributaries (see map). While occasionally containing pools of water, the main *wady* flooded only once or twice in a century, according to reports given to Doughty (2:338, 420, 500). From the southwestern corner of this immense plateau Doughty entered a "craggy mountain region" and passed through a high stony valley into quite "another nature of Arabia," the coastlands known as Tehama (2:509–15).

As well as bringing out an acceptable regionalization of northwestern Arabia in terms of terrain and ultimately geology, *Arabia Deserta* reveals Doughty's sense of the relationships between physical conditions and the pattern of human activity. It is thus possible to recognize regions in the fullest sense understood by nineteenth-century geographers. The distinctive human activities found in each of the physical regions outlined

above emerge in the course of the narrative. In general Doughty reveals
variations on a combination of pastoralism and oasis cultivation. Opportunity and constraint were provided by the precise physical setting. Thus,
the harsh terrain of the *harras* was nearly empty of human activity, apart
from some transhumance grazing of animals by people who came up from
the Tehama during the "light and airy" summer months but retreated
again before the "intolerable cold" of winter (1:458, 472–77). At least
some of the valleys, though, supported cultivation "amidst that huge
waste of harra stones, in the ground next the wells" (1:487–88). The
largest extent of cropland seen by Doughty in this region lay in the dank
Kheybar valleys, pressed "like a palm leaf, in the Harra border" and where
irrigation water came from numerous springs (2:92, 110). The crystalline
plateau provided good grazing, as already noted, but there were various
poor corn villages here and there. Larger oases, with date palms, were
described in el-Kasim (2:336–38) and the vicinity of Hayil (1:633–34).
Although some nomads were found in the sandstone hills, wavering dis-
persedly, "seeking pasture in the midst of this hollow fainting country"
(1:368), the environment was incapable of supporting extensive grazing
(1:395). A few oases were seen, especially along the eastern edges of the
harras where dry stream beds provided cultivable land and access to water
(1:86, 112–13, 182–87). On the edge of the Nefud was the oasis of
Teyma, occupying the floor of a former seasonal lake (1:329, 340, 569–
72). In all these regions, irrigation was essential to cultivation and imposed a particular rhythm on the way of life. The limestone uplands bordering the Jordan were a contrast. They supported great flocks of sheep as
well as pockets of rainfed cornland which produced "plentiful harvests"
(1:55–78). These excerpts make clear that Doughty had a sense of the
areal variation present in the parts of Arabia which he crossed. He chose
not to make them the basis of a systematic account or to attempt any
formal explanation of the physical-human correlations which he saw. The
drama of the travel narrative predominates in *Arabia Deserta*.

HUMANISTIC AND PERCEPTION GEOGRAPHY

During the second half of the twentieth century geography moved away
from the physical determinism which had informed so much of its work in
the latter part of the previous century. The reasons need not detain us
here. Areal differentiation is still tacitly recognized as of basic importance,

but regionalization is no longer based solely on topographical and ultimately geological data. Social and economic criteria are more usually employed. Since the late 1950s geography has seen itself as a spatial science,
concerned with the social and economic effects of distance and with the
geometrical configuration of human phenomena. Statistical analysis and
mathematical modeling are essential to its aspirations. In fact, the subject
has changed its character so much since Doughty's time that modern geographers would probably not wish to appraise *Arabia Deserta* only in
terms of its contribution to regional geography. Its geographical value
today lies primarily in two directions. The first is its character as a description of a particular personal encounter with Arabia. The second is its
utility as a source for the historical geography of the peninsula, or part of
it, in the last quarter of the nineteenth century. Partly as a reaction against
the mechanistic and depersonalized character of spatial science geography,
a growing number of geographers now interest themselves in how people
have perceived their environment, structured it in their minds, and expressed their reactions to it. *Arabia Deserta* is a prime candidate for this
type of study. Several difficulties beset the task. Although based on diaries, the book is a retrospective, considered account of Doughty's travels
rather than a spontaneous description of events shortly after they happened or a record of immediate impressions. It is an account of a spiritual
quest, at least as much as the chronicle of an actual journey (Ta, 64–90).
The material is less important than the way it is presented.[12] The original
experience has been deliberately heightened to increase the sense of
drama. A note of bitterness runs through the whole work (Ta, 43), perhaps the inevitable result of the trials and tribulations which must often
have sapped the author's spirit even in remembrance as well as in actuality.
Despite the problems, though, four humanistic themes emerge from the
pages of *Arabia Deserta*.

   The first and foremost is Arabia itself, the people and the land. Against
their harsh personalities, Doughty tests his own. *Arabia Deserta* shows
him exposed not only to the essential structure of the earth, but also
stripped to his basic humanity. He contends with an environment which
almost overwhelms him and deals with a people whose personal hardness
is a result of their own battle for survival in a harsh land. Doughty's belief
in the essential goodness of man survives his worst experiences, despite
the bitter dregs; it is vindicated by the many personal kindnesses shown to
him as the passive stranger and guest. The *Nasrany* Khalil (Doughty's

persona in *Arabia Deserta*) refuses to disguise or renounce his Christian
faith, even though the privations of Arabian travel must have sorely tried
it and the people humiliated and persecuted him for his rugged per-
sistence. The land and the people continued to fascinate, despite bone
weariness and illness.

Through his account of his mental and spiritual struggle with Arabia
comes Doughty's second, subordinate theme. This is what Bevis calls his
exceptional responsiveness to topography.[13] Doughty must have been
deeply affected by what he saw. His writing not only evokes vivid images
for the reader, as we have seen, but also conveys the emotional impact of
particular landscapes, onto which he often transfers his mental state.
These are of interest to the student of perception. When Doughty writes
about the *harras,* he talks of being "engaged in the many basalt coombs
and crooked folds" (1:425) and of the "vast bed and banks of rusty and
basaltic bluish blocks . . . stubborn heavy matter, as iron, and sounding
like bell-metal: lying out eternally under the sand-driving desert wind
. . ." (1:427). By contrast, the "low ranging hills" seen to the east of Shobek in the early elated days of his journey were "fresh" (1:70). The uplands
farther south, though, soon became "a dead land, whence, if he die not,
he [the traveller] shall bring home nothing but a perpetual weariness in
his bones" (1:95). The *fjelde*-like landscape encountered when he was ill
and nearing what was to be the end of the journey was a poignant reminder of those days, some fifteen years before, when he researched the
glaciers of Norway (2:515; H, 5–7).

The third theme, again related, is the harshness of the physical environment of Arabia. It is conveyed through adjectives, reused time and again,
and by brief descriptions. The sandstones are "inhospitable" and "horrid"
(1:90, 172), while the aspect of the *harras* was "direful" to an extent
undreamed of (1:452; 2:525). Much of the terrain, of whatever kind, is
described as "waste" or "wilderness," sometimes as "an iron wilderness" or
an "iron desolation" (1:425, 452). "No sweet chittering of birds greets the
coming of the desert light, besides man there is no voice in this waste
drought" (1:286). Doughty reports how he often crossed a "dazzling" wilderness, "stricken by the barren sunshine, the brain . . . swooning"
(1:484) or travelled in "a scalding tempest of sun's rays, which strikes up
again, parching the eyeballs, from the glowing sand" (1:423). The air
"was like a flame in the sun" (2:288). The night, despite its chill, was
often "a most sweet respite" (1:424). Occasionally, the eyes and spirit were

further refreshed by a "pleasant wooded place" or "a delicious green grove of fruit-bearing wild fig-trees" and the "green pageant" of an oasis, beautiful "after the burning barren dust of the desert" (1:118, 487–88, 555). Even when there was rain, it came down "shrill and seething, upon the harsh gravel soil" (2:330) and "a cold wind breathed over the desert" (1:209, 613).

Finally, Doughty perceived Arabia as like the sea. Other people have made the same comparison, but in *Arabia Deserta* it is "elaborated and extended into a pervasive metaphor."[14] Not only are the mountains, seen in the distance or travelled beside in the desert, frequently described as "coasts" (Tr, 63), but plains are represented as "beaches," whether "that flint beach, which lies strewn over great part of the mountain of Esau" (1:67), or "a flaggy pavement of sandstones rippled in the strand of those old planetary seas" (1:97), or "a bare and black shining beach of heated vulcanic stones" (1:425). The vale between Jebel Ajja and Jebel Selma was as "barren as a sea-strand" (1:635). Like the sea, much of Arabia seemed empty and solitary to Doughty. But it was not trackless. He frequently came upon an "old, worn camping ground" (1:428; 2:295) and noticed, when crossing the crystalline plateau, how "The country is full of cattle paths—it may be partly made by the wild goat and gazelles" (2:495).

HISTORICAL GEOGRAPHY

Arabia Deserta is an account of a journey through part of northwestern Arabia during a particular two-year period. Its value as a historical source is discussed in another chapter of this volume. Here an attempt is made to evaluate it for purposes of reconstructing the historical geography of Arabia, especially its settlements and economy. At first sight the credentials are impeccable. Doughty was, after all, a first-hand observer. He seems to have paid meticulous attention to detail and claims to have checked his sources (1:469). Doubts arise from Doughty's use of language and the possibility that the search for effect has led to poetic license. These are not entirely settled by the commonsense retort that no artistic purpose would be served by embellishing the account of settlements and land use, for Doughty clearly reacted as subjectively to settlements, for example, as he did to the physical landscape. For instance, Tebuk was "built of raw clay, appears of an ochre colour, pleasantly standing before a palm-grove, in a world of weary desert" (1:112), while el-Ally was described as "narrow, upon the wady side, under the Harra" (1:194). As he came over a fold of the Nefud, Doughty saw "a great clay town built in this waste sand with enclosing walls and towers and streets and houses! and there besides a bluish dark wood of ethel trees, upon high dunes . . . I saw, as it were, Jerusalem in the desert!" (2:339). Another cause for concern is that, as Hogarth revealed, the diaries which Doughty kept and on which he drew for *Arabia Deserta* contain alarming gaps, notably during his three-month stay in the Kheybar oasis (H, 68, 82, 84). It is difficult to imagine that he could recall every detail of what he saw or heard, while it would have been unwise, as he admitted and other travellers have discovered, to make notes in the presence of many of the ordinary people of the country (1:629). The only way of checking Doughty's reliability is to compare his descriptions with those of other European travellers. These should be as nearly contemporary as possible in order to minimize any differences which may have developed over time in the phenomena being described. Unfortunately, the scope is limited. Doughty's routes were virtually unique and few travellers penetrated the interior of Arabia as far as he did until the twentieth century. Hayil alone offers the possibility of serious comparison for, as the capital of the emir Ibn Rashid, it attracted several European travellers in the 1860s and 1870s. Amongst these were the English Jesuit and former soldier William Gifford Palgrave (1826–88), who claimed to have reached the town in 1862, and the Blunts, Wilfrid (1840–1922) and his wife, the Lady Anne (1837–1917), who arrived there just nine months after Doughty (January 1879).

Doughty provided a sketch plan of what might be called, rather grandly, the central business district of Hayil and produced a single consolidated account of the town, though he visited it twice (1:636–70; 2:19–61). It is not as detailed as his description of Aneyza (2:363–475). Stripped of the personal details of his story, the account can be summarized in a brief space. The town lay in a vale between two mountains. It was sheltered to the north by the "bergs" of Sumra Hayil, which made the town stuffy in summer, and apparently surrounded by date palms. There was a nomadic encampment outside. It was walled and dominated by the "whitened donjon of the *Kasr*," or castle, belonging to the emir. In front of it was a long public square and facing the *kasr* was a line of nine *makhzans* (guestrooms). Doughty thought Hayil a "clean and well-built clay town," with the streets "well set out" and lined with one-storied houses. The streets were clean ("the draffe is cast out into certain pits and side places") and instead of an apparently expected air of decay there was one of newness, thriving, and spending. The public *suk* (market) was two hundred paces long and lined on both sides with shops, more than 130 altogether ("small ware-rooms, built backward into which light enters by the doorway"). Most of the tradesmen were foreigners, but Doughty saw local women under a porch selling dates and pumpkins and noticed that near the end of the *suk* was the cornmarket and the place where camel-loads of firewood and wild hay were sold. There were a number of artisans—workers in wood, metal, and gypsum plaster, as well as builders and carpenters. Doughty learned that the local women sewed and embroidered and plaited palm mats. Just above the *suk* was the butchers' market, in a court. Hayil was divided into eleven wards. Doughty heard that there were four common schools. The population of this capital of an extensive (90 × 170 leagues) but thinly populated territory (hardly 20,000 settled and 14,000 more or less nomadic) was estimated at about 3,000. When the emir was away, as on Doughty's second visit, most of the shops were shut since there was no business to transact, and the town seemed "a dead and empty place" (2:271). It was perhaps this element which led Doughty to characterize "Hayil as a half Beduin town-village, with a foreign suk," especially compared with Boreyda, which was "a great civil township of the midland Nejd life" (2:348).

Palgrave has been accused of inaccuracy and H. St. John B. Philby even doubted whether he reached Hayil at all.[15] Doughty and the Blunts accepted his claims and the circumstantial details do suggest that he set foot in Ibn Rashid's capital. His account of the Hayil he saw more than fifteen years before is less systematic than that by Doughty[16] and can be distilled to a short statement. Palgrave agreed with Doughty on several points. Thus, he was impressed by the appearance of the town. He noted a few Beduin tents clustered close to the rampart, the dominance of the castle with the open space in front, and the proximity of the market. But he gave a few more details on certain items and produced a plan of the whole town. His soldier's eye recorded the height of the fortifications and the presence not just of towers but of "bastion towers." He observed the grand scale of houses belonging to the emir's principal officers and the location of the large public mosque, marked by Doughty on his plan but not described in the text. Palgrave also differentiated in the *makhzans* between "warehouses and small apartments" and noted that the quarter near the castle was relatively new, dating only from the accession of the present dynasty. By contrast with Doughty, though, Palgrave tells the historical geographer very little about the *suk* beyond its being new and full of activity. He put the population at 20,000 to 22,000, which seems unrealistic when large cities like Baghdad and Damascus had populations estimated at about 80,000 and 140,000, respectively, in the 1870s.[17]

The Blunts stayed for ten days and Lady Anne's description of the town as such is extremely short. This is mainly because she and her husband agreed that discretion was needed amongst religious fanatics and, consequently, she remained very much indoors, avoiding passing through the streets except when invited to the *kasr*.[18] All that Lady Anne tells us, in fact, is that she did not find the town "particularly imposing" when they approached it; most of the houses were hidden in the palm groves and the wall was little more than ten feet high. Like Doughty she was struck, however, by "the extraordinary spick and span neatness of the walls and streets" which gave "almost an air of unreality."[19] The rest of her account contains no description of the town's layout, nothing about its economic activity, and no references to public buildings apart from the *kasr*, which she described as "almost a town itself."[20] There is certainly nothing to contradict Doughty.

If Doughty's account of Hayil can be accepted as reliable, as I think it can, then the historical geographer is inclined to believe what he says about the thirty or forty other settlements mentioned in *Arabia Deserta* and about land use and economy. This is especially true for the large, almost set pieces which Doughty has embedded in his work. These include, in addition to Hayil, the oasis of el-Ally which he visited early in his Arabian travels (1:181–89, 194–96, 526, 555) and el-Kasim (2:336–38), where he went toward their end and stayed in Aneyza (2:363–76). In almost every district he crossed, Doughty noted how potsherds, broken glass, and a few building stones and bricks betrayed the sites of deserted settlements (1:154; 2:420–21). Oasis cultivation in Arabia, he observed, was "hardly less skilful than that we see in the *ghrûta* of Damascus" and he went on to give a brief outline of agricultural practices (2:416). He understood the devastation brought by "clouds" or "pillars" of "wreathing and flickering" locusts (1:380–81) and the nearness of famine when the rainfall was so variable from year to year (2:132). Early on he appreciated the effects of distance and transport costs on trade in cereals (1:56), but he went on to record the dependency of Hejaz on the *Haj* caravans (1:238–40), the commercial influence of Mecca on the interior (2:488, 561), and the existence of important trade links between the inland settlements of Arabia, on the one hand, and Iraq and Kuweyt, on the other (1:630, 656; 2:20, 23, 58, 65, 337, 375, 409, 418–19). All this—and much more—is important evidence for the spatial dimensions of the socioeconomic patterns of northwestern Arabia in the last quarter of the nineteenth century. It should be more widely exploited to reconstruct the life of the region on the eve of important changes brought about, even before the discovery of oil in the Eastern Region of what is now Saudi Arabia, by the Hejaz Railway from Damascus to Medina (completed 1906) and the expansion of the Wahabies under Ibn Saud.

CONCLUSION

The diversity and richness of *Travels in Arabia Deserta* make it an immense quarry for geographers. As well as being a source of valuable information about a certain part of Arabia at a particular time, it is a marvelous exemplar of one man's struggle to express his feelings about the terrain of the peninsula and convey at least something of the impression which it made upon him in the different moods generated by experiences of travel and people. At the same time, readers become keenly aware of areal differentiation in the small part of Arabia which Doughty crossed and of the reality of topographically—and geologically—based regions. In addition, they are brought to an appreciation of the effects of environment (both positive and negative) upon the life of the people, as well as the constraints imposed by distance upon the character and significance of trade. Re-reading *Arabia Deserta* brings one close to the well-springs of the geographer's endeavor—the wish to know, understand, and describe the diversity of the earth's surface in all its fullness.

NOTES

1 A, 103; Richard Bevis, "Spiritual Geology: C. M. Doughty and the Land of the Arabs," *Victorian Studies* 16, no. 2 (1972): 163–81; David George Hogarth, *The Penetration of Arabia: A Record of the Development of Western Knowledge Concerning the Arabian Peninsula* (London: Lawrence and Bullen, 1904), 272; H, 130–31; Ta, 28, 83–85.
2 Alois Sprenger, *Die alte Geographie Arabiens* (Bern: Commissionsverlag von Huber, 1875); Ta, 28.
3 Hogarth, *The Penetration of Arabia*, 289–91; H, 101.

4   *Globus* 37 (1880): 201–3; 39 (1881): 7–10, 23–30; 40 (1881): 38–41; 41 (1882): 214–18, 249–52.
5   *Petermanns geographische Mitteilungen* 27 (1881): pocket.
6   Alois Musil, *Northern Hegâz*, 1 : 500,000. Oriental Explorations and Studies, no. 1 (New York: American Geographical Society, 1926).
7   John Norman Leonard Baker, *The History of Geography* (Oxford: Blackwell, 1963); Robert Eric Dickinson, *The Makers of Modern Geography* (London: Routledge and Kegan Paul, 1969); Edmund William Gilbert, *British Pioneers in Geography* (Newton Abbot: David and Charles, 1972).
8   G. Tatham, "Geography in the Nineteenth Century," in *Geography in the Twentieth Century*, ed. Griffith Taylor (London: Methuen, 1951), 28–69.
9   Bevis, "Spiritual Geology," 173. The quotation is from Sir Richard Francis Burton, *Personal Narrative of a Pilgrimage to Al-Madinah and Meccah*, memorial edition (London: Tylston and Edwards, 1893; repr. New York: Dover Publications, 1964), 2:131.
10   David George Hogarth, *The Nearer East* (London: William Heinemann, 1902), 64–73, and *The Penetration of Arabia*, 278–94.
11   Hugh Scott, Kenneth Mason, and Mary Marshall, *Western Arabia and the Red Sea*, Geographical Handbook Series (London: British Admiralty, Naval Intelligence Division, 1946), 37–42; William Bayne Fisher, *The Middle East*, 6th ed. (London: Methuen, 1971), 473–77 (first published 1950).
12   Robin Bidwell, *Travellers in Arabia* (London: Hamlyn, 1976), 93.
13   Bevis, "Spiritual Geology," 166–67.
14   Ibid., 167.
15   Harry St. John Bridger Philby, *The Heart of Arabia* (London: Constable and Co. Ltd., 1922), 2:117–56, particularly 136.
16   William Gifford Palgrave, *Narrative of a Year's Journey through Central and Eastern Arabia (1862–63)* (Cambridge and London: Cambridge University Press, 1865), 1:102–67.
17   Haim Gerber, "The Population of Syria and Palestine in the Nineteenth Century," *Asian and African Studies* 13 (1979): 57–80; Robert Mantran, "Bagdad à l'époque ottomane," *Arabica* 9 (1962): 311–24.
18   Lady Anne Blunt, *A Pilgrimage to Nejd*, 2nd ed. (London: John Murray, 1881; repr. London: Frank Cass, 1968), 1:227.
19   Ibid., 1:212.
20   Ibid., 1:231.

PHILIP C. HAMMOND

Charles M. Doughty as a Source
for Nabataean Archaeology

When Charles M. Doughty began his two years of wandering through
Arabia Deserta in the late nineteenth century, little was known about that
mysterious pre-Islamic Arab people called the Nabataeans. Although a
few of the classical writers—especially Diodorus of Sicily, Strabo, Josephus, and others[1]—had touched upon their early history, the Nabataeans
would not emerge into the reality of historical fact until the works of
Albert Kammerer and Jean Cantineau and the excavations of George
Horsfield,[2] which finally permitted the identification of their multi-
tudinous sites by ceramic as well as epigraphic means.

Nabataean script, as a sign of Nabataean presence in inscriptions and
graffiti, had been recognized by the early epigraphists and was relatively
well established as a known and translatable language by Doughty's time.
As he points out (1:32, fn. 2), the *Corpus Inscriptionum Semiticorum* (the
scholarly world's "official" collection of Semitic inscriptional materials)
was already in the process of publication by the Paris Académie des Inscriptions by the time he arrived back in England, as a consequence of
explorations conducted in Coele-Syria and Arabia before his own visit.[3]

The sporadic references to the Nabataeans and the body of inscriptional
materials being collected in what is now southern Syria, Jordan, Sinai,
and northern Saudi Arabia had, before Doughty's travels, provided the
skeleton upon which subsequent research would build the flesh of a living
culture. This was done by historical analysis at first and, more currently,
by the results of archaeological research.

We first see the Nabataeans, in the early classical period, emerging at
the beginning of the fourth century B.C. as a gradually sedentarizing
Beduin group, apparently moving into the area of modern Jordan from the

Arabian peninsula. Petra became their stopping place and soon became a semifortified stronghold, achieved by nature and strategically placed walls and guard-points. By the first century B.C.–A.D. they had become masters of the vast trade routes stretching from the Arabian peninsula northward to Damascus and the seaports feeding the western world. As once-nomads, they became the controllers of the caravan trade, whose beginnings reached as far as China and whose markets were the streets of Alexandria and Rome. By the first Christian century they had over a thousand depots, transfer points, settlements, and agency offices throughout the southern Coele-Syrian area. Politically they became a hereditary monarchy, with ties to the major kingdoms of the day: Ptolemaic, Seleucid, Jewish, Parthian, and Roman.

Petra flourished as one of the "great" provincial capitals, complete with theater, temples, market places, and all the other necessary public and private installations required of urban sophistication in that period. Most sensational, however, were the monumental rock-hewn tombs which surrounded the living area and remain today as virtually the only sign of their occupation of the site. Archaeological excavations, including my own, are beginning to reveal other architectural evidences, but an entire city is an awesome task to uncover except in bits and pieces over years of work.

It is not extensive inscriptions or casually scratched remarks by passersby that form the outlines of a people. It is only the amassing of data—be it direct or indirect—that permits us to "see" an ancient culture. Even a complete history, by a contemporary or an observer, cannot fully sketch in the life that is lived beyond the pages of a commentary. Hence, archaeology must become the modern tool for securing the data, reconstructing the culture history, and finally interpreting the process by which that culture history was created and shaped and came into full flower.

But here a clear definition of what archaeology means today must be laid out. The Middle East has been notorious for a kind of archaeology which deals in things and not in the life and culture of people. Under the impact of the rise of anthropology in the early 1920s, as envisioned by A. L. Kroeber and others on the American scene,[4] archaeology began to change in the New World, and it is slowly making that change in regard to its self-image in the Old.[5] Still further, as archaeological data began to expand, the single individual, as an archaeologist, began to seek the assistance of colleagues in a wider and wider range of disciplines. With such a broader definition of archaeology as a multidisciplined study of ancient culture, a different scale can be used for the evaluation of Doughty's contributions as a source for the archaeology of the Nabataeans.

It is perhaps the epigraphist (that is, the expert in ancient languages and inscriptions) of a modern archaeological team who turns to Doughty's work first. Although all of the inscriptions which Doughty secured in the field are now in the *Corpus Inscriptionum Semiticorum,* in a special volume, *Documents épigraphiques,* edited by Ernest Renan (1:32, fn. 2) and appendix (1:224–27), the descriptions of their locations, the settings in which they were found, and his own subjective reflections concerning them are necessary parts of their interpretation, and for this the student must consult *Arabia Deserta.* Still further, Doughty furnished something in the way of a demographic or distribution map of ancient peoples and the routes they followed in his notes concerning the inscriptions he found. Regrettably, Doughty could not read Nabataean or any other of the ancient scripts he found evidenced. Doughty never learned Nabataean, and he had only a rudimentary knowledge of Hebrew.[6] Arabic really remained his chief tool and only claim to Oriental expertise. Yet he contributed to the field by careful copying, the making of actual reproductions of inscriptions (via "squeezes," using wet paper to secure a physical impression of the texts), and by seeking out the expert epigraphists of his day to whom he almost gratuitously handed over his hard-won efforts. The story of Doughty's experiences in the course of attempting to secure publication of the epigraphic materials is admirably set out by Hogarth:[7] the tedious correspondence with Sprenger in Germany, the disappointments of his communications with Halévy in Paris, the refusal from the British Museum, along with the initial delay from the time the materials were retrieved from the British Consulate in Damascus (1879) until the *Corpus* volume was finally published in 1884. Despite these obstacles, relatively fast publication (for the scholarly world, that is) resulted from his actions and the academic communities were made aware of the data.

Because of his long periods of residence in certain areas (Teyma for a month and in the vicinity of Medain Salih for twice that period)[8] and his return to others, Doughty was able to seek out little-known inscriptions on the basis of local informants and to spend the time necessary to conduct the searches. Too often, epigraphic surveys have failed owing to lack of information concerning the location of locally known inscriptions or to the absence of time to search for scattered and often difficult-to-access examples, even if reported to the surveyors. Doughty had time, friends, and the energy to exhaust as many possibilities in an area as were made known to him. His mode of travel, by camelback, was also an asset, since modern vehicular travel is often too fast to allow the traveller to notice the signs of ancient writings which lie hidden behind boulders and scrub or deep in the side *wadis* (riverbeds) of the Middle East.

Finally, modern reuse of ancient building materials (going on in his time as well) has often led to the destruction of valuable epigraphic materials. A common habit in the Middle East has been the reuse of inscribed blocks in modern house walls with the inscribed faces turned inward out of sight. Doughty recorded what he saw, and those inscriptions can therefore never be lost.

Site survey, a major effort of archaeologists today, was a second major contribution of Doughty's wandering. In his day the Nabataean area sites of Umm Jemal, Maan, Petra, Teyma, and Medain Salih—quite familiar now—were virtually unknown to the western world. It would be almost another quarter-century before scholars would penetrate the trans-Jordanic and northern Saudi Arabian areas to investigate really thoroughly the sites Doughty described.[9] The enormous value of his initial work at those then almost inaccessible sites was applauded by the scholarly world upon the publication of his descriptive and evaluative insights, as the appendix comments of de Vogüé (1:673 ff.) indicate. No better work, for example, has been done at Medain Salih, which Doughty "discovered," since his own visits there, although Charles Huber and Julius Euting worked there soon after (H, 41, 60, 106).

Once again, the availability of adequate time to spend in the area, local informants and friends to assist exploration, and the inquisitive mind of Doughty made for a combination not available to many scholars even today. But the importance—still unrealized by proper excavation—of Medain Salih as Nabataene's major southern site was evident to Doughty because of its sheer extent and monumental carvings and inscriptions. Although now somewhat more properly placed, architecturally and otherwise, in the scheme of Nabataean studies as a result of the work of Jaussen and Savignac, Doughty's descriptions and sketches provided a base for the study of Medain Salih still usable today. His uninformed (but correct!) suggestions (1:31, 158–60, 231 ff.; 2:554) concerning the use of certain of the carved installations, his discussions with local informants, and his exploration of the area itself all stand unchallenged as proper survey details.[10]

Parallel in value to Doughty's descriptive notes on Medain Salih are those he made concerning Teyma and its environs (1:328–44, 574–616). Here also his data furnished a wealth of information about a little-known site which still guides exploration. Likewise, as a description of a still unexcavated site, those notes have had very little added to them in the past century. Umm Jemal (1:50), Petra (1:78–82), and other areas have subsequently been subjected to various degrees of scholarly investigation and excavation, but Doughty pointed the way and focussed attention upon their importance.[11] Maan's "old town" still needs closer attention (1:71–74), and the camel routes from Maan need to be followed once again, with Doughty leading the way (1:96 ff.).

On the negative side, for which Doughty can in no way be held responsible, is the fact that he could not identify a Nabataean site if no inscriptional material was present. That regrettable situation was unremedied until advances in technique and the excavations at Petra in 1929 and following years provided archaeology with ceramic markers concerning the presence of Nabataean occupation.[12] Knowledge of precise ceramic dating would undoubtedly have increased the value of Doughty's investigations to an unbelievable degree, since he wandered where few others have been since. This same problem also beset the survey work of Alois Musil, Albrecht Alt, T. E. Lawrence, C. Leonard Woolley, and many others until Nabataean presence was detectable on the basis of pottery as well as script.[13]

On the more traditional side of archaeology, Doughty brought back "samples," especially from Medain Salih (1:212–13), of resins, cloth, leather, coins, and similar materials, along with his sketches, site plans, ceramic and numismatic notes, epigraphic squeezes, geological remarks, and extensive data on flora and fauna observed everywhere he went. Unfortunately, the state of archaeology in his day left much of that material either unpublished or unintelligible to those to whom it was given for analysis (1:228–29). The sole exception was the epigraphic material, as noted above.

What does remain—and remains to a great degree still untapped—are the materials scattered not only throughout his text but also in the pages of his "Index and Glossary of Arabic Words" (2:576–696). Perhaps those who have been engrossed in Nabataean studies, myself included, have consistently sought out Doughty's more "accessible" archaeological data from the text of his volumes and unthinkingly ignored the wealth hidden in the index and glossary. My default in this regard may, perhaps, serve as a general example of this sin of omission. In pursuing Nabataean studies in general, I paid due attention to Doughty's descriptions of places where he reported inscriptions in order to trace the geographical boundaries of Nabataean occupation, but little attention to the entries in Doughty's index, other than the page numbers of the sites he noted. It has only been after further research that the inestimable value of the geological notes, travel routes, comments on village versus Beduin life, floral and faunal types, and the host of other valuable data in the index has been realized, many decades after Doughty jotted them down. Yet, at the same time, in excuse for our failure, it may be that the traditionalism of archaeology in the Middle East is at fault and we have only just recently realized the necessity for the incorporation of cultural and interdisciplinary study, in the broadest sense of the terms, as part of the archaeologist's duty.

The British military strategists during World War I did realize the importance of both Doughty's text and the index, however. Hogarth,[14] in reporting on the matter, notes the close study of Doughty by the Cairo office and the almost page-by-page absorption of his descriptions and references by T. E. Lawrence. For the latter, such knowledge as Doughty transmitted was the priceless key both to sheer survival in the desert and to the ability to comprehend the mind of the Beduin and secure their aid in behalf of the Allied efforts in the Middle East. It is therefore incumbent upon anyone seeking Doughty's contributions to Nabataean archaeology today to point out the ethnographic or "cultural" contributions he made.

Very little changed in the Middle East from the first century A.D. (and before) to the late nineteenth century except religion and politics. In the latter case, the rule of the Turks was very little different from that of any of the other "foreign" governments inflicted upon the Coele-Syrian area since the dawn of history. Hence, by analogy (a perfectly good basis for observing palaeoculture in modern cultural anthropology), the Beduin and town life Doughty reported were little different from that to be expected during Nabataean times. What few "modern," western technological changes were known to the larger urban centers of the Middle East in Doughty's time were still far in the distant future of the area as a whole. Hence, what he has to report can be (carefully) extrapolated to visualize the life of the Nabataeans, at least to some degree. Perhaps only in regard to the role and place of women do we find Islam having introduced change, but Islam, as a "national" religion, was very little different from Judaism, Christianity, or the multitude of "pagan" cults of Nabataean times in regard to its effects upon the lifeways of the people. Hence, when we read Doughty's descriptions of Beduin camp-life (1:346–400, 431–565; 2:249–319) we can visualize the same kind of existence for the pre-sedentary Nabataeans as they made their way along the peninsula up to Petra. The same tasks, the same animals, the same methods for finding water, the same routes, and probably the same desert protocol which Doughty saw then are the analogies for Beduin of all ages in the Middle East. It is only recently that mechanization, radio, television, "permanent" (government-built) housing, medical services, and other changes have brought an end to the unchanged and unchanging wanderers of the desert lands. When I first began my thirty-year contact with Petra, Doughty was the key to understanding the life of the local Beduin and being accepted by them. Only in the last decade has marked change occurred and Doughty's words become old-fashioned and less relevant.

Similarly, when we read about village life (1:566–616, 636, 672; 2:15–184, 336–456) and its customs we can again see the Nabataeans settling into sedentary life at Petra and changing lifestyle to suit the change in life pattern. Archaeologically we can get a glimpse of this as we look at the private dwellings excavated in the last ten years under my direction at that site. Once within walls, the Nabataeans had to accommodate to such fixed living. Thus we find cupboards filled with the imported "china service" a Beduin family could not have transported from place to place while still nomadic. We find walls decorated with painted plaster—obviously impractical while dwelling in tents. We find a wide variety of cooking vessels and eating vessels, unnecessary and untransportable by a wandering people. We find hoards of coins, showing the need for more than Beduin barter. And we find public buildings of great magnificence—the heritage and pride of townsmen and urbanites, unlike the crude stele and shrines of the desert Beduin. Dozens of other examples can be shown and reflected back from Doughty's comparison of town and country in his own day.

Doughty was not a systematic ethnographer; that "science" would await the dawn of American anthropology in the first quarter of the twentieth century.[15] Yet, by recording what he saw, heard, and could infer in the world around him, he gives adequate data for reconstructing the life of the Nabataean period as well as of his own period of observation. It was Doughty's work that became a modern textbook for T. E. Lawrence[16] and it can be so used for anthropological archaeology today if it is properly employed.

But the data are widely scattered throughout Doughty's main two volumes. Only in the index and glossary is there any organization and that, unfortunately, is dependent only upon the definitions of Arabic words and personal names. Sifting through and putting into more useful order the myriad ethnographic contributions there—and throughout the whole of Doughty's work—would tax the limits of this paper and the energy of even the most assiduous student of cultural anthropology. However, there are certain segments of *Arabia Deserta* which are more accessible, in a manner of speaking, and which suggest an untold richness of data for future study. These areas are ones which but skim the top of the unrealized bounty available throughout the volumes.

TRAVEL

The communication lines of the Middle East have remained constant since the geomorphological changes in the area created them. A glance at the biblical descriptions of routes, when compared to modern road maps, confirms this. Perhaps the most well known example of this constancy of communication lines is that still called today the "King's Highway," leading from Akaba at the tip of the Red Sea northward toward Jerusalem on the eastern bank of the Jordan. This was the traditional route wished-for by Moses, the conquest route of King David, the Great Nabataean Highway, the fortress line of the Latin Kingdom, the access of the Moslem conquest—and a black-top road today!

But in the great uncharted expanse of the desert areas one might expect that travel was without routes or tracks, let alone the modern equivalent of a road. Yet Doughty suggests quite a different picture and reconfirms our glance at the Bible, the Assyrian records, the conquest lines of Egypt, or Peutinger's Table.[17] Routes do exist, dependent upon water supply, terrain configuration, the quality of the under-foot soil or rock, and a number of other factors. Doughty points this up time and again in his discourses on travel. Some he refers to specifically (the "old gold and frankincense" route; or the road from Arabia Felix), but most are simply the normal routes between one place and another, be it a pasture, a water-hole, or an inhabited town (1:51–66, 116–24, 402–3, 407).

Linked to these data are bits of information regarding how Beduin find water, how long a specific journey is expected to take (i.e., camel endurance distances and times), how "routes" are kept by landmarks, and similar details. The Nabataean cultural analyst is informed, for example, however obliquely, that communication between Petra and Damascus (ca. 220 miles) required only three days by camel back, whereas el-Hejr and Teyma could keep in touch daily (2:553). When political control or even cultural interchange is discussed, time becomes a factor, along with the routes involved.

Associated with travel is the matter of travel animals, and here Doughty supplies us with information concerning the types, care, and breeding of camels, horses, and donkeys, the Middle East's main vehicular resources until the coming of the automobile, steam train, and airplane of today.

DESERT LIFE

The life of the Beduin is described throughout Doughty's volumes in considerable detail. With the rapidly disappearing modern analog to ancient nomadic pastoralists via sedentarization (both voluntary and compulsory) in the Middle East, such a picture of desert life as Doughty bequeathed the cultural specialist is fast fading away. In the quarter-century which has elapsed since I first visited Petra, Beduin life has undergone dramatic change. Tents gave way to the caves of Petra, bare stone walls were first whitewashed and then decorated with photographs, piled-stone entrances received salvaged doors, the transistor radio came and has given way to television sets, and now the government's "resettlement" plan has brought concrete block houses far from the Petra basin.

Since the classical writers[18] tell us that the Nabataeans were once pastoral nomads prior to sedentarization, this picture is relevant to them as well. Still further, Doughty's reports of Beduin-become-townspeople are also relevant in attempting the study of the rise of the Nabataean state and the study of the Nabataeans as merchant-caravaneers throughout the area after the "state" was formed and after it "fell" to Rome in A.D. 106. The graffiti all along the caravan routes of Sinai and Egypt are adequate testimony to the need for knowing how Beduin live—and move around! Modern "process" interest in the "how" of ancient peoples has finally reached the Middle Eastern archaeologists and their search for understanding the ancient world. That "how" must search out the analogs and attempt to fit known ancient data to them. Doughty's information thus becomes a first-hand look at ancient pastoral-nomadic lifeways as well as simply a description of what he saw around him in a much later time.

TOWN AND VILLAGE LIFE

Although the small town in the Middle East today resembles Doughty's examples, the introduction of television, radio, and telephone communication has homogenized daily living as well as had an effect upon language and other specifics of culture. Doughty, on the other hand, had the opportunity of long-term observation of such settlement patterns and did note variations between customs, language usage, crops grown and the methods employed, among many other details (1:171–72, 183, 194, 337, 597, 603, 688, 416, 466, 638, 644; 2:53, 59, 165, 317, 322, 355, 452, passim). Some hints of settled life have been forthcoming from the domestic site recently excavated at Petra,[19] but little is known, even in general, of how the Nabataeans lived once sedentarization took place. Once again, Doughty supplies at least some analog features. Doughty's observations concerning town size related to arable land available (1:211–12), are but one aspect possible of further examination concerning the multitude of sites now known to have been occupied by the Nabataeans.[20]

INSTITUTIONS

The customary life, including social structures, customary behavior, belief system development, decorative preferences, cosmological perception, and related aspects, of both Beduin and sedentarized people in ancient times comes to the archaeologist by inference if documentation does not exist. In the case of the Nabataeans, very few of these aspects are available directly and must be patched together from, up until now, a very scanty archaeological record as a result of actual excavation. The excavations I have conducted since 1973 at Petra are at least one example of this patchwork. Most especially of importance have been the materials recovered from the Allat temple (popularly, the "Temple of the Winged Lions"), one of the first examples of a Nabataean cult-place preserved by the debris of a natural catastrophe. At that site architecture, architectural technology, decorative motifs, small objects, stratigraphy, pottery, and a multitude of clues have permitted the beginning of a better understanding of Nabataean religion. Doughty's comments regarding many of the institutionalized aspects of Middle Eastern life, both in the desert and the town, can thus be helpful in two directions: an analogical backdrop and, more directly, a data-base for interpretation of material remains. If Strabo had been able to avail himself of Doughty's notes he would not have imposed the sociopolitical label of "democratic" on the kings of Nabataene, but would rather have understood that a monarch would follow the proper customary hospitality to guests, even if he were a tyrant! Doughty encountered this strange paradox time and again as his various hosts, Beduin and townsmen, though hating an unbelieving foreigner, still served the guest-cups of required hospitality.

HYDROLOGY

Doughty's interest, often quite necessary from self-preservation motives in his travels, in watering places, wells, and irrigation systems is also of interest to research concerning Nabataean hydrological endeavors. At Petra and elsewhere, the ruins (and today, often restored examples) of Nabataean water systems have led some specialists, including myself, to place the Nabataeans high on the list of hydraulic engineers of antiquity.[21] By seeing as it were through Doughty's eyes (1:350, 368, 600; 2:95, 205, 239, 329, 370, 379, 574) how systems were used prior to modern pumping machinery, some conception of how ancient (and Nabataean in particular) systems were developed, maintained, and improved in the generally arid areas becomes real.

NATURAL HISTORY

As late as Doughty's time, some species of plants and animals were still present or recently remembered in the areas of his travels. Although he is by no means a definitive source of data, he is a good accompaniment to other natural history studies. The latter very often note only present species and do not pick up, as Doughty did from the interminable conversations he had, what was recently or possibly anciently present (1:174). Still further, Doughty used his knowledge to suggest uses of natural resources (e.g., the kind of wood used for doors at Medain Salih, [1:158]) in ancient times, natural food resources (1:66, 173, 195, 319, 338, 377, passim; 2:108, 230, 317, 466, passim), medicinal plants (1:297, 472, 510, 644), plant-food preparation methods (1:172, 624; 2:200, 239), plant and tree growing methods (1:164, 185, 194; 2:81, 341, 380, passim), and related topics. Agronomists and demographers may also find in Doughty's notes clues to floral and faunal types, including crop production and land use, and their relation to population size in ancient times. His geological background emerges in this regard also, in references to soil types encountered, as well as in his specific geological descriptions (1:59, 90, 451; 2:77, 78, 269, 493). The latter are spread throughout his writings, and the brief "geological notes" (2:575–76) he presents as his formal geological contribution hardly do justice to the recurrent references elsewhere in the volumes. When Nabataean stone-work, to take but one example, is examined, the archaeologist is often left with little available data concerning specific stone sources that are not apparently present in the immediate area. Therefore, I am indebted to Doughty's suggestion that a possible quarry exists near Dhat Ras (1:59–60), a fact no one else seems to have observed and which appears nowhere else in the literature. Investigation of this quarry may answer the question as to the source of the crystalline limestone ("marble") so common in Petra's decorative architecture. Since a larger-than-life statue of Hercules in that "marble" was found during the excavations of the Main Theater in 1961–62,[22] the presence of a close source for large pieces of such a material is indeed relevant to the question of Nabataean lines of supply.

CONCLUSION

When the "Index and Glossary of Arabic Words" appended to the second volume of the *Travels* is first opened, Doughty's sole purpose seems to be the definition of every word he ever encountered. In a language that purportedly has as many words for a camel as it has for sword types, such a contribution may seem appropriate to the linguist alone. However, in his "definitions" Doughty has encompassed a mass of anthropological data. Kinship analyses, societal patterns, pharmaceutical information, geological facts, floral and faunal types, genealogical relationships, history, bibliographical resources, site names, tribal customs, architectural details, climatic details, customs, and a variety of other sometimes esoteric knowledge spill forth from the Arabic words and indexed citations Doughty lists. Even the Arabic per se is delightful—and informative, since the modern radio, television, and newspaper have so eradicated the speech of the Beduin.

Much contained in the index and glossary is irrelevant to Nabataean issues, but, on the other hand, much can again furnish analog material. Sorting the useful from the nonuseful in this regard is, as noted above, beyond the scope of this chapter. Yet the body of material exists and its potential should be investigated.

If the Nabataeans were "Arabs," then Doughty's work must be seen by Nabataean researchers in terms of T. E. Lawrence's recommendation: "in a few of its pages you learn more of the Arabs than in all that others have written" (1:27). That same verdict may well be echoed by those of us in Nabataean studies. Since Doughty's time more has been learned about the Nabataeans, but most of this new learning has been in the realms of language (grammar,[23] new inscriptions[24]), site locations,[25] generally identified by pottery remains, the pottery itself,[26] architecture,[27] and now my own deliberations on the culture. Theories have also appeared in regard to origins and the processes of state formation and political position of the people.[28] But when the matter really comes down to those details less obvious from the material remains or the scant documentation, we in the field of Nabataean studies must acknowledge our debt to Doughty's intrepid trek through the perils and hardships of ancient Arabia Deserta and to the written legacy of *Arabia Deserta*.

Finally, and perhaps by no means less of a contribution to all archaeology, Doughty attempted to teach us to write intelligibly in our native language. In these days of professional jargon and archaeopedantry, such a legacy may well be appreciated as a goal to be sought after with renewed diligence.

NOTES

1   Diodorus of Sicily, [*Works*], trans. C. H. Oldfather, Loeb Classical Library (London: W. Heinemann, 1953), book II, iv; III, 42, 43, 48; XIX, 94–96; Strabo, *The Geography of Strabo*, trans. H. L. Jones, Loeb Classical Library, vol. 7 (London: W. Heinemann, 1930), 16.4.20–24, 26; Josephus, *Antiquities of the Jews*, trans. W. Whiston (Grand Rapids: Kregel, 1960), book XII, 5; XIII, 1, 5, 8–9, 17, 21–24; XIV, 2–7, 9, 18, 25–26; XV, 4–9, 11; XVI, 2–3, 8–10; XVII, 3–4, 10–13; XVIII, 5, 7, 21–22; XIX, 5, 9; XX, 1–3, 7–8; XXX, 2, and *Wars of the Jews*, book I, 2–6, 9, 12, 14–15, 17, 28–31; II, 4, 8, 10–13, 17; IV, 8; V, 13; VI, 8, 15; also 1 Macc. 5:8, 24; 9:36–42; 11:16; 2 Macc. 5:8, 10–12.

2   Albert Kammerer, *Petra et la Nabatène* (Paris: Paul Geuthner, 1929); Jean Cantineau, *La Nabatéen* (Paris: Ernest Leroux, 1930); George Horsfield, with Agnes Horsfield, "Sela-Petra, the Rock of Edom and Nabateae," *Quarterly, Department of Antiquities of Palestine* 7 (1937), 8 (1938), 9 (1941).

3   Doughty's own contribution to this collection was published as *Documents épigra-phiques recueillis dans le nord de l'Arabie par M. Charles Doughty,* ed. Ernest Renan (Paris: Académie des Inscriptions et Belles-Lettres, 1884).

4   Alfred L. Kroeber, *Anthropology* (New York: Harcourt, 1923).

5   Gordon R. Willey, "One Hundred Years of American Archaeology," in *One Hundred Years of Anthropology,* ed. J. O. Brew (Cambridge: Harvard University Press, 1968), 29–53; Glyn Daniel, "One Hundred Years of Old World Prehistory," in ibid., 57–93. Since those two summary articles, dozens of volumes have appeared to carry developments still further.

6   Ta, 136–37.

7   H, 95 ff., 102–6.

8   H, 41–54, 60.

9   E.g., Antonine Jaussen and Raphael Savignac, *Mission archéologique en Arabie,* vol. 1 (Paris: Ernest Leroux, 1909), vol. 2 (Paris: Paul Geuthner, 1914); Rudolf Ernst Brünnow and A. von Domaszewski, *Die Provincia arabia* (Strassburg: Karl G. Trubner, 1904); and see, most recently, F. V. Winnett and W. L. Reed, *Ancient Records from North Arabia* (Toronto: University of Toronto Press, 1970), vii–viii (with bibliography).

10 See also H, 47–48, 208–9 citing letters describing Medain Salih and comparing it with Petra; Winnett and Reed, *Ancient Records,* 42–53 and 53, note 106; Alois Musil, *Arabia Petraea,* 3 vols. (Vienna: Alfred Hölder, 1907, 1908); Albrecht Alt, "Aus der 'Araba, II, III," in *Zeitschrift des deutschen Palästina-Vereins* 58 (1935): 1–74; C. L. Woolley and T. E. Lawrence, *The Wilderness of Zin,* Palestine Exploration Fund Annual—1914–1915 (London: PEF, 1915).

11 Winnett and Reed, *Ancient Records,* 22–36, the most modern scientific account and parallel references. The list of investigators who have visited or studied the land east of the Jordan is now exceedingly extensive. At Petra alone, since Horsfield's day, that list includes W. F. Albright, Murray, Ellis, Parr, Kirkbride, Lindner, myself, and the Department of Antiquities of Jordan, to name but a few.

12 George and Agnes Horsfield, "Sela-Petra, the Rock of Edom and Nabatene," vol. 3, "The Excavations," *QDAP* 8, no. 3 (1938): 92.

13 The survey efforts of Musil, Alt, Lawrence, and Woolley, as well as others, previous to 1929 lacked the ceramic "key" to identifying Nabataean sites in the absence of epigraphic indications and generally identified Nabataean surface pottery fragments as Byzantine or even Roman.

14 Hogarth (H, 184) notes that *Arabia Deserta* came into "daily use" at the British headquarters in Cairo as a "source book," and elsewhere notes that Lawrence had practically memorized the work, so vital was it for his introduction to the Arabian area.

15 Fred Eggan, "One Hundred Years of Ethnology and Social Anthropology," in J. O. Brew, ed., *One Hundred Years of Anthropology* (Cambridge: Harvard University Press, 1968), 125, suggests that Frank H. Cushing "was probably the first professional ethnologist," but recognizes the perhaps more specific place in that role established by Franz Boas in the present century (128–30).

16 Hogarth (H, 174–75) notes the contact with Doughty made by Lawrence and his pre-military enthusiasm for *Arabia Deserta.*

17   Peutinger's Table is a thirteenth-century copy of a third century A.D.(?) map of the
     Roman world. Since the Romans were interested in communication lines, those were
     carefully noted—as was Petra.

18   Strabo, *Geography of Strabo*, 16.4.26, gives a somewhat distorted picture of the seden-
     tarized Nabataeans, but his account does seem reflected by Doughty's accounts of
     settled village and town living in his day.

19   Though not yet fully published, Site I of the American Expedition to Petra, excavated
     between 1974 and 1977, will furnish considerable detail in regard to domestic living
     at Petra. See P. C. Hammond, "Excavations at Petra, 1975–1977," in *Annual of the
     Department of Antiquities, 1977–1978* (Amman, 1978): 82–84.

20   Nelson Glueck, *Deities and Dolphins* (New York: Farrar, Straus and Giroux, 1965), 6,
     notes that "literally hundreds" of Nabataean sites can be identified by their surface
     pottery sherds.

21   P. C. Hammond, "Nabataean Water Works in the Desert," *Natural History* (1967):
     37–43.

22   P. C. Hammond, *Petra, The Excavations of the Main Theater* (London: Quaritch, 1966),
     69–70.

23   J. Cantineau, *Le Nabatéen, I, II* (Paris: Ernest Leroux, 1932), remains the most useful
     grammar available still today.

24   A considerable number of new inscriptions have been discovered since Doughty's day
     and since the *Corpus Inscriptionum Semiticorum* was published. These are, unfortunately,
     still scattered all over the literature and only a new edition of the *CIS* will bring them
     together.

25   Glueck's estimate of known Nabataean sites (note 20 above) was enlarged by his own
     work in the Negev of southern Israel later and sites are still being "found" today. Our
     own work at the Egyptian Delta site of Tell El-Shuqafiya will add another previously
     unrecognized cult-site when permission is granted for the publication of an inscrip-
     tion reputed to have found its way to a local museum from there. See also P. C.
     Hammond, *The Nabataeans—Their History, Culture and Archaeology* (Lund: Paul
     Åstrøm, 1973).

26   Although Horsfield, Glueck, and others published and discussed Nabataean ce-
     ramics, my Ph.D. dissertation ("A Study of Nabataean Pottery," Yale Graduate
     School, 1958) was the first to attempt broad classification, technological analysis, and
     pattern typology of the fine, thin red wares in particular. Since that time, Karl
     Schmidt-Korte, Nabil Khairy, and others have reexamined the corpus and made fur-
     ther advances in our understanding of the technology involved.

27   Studies of Nabataean architecture began with Gustaf Dalman's *Petra und seine Fels-
     heiligtümer* (Leipzig: G. C. Hinrich, 1908), as well as the monumental survey of Petra
     by Rudolf Brünnow and Alfred von Domaszewski noted above. Sir Alexander Ken-
     nedy, *Petra, Its History and Monuments* (London: Country Life, 1925) carried on the
     attempt to establish chronology and to trace stylistic origins. Since then a number of
     scholars have reattempted the same tasks, but the entire question is still considerably
     in debate.

28   The trend today is toward the theoretical approach, especially in regard to the role of
     the Nabataeans in the Roman Empire, as well as their own movement from nomadic
     pastoralism to political statehood.

REGINALD SHAGAM AND CAROL FAUL

Charles Doughty as Geologist

The authors of this chapter do not have a firsthand acquaintance with the area of Charles M. Doughty's travels in Arabia, but one of us (R. S.) has seen that portion of Sinai travelled by Doughty prior to his Arabian explorations, and the other has seen rocks in Egypt equivalent to those Doughty observed in what is now Saudi Arabia. The fundamental framework of the geology in those regions is virtually identical with that in the area of Doughty's geologic map, so we set about reading *Arabia Deserta* with pleasurable anticipation. But as we read our disappointment grew, partly as a result of the low caliber of Doughty's geologic observation and even more because of his almost complete lack of interpretation of his findings. Thus, although the very language and epic sweep of *Arabia Deserta* prove his artistic originality, we are forced to conclude that as a geologist Doughty was dull and unimaginative. We will justify this conclusion by critically analyzing Doughty's contribution to the study of Arabian geology, especially in the framework of his own generation, while remaining sensitive to the hardships of his journey that impeded scientific work.

GEOLOGY AND ARABIA

An outline of some geologic terms and history is necessary as a basis for subsequent discussion. Igneous rocks are those which crystallize from molten material (magma). They may be volcanic if the magma erupted at the earth's surface, or plutonic ("of Pluto"; i.e., infernal) if the magma cooled and solidified at depth in the earth's crust. Sedimentary rocks may be formed of eroded fragments (shales, sandstones) or marine organisms cemented by calcium carbonate (limestones); some are composed of silica precipitated from solution (flints). Rocks of whatever origin, subsequently modified by elevated temperature and pressure in the plutonic environment, are termed metamorphic. Deformed rocks in which original planar

layers develop wavelike forms are said to be folded. Earth fractures separating crustal blocks which show a displacement (horizontal or vertical) of
one with respect to the other are termed faults. The younger (later) stages
of earth's history are collectively referred to as Phanerozoic ("abundant
life") time, in which the oldest subdivision is the Cambrian period. Rocks
underlying (and therefore older than) those of Cambrian age are simply
grouped as Precambrian in age. Other more complex features are described and illustrated below as needed.

A much simplified geologic history of Arabia[1] may be viewed as a
"drama" in five acts, as illustrated in figure 1. The enormous vertical
displacements of the earth's crust during the geologic history of the continent are evident when we use sea level as a datum for the sequence of
diagrams, each representative of one of the "acts." In Act I (900 to 540
million years ago) the Precambrian rocks are folded and contorted, especially at depth. The effect of uplift and erosion represented by Act II
(540 to 500 million years ago) is to remove five to fifteen kilometers of
crust so that rocks once subjected to high temperatures and pressures at
great depth come to be exposed at the earth's surface. In later subsidence
of the crust (Act III) those rocks are covered by deposits of sand, now seen
as horizontal layers of sandstone. The plane of contact between the sandstones and the underlying intensely deformed igneous and metamorphic
rocks is known as an unconformity (specifically, the "basal unconformity"
because it is the lowest of several in Arabia). Unconformities thus represent hiatuses in the geologic record and in this case an enormous convul-
sion in the geologic history of the earth. The contrast between flat-lying
sedimentary rocks above and contorted igneous and metamorphic rocks
below is obvious, as may be seen in figure 2a, a photograph of the same
basal unconformity as it appears in southeastern Sinai.

Acts III (500 to 110 million years ago) and IV (110 to 40 million years
ago) illustrate accumulation of sands at or just above sea level followed by
a marine transgression over the continent during which fossil-rich limestones with interbedded layers of flint were deposited. Actually there were
several such marine incursions in the range of about 300 to 130 million
years. We depict only that of Act IV because it was the most recent such
event and hence those limestones and flints are the best preserved and
cover extensive tracts of the land surface.

During the time represented by Act V (40 million years ago to the
present) the Red Sea was formed when Arabia and Africa sundered. It was

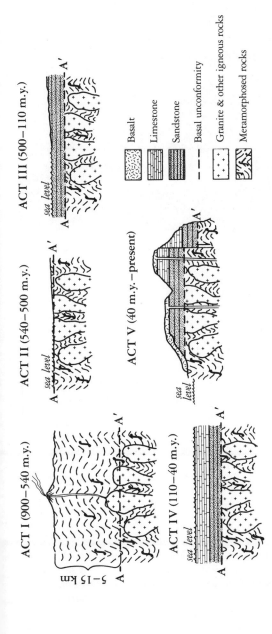

FIGURE 1. Diagrammatic representation of the geologic history of Arabia as a "drama" in five acts (see text for definition of terms). Act I: intense folding and metamorphism (sigmoids) of the crust at depth accompanied by the intrusion of granite magma (crosses). Act II: major uplift of the crust causes intense erosion to the depth A–A' of Act I—the land is worn to a near planar surface (peneplain) tilted gently to sea level. Act III: sands accumulate at or just above sea level in an environment hostile to organisms. Gentle subsidence of about 3 km occurs as the sands accumulate and are lithified to sandstone. The plane of contact between the sandstones and the Precambrian plutonics is the basal unconformity. Act IV: the sea transgresses over the continent, abundant marine invertebrates inhabit the shallow waters and are eventually incorporated into limestone deposits (with some flints) which accumulate to a thickness of about 1–2 km. Act V: pronounced uplift (although far less than in Act II) causes the sea to drain off the continent and erosion begins again. Some limestone/flint and sandstone layers are worn away and in places the Precambrian plutonic rocks are again exposed at the land surface. About 25 million years ago great fractures rent the crust, permitting lava to erupt and flow out over the land surface, covering limestones, sandstones, and Precambrian plutonic rocks in different areas. Preceding and following the eruptions faulting occurred and crustal blocks on one side were uplifted, down-dropped, or moved horizontally. Where fault displacements are vertical, the relative movements are recognizable by corresponding displacements in the basal unconformity.

a

b

Sandstone

unconformity

Precambrian

Precambrian

fault

FIGURE 2. View of the basal unconformity near Dahab, southeast Sinai (2a). Features
present are indicated on the accompanying sketch (2b). Movement of the fault shown
diagrammatically in the sketch (actually out of sight behind the hillock in the bottom
right corner of the photo) resulted in uplift of the distant mountain of Precambrian rocks
in the bottom right background of the photo. The dashed line represents the unconformity
long since removed by erosion along with the overlying sandstones. Conceivably Doughty
visited this locality in Sinai; he clearly shows the sense of the geologic relationships in the
west (right) end of his Diagram 1 in the appendix to *Arabia Deserta* (2:576), reproduced in
our figure 7b. Amazingly, there is no reference to this or any other unconformity in his text
and apparently he did not realize that displacements in the elevation of the basal unconformity were the result of faulting.

a time of regional tension with development of deep crustal faults which permitted basalt magma to rise to the surface. Most notable of the faults with large displacements is the Jordan Rift, along which there was movement of more than one hundred kilometers of one side with respect to the other. Numerous additional faults with smaller displacements occur in Saudi Arabia parallel to the coastline of the Red Sea or to the more northerly trend of the Jordan Rift. Where the relative movements on faults has had a pronounced vertical component, crustal displacements may easily be recognized by displacement of the basal unconformity—a reference plane par excellence as shown in figure 2b.

An unconformity less severe than the one at the top of the Precambrian rocks is shown in Act V: erosion resulting from uplift of the continent removed significant thicknesses of the horizontally layered sedimentary formations so that when the *harra* (lava field) basalts erupted at the earth's surface they flowed over different rock units in different areas. In this case intense deformation of the rocks underlying the basalts did not occur prior to the cutting of the unconformity by erosion. As a result, the horizontal layering of the lavas conforms with that of the underlying sedimentary formations except where lava cascaded over cliffs.

Thus, the sequence of rock layers in Arabia is metamorphic and folded rocks as basement with an unconformity at the top, horizontally layered sandstones above, limestones with flint, and finally a capping basalt.

DOUGHTY'S GEOLOGIC PREPARATION

The formal training and experience in earth sciences of the man who was to describe the geology of this region in *Arabia Deserta* are outlined in Hogarth's biography (H, 1–36). As a boy, Doughty collected fossils and rocks in the chalks of the Sussex Downs. He studied geology at Cambridge and prior to graduation in 1866 took a year off to study glaciers and glaciation in Norway. The years 1870–76 were devoted to "studious travel" (H, chap. 2) mainly in Mediterranean Europe with brief forays into North Africa (Tunisia and Algeria) and ending in the Middle East. Although the principal aims of his travels were apparently not geologic, he did take advantage of opportunities to observe earth processes and materials (H, 19). He visited Vesuvius during an eruption (described in 1:466–68), climbed a dormant Etna in Sicily, examined the Rock of Gibraltar (granite), and made some observations and sketches of the Atlas Mountains in Algeria.

He arrived in the Middle East in the first half of 1874 and, except for a few months in Vienna in late 1875, spent much of the approximately two and one half years before his departure for Arabia in extensive travels through what are now Lebanon, Syria, Jordan, Israel, Egypt, and Sinai. As noted, the geology of much of this extensive region differs little from that of the Arabia through which he journeyed. In particular, three months spent in Sinai around February to May 1875 served as a training exercise for what he was to see in Arabia.

Clearly, Doughty had both solid formal training and wide field experience as a geologist prior to his setting off for Arabia. His instruments for the journey included aneroid barometer, telescope, pocket sextant, thermometer, compass, tape measure, and watch. With the aneroid he measured altitude as many as five or six times daily (amazingly, the instrument survived the whole journey). Doughty computed distances by the time of travel, assuming an estimated standard pace of 2.5 miles per hour for a camel caravan. After his watch failed he computed distances by camel journeys and diligent cross-checking of camel marches (1:54). His map was constructed by "reckonings from Ma‹an, Medina, Hâyil, Jidda," whose positions he took from Heinrich Kiepert's *Karte zu Ritter's Erdkunde* (2:643).

DOUGHTY'S ACHIEVEMENT IN GEOLOGIC MAPPING

When intensely deformed rocks are planed off by erosion, as occurred in Act II of our drama, a distinct regional structural "grain" is apparent in outcrop (see figure 3), much as the vascular system of trees defines a grain in planks. Where the rocks overlying the unconformity were removed by erosion, that grain in northwestern Saudi Arabia is oriented roughly northwest-southeast. The concept of grain, however, cannot be applied to the flat-lying cover of sedimentary rocks (figure 3). The map distribution of such flat-lying rocks is simply a function of past erosion. Thus, those of Doughty's journeys (for example, the Aneyza-Jidda leg) which took him across the grain of the oldest rocks provided the best opportunity to see the varieties of Precambrian plutonic igneous and metamorphic rocks and structures. The rocks above the unconformity, however, he would best observe as he ascended and descended topographic highs such as the lava fields.

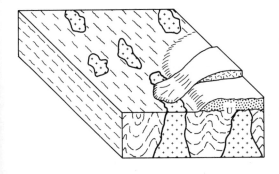

FIGURE 3. When highly folded rocks are subjected to erosion a distinct regional "grain" appears in the surface exposures. As indicated in the bottom right portion of the surface of the block, no such "grain" occurs where horizontally layered rock formations outcrop. Dashed lines represent the foliation of metamorphic rocks, crosses = granite, dots = sandstones, dashes = basalt lavas, U = basal unconformity.

The rock formations Doughty mapped are basically those outlined in our "drama": a lowermost (i.e., oldest) unit of plutonic igneous and metamorphic rocks separated by the basal unconformity from the monotonous layered sandstones, which are overlain in turn by limestones with interbedded layers of flint. The youngest rock layer comprises the basalt of the lava fields. The last are so recent that, having undergone little erosion, their current distribution may differ little from their original maximum extent. But where the significantly older sandstones and limestone/flint units are exposed, they have undergone a greater degree of erosion, at places exposing Precambrian plutonic rocks.

How well Doughty succeeded in his geologic mapping may be gauged by a comparison of our rendition of his map (figure 4) with our highly simplified version of a map published in 1962 by the U.S. Geological Survey and the Arabian-American Oil Company (figure 5).[2] For comparison to Doughty's map we have grouped different rock units on the 1962 map to conform to those selected by Doughty; the grouping was necessary because the newer map is much more detailed. In the Precambrian plutonic terrain we have differentiated between igneous rocks (mostly granite, symbolized by crosses) and metamorphic rocks (sigmoids).

Initially Doughty's map and the 1962 map appear distinctly different, but closer inspection suggests otherwise. Apparently the geographic base map used by Doughty (Kiepert's) was in error. On figure 4 we have shown

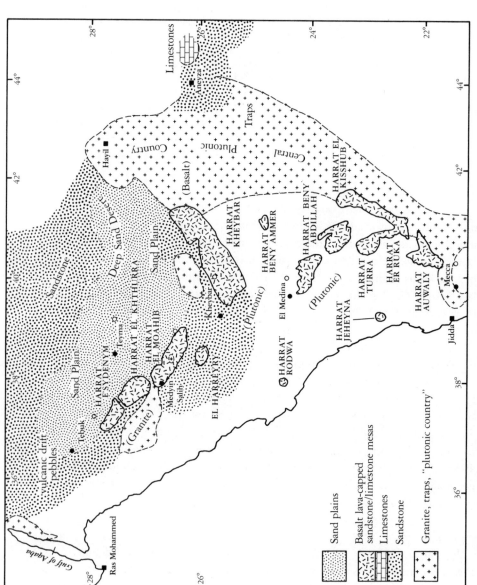

FIGURE 4. Simplified rendition of Doughty's geologic   Doughty; closed circles are the correct locations, as placed on

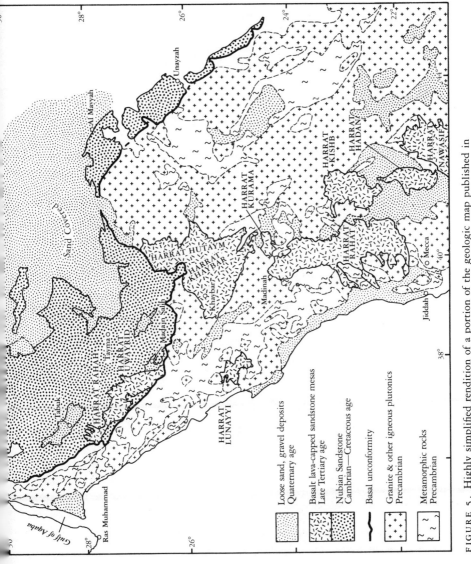

FIGURE 5. Highly simplified rendition of a portion of the geologic map published in 1962 by the U.S. Geological Survey and the Arabian-American Oil Company.

the settlements as he placed them (open circles) and their locations on the 1962 map (closed circles). The Red Sea coastline of Arabia is almost identical on the two maps and it would be logical to assume that the early cartographers used the coastline and Jidda as base line and standard reference point, respectively, and that errors in mapping would increase progressively eastward with distance from the coast. This is not always the case: the location of Aneyza, the easternmost town, is close to correct, whereas Mecca, the nearest point of all to Jidda, is mislocated by more than twenty-five miles. Because of such errors there is a nonuniform distortion in Doughty's geologic map for which one cannot blame him.

In a local context, his mapping was generally correct. Compare, for example, the location of his Harrat e'Sydenym in the northwestern part of the map with respect to Tebuk, and the location of the same but differently named Harrat Rahah to Tabuk on the 1962 map. They are virtually identical. The marked differences in the total outlines of the *harras* on the two maps reflect clearly the difference between the near-total access enjoyed by modern mappers and the restricted access of a century ago. We must keep in mind that Doughty had virtually no choice in the routes he travelled; the very harshness of the terrain and fear of marauders dictated that he stay with and follow the routes (from water hole to water hole) chosen by his nomadic Beduin hosts of the moment. They obviously chose the easier lower ground where rock exposure is often obscured below the cover of sand dunes or the gravel wash of the *wadis* (dry river beds). Furthermore, he had to ride at the pace set by his hosts in many cases and could not linger to examine outcrops in detail.

Much to Doughty's credit—given the difficult conditions, including the lack of a support team, under which he worked—his observations and mapping of the areas he travelled are correct. Note, for example, the re-entrant notch he shows on the northwest side of the Harrat Kheybar. Exposed in the notch are sandstones as shown on both maps; but in the adjacent area to the west and southwest the maps differ. Doughty shows the sandstones extending to the southwest and enclosing an oval area of granite, whereas the 1962 map shows that entire region as Precambrian granite with some metamorphic rocks. Doughty was simply following standard geologic mapping procedure (then as now) in extrapolating from his line of march and observation in order to fill in open spaces on the map. Because of the absence of grain in the rocks above the basal unconformity and the fact that distribution of the younger rocks is simply a function of erosion, Doughty was particularly prone to error. Accordingly, the high northwest rim of Harrat Kheybar which he had observed on his approach from Hayil closely resembles that shown on the 1962 map, but the remaining borders, where he did not venture, are inaccurately shown on his map. Such uncertainties are clearly indicated by a washing out of tones of grey on Doughty's published map and by his not using the dashed line he normally employs to indicate boundaries of rock units. Similarly, he depicts as a cluster of small southern *harras* what is actually a continuous basalt outcrop as shown on the later map.

We find a marked contrast between Doughty's map and that of 1962 concerning the lowest layer of the geologic cake, the Precambrian plutonics. Where the new map distinguishes between igneous and metamorphic rocks, Doughty shows the extensive region between Harrat Kheybar and Aneyza as "Central Plutonic Country." Basalts identified in this region are clearly coeval with the young basaltic event of the *harras,* but his use of the additional term "traps" is not clear. "Trap" is an old term synonymous with basalt. He might have meant it to refer to a plutonic variety of the *harra* basalts, but we suspect that some of the darker Precambrian metamorphic rocks may have been mistakenly identified by Doughty as traps. In this region the concept of structural grain was useful for Doughty to observe the different kinds of rocks; he crossed the area on his initial journey east to Hayil, then en route to Harrat Kheybar, and again on his final trek to Jidda. Given his logistic and other problems, it would have been unreasonable to expect any finer detail in that portion of his map. Between the *harras* and the Red Sea coast his map shows only the patch of granite west of Harrat el-Khthurra which is again differentiated into metamorphic and igneous components on the modern map. Here, however, it was simply the lack of opportunity to observe that caused error—he saw the granite only from a distance (1:98), and on his final journey to Jidda and safety he was in ill health and of necessity concerned first and foremost with his own survival.

Thus, despite some easily explicable differences, we find a clear similarity between Doughty's and the newer map, the basaltic *harras* on both maps forming an irregular arcuate spine separating eastern and western regions of plutonic outcrop, and the sandstones and limestones dominant in the north and parts of the east. Allowing for the inaccuracy of his base map, Doughty's work represents an excellent reconnaissance effort.

Before we leave this discussion of Doughty's map, however, we must point out one significant geologic error which is less excusable than the others mentioned above. A small patch of granite is shown enclosed within Harrat el-Moahib, west of Medain Salih. The text describing that area of his travels (1:421–82) makes no reference to granite outcrop although Doughty notes (1:451) that he found a block of granite brought up by lava from below and that the nomads said that such rocks occur not far below the surface of the Harra. From his map it appears that his route passed a few miles distant from the granite outcrop, suggesting that he did not actually stand on the outcrop. Three major interpretations of this granite are most likely, as shown diagrammatically in figure 6a, b, and c. Two explanations (a and b) involve effects of erosion or faulting and erosion and can be rationally viewed in the framework of Act V of figure 1. A third and most extraordinary possibility is that granite magma intruded through the unconformity and the overlying sedimentary rock and basalt sequence (c). In terms of the theoretical "drama" illustrated in figure 1,

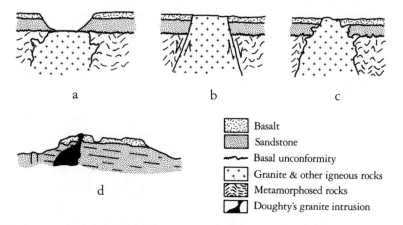

Basalt
Sandstone
Basal unconformity
Granite & other igneous rocks
Metamorphosed rocks
Doughty's granite intrusion

FIGURE 6. Possible explanations for the small patch of granite outcrop in Harrat el-Moahib on Doughty's geologic map. a: Erosion locally exposes underlying Precambrian granite at the surface. In this case the line delimiting the granite on Doughty's map would represent the circular trace of the basal unconformity. b: The granite is uplifted along bordering faults; subsequent erosion results in a flat land surface. c: Late (young) intrusion of granite magma through the Precambrian plutonics, the unconformity, the sandstones (and limestones), and even the lava capping of the Harra. This was the solution Doughty shows in the uppermost cross-section of his map sheet, here reproduced as d. The granite is minuscule at the scale of his map but, far from a petty blemish, it is a blunder of magnitude as explained in the text. According to the 1962 geologic map, no such granite outcrop occurs so none of the solutions illustrated are pertinent.

such a granite would have to be very recent—only about 10 million years old at most. This would be extraordinary because other granites in the area are much older and lie beneath the basalt and sedimentary rock layers. The west (left) end of the top cross-section on the map sheet (our figure 6d) astonishingly implies the last interpretation noted above (figure 6c). Under Harrat el-Aueyrid (= el-Moahib) he shows clearly a steeply conical body of granite that can only be interpreted as intruding through the sandstones to the base of or into the very young lava capping. This can be seen with difficulty in the black-and-white print in the Dover edition of *Arabia Deserta* but it is clear beyond doubt in the colored version of the map and cross-sections in the Random House edition.[3] Why Doughty did not comment on his map's implication is a mystery, but in any case it appears from the modern map that no such body of granite exists; Doughty must have misjudged from afar the form and color of a distinct variety of the lavas. With this one exception the errors on Doughty's map are excusable; it is a commendable effort for the time and circumstances.

CRITICISM OF DOUGHTY'S GEOLOGIC INTERPRETATIONS

A geologic map, however, is only a convenient device for portraying at a glance the essential geologic features of a given area. The true test of professional competence comes in the ability of the geologist to integrate the map data in some unified hypothesis which answers to our continual striving for an understanding of our planet. We would look for that in the text and cross-sections accompanying the map.

In evaluating Doughty's text and cross-sections, we must take into account the fact that he *did* have the time and resources necessary for analysis of the data he gathered with such difficulty in Arabia. He began to write *Arabia Deserta* soon after returning to England from Bombay in December 1878, and although he spent time on a return visit to Damascus and a stay in Italy, he returned to live in England for several years until the publication of his book in 1888. Clearly he had the opportunity to think about the significance of his geologic findings in spite of the distraction of repeated disputes with members of the scientific establishment and publishers and the fact that it took him years to recover physically from the ordeal of his Arabian journey. Therefore, a geologist reading *Arabia Deserta* reasonably expects some attempt at synthesis and hypothesis; but Doughty gives us few such contributions.

His most numerous and perceptive observations concern the *harra* basalts—the youngest layer of the geologic cake and clearly his first love. We find scattered observations concentrated in volume 1, chapters 13–16 (1:429–87), and in volume 2, chapters 3, 4, 7–10, and 16–18. Primarily Doughty gives us simple but sound observations: tongues of lava overriding those below and frozen in the act; collapsed lava tunnels; "lava . . . wreathed as it were bunches of cords" (2:88), a good description of ropy lava. Jagged, knife-sharp, blocky surfaces are clearly the type of lava called *aa* (the standard term, of Hawaiian origin). Dykes and veins of lava intruding through the sandstones are vividly described (1:440, 466). Diagnosis and geological theorizing, however, are almost completely lacking. An exception is his suggestion that columnar-shaped basalt canted to one side (rather than in the more common vertical orientation as at Giant's Causeway, Northern Ireland) could reflect cooling from below as the upper levels of the lava continued to flow (1:442). This inference is almost certainly incorrect as the columns are probably the product of contraction upon cooling after complete solidification of the basalt. But it does reveal the mind of a geologist at work.

About the next lower (older) geologic level, the limestone/flint rocks, Doughty gives us almost nothing outside of a few passing comments in the opening chapters about the way from Damascus to Petra, although in rare instances he refers to metamorphism—the burning of limestone by the basalt flows (1:427, 471).

He grants us somewhat more information about the next unit below, the sandstones, but almost all at the most elementary and incomplete descriptive level. Wind erosion resulting in weirdly shaped pillars attracts his attention and they appear in frequent sketches (1:285, 347, 407, 409, 410). But the only trace of geologic thought related to them appears on 1:172, where Doughty implies erosion of soft rock between vertical joints (fissures) on the basis of his having noted that stratification can be matched from pillar to pillar.

On the lowest and oldest rocks, the Precambrian plutonics, he gives us virtually nothing. He encountered these rocks on his journeys to and from Hayil, and especially on the final Jidda-Aneyza leg. Aside from the words "granite" (sometimes modified by "red," "rosy," or "grey") and "traps," he does not offer even local, let alone grand-scale, hypotheses. In the map and text he mistakenly distinguishes between "traps" and "basalt." The multicolored varieties of some traps (2:240) suggests to us, as indicated above, that he mistook metamorphic rocks for coarse-grained plutonic varieties of basalt known as gabbro, dolerite, or diabase.

Thus, Doughty contributes only minimal attempts at overall integrated hypotheses of the geologic history and evolution of Arabia. The definition of the kind and sequence of the four principal geologic layers is provided in Doughty's appendix (2:575–76), but only in the most superficial and arbitrary form; this appendix is a poor afterthought. Otherwise, there remain a few scattered inferences drawn locally. For example, from the fact that lava caps some isolated sandstone pillars he infers subsequent headward erosion of valleys (1:478); on the route from Medain Salih to Teyma he interprets a broad, flat expanse of clays, loam, and salt as representing an extensive lake bottom ("in other time of the world [it is likely to have been] a winter meer" [1:340]). We understand that by "other time" he intends the Pleistocene Ice Ages, and the inference is astute. He also suggests the lowering by erosion of sandstones not protected by the overlying cover of resistant *harra* basalt (1:465). An important observation he did not elaborate upon is his discovery that the cover basalts in places rest on sandstones and in other places on the plutonic crystalline rocks (2:506; see figure 3). On the whole, Doughty offers geologic thought at a very elementary level.

DOUGHTY AND OSCAR FRAAS COMPARED

Along with his lack of interpretation, Doughty's ignorance of the pertinent literature is surprising and distressing. Oscar Fraas had published in 1867 a treatise on the geology of Sinai and extensive tracts of what are now Israel, Jordan, Syria, and Lebanon.[4] It is the very model of a professional report. The same region was travelled by Doughty before he left for Arabia. Indeed, the three cross-sections in Doughty's appendix to volume 2 concern the geology which Fraas had described in his report in far greater detail.

Unfortunately, Doughty's known proclivity toward willful neglect of his contemporaries' work in exploration and literature[5] also seems to apply to geology as well: in spite of the fact that Fraas's work was published nine years before Doughty's Arabian journey and twenty years before the publication of *Arabia Deserta,* Doughty's book contains no reference to Fraas.

It is very unlikely that Doughty could have wandered as he did through
Sinai and the Levant without becoming aware of Fraas's journeys. The
appearance of strangers in backward areas is immediately noted and remembered. Lawrence, in his preface to *Arabia Deserta,* notes his encounters more than thirty years later with Arabs who remembered Doughty
(1:19). Yet on his visit to Vienna from Damascus in 1875 Doughty apparently made no effort either to get in touch with the Austrian Fraas or to
find his published work. If too pressed for time then, he surely had the
opportunity to seek out this work when he was back in England during
the many years before the publication of his book.

Doughty's references in *Arabia Deserta* to Albrecht Zehme's and Alois
Sprenger's books prove that he could read German; but Fraas's primary
field research, unlike Zehme's and Sprenger's library studies (of Arabian
exploration and geographic history, respectively), may have posed more of
a threat to Doughty's wish to be first to actually explore certain regions.
He emphasizes this desire with regard to his archaeological finds and aspects of his geology, referring for instance to "the situation of the southern
Harras, . . . which, with the rest of the vulcanic train described in this
work, before my voyage to Arabia, were not heard of in Europe" (2:378).

Fraas described faults (*Verwerfungsspalten;* i.e., fissures with an offset) as
the reason that one remains in the same horizontal rock formation even
though the terrain drops steeply (Fraas 1867:60). He ascribed the Jordan
Rift to downthrow (*Versenkung*) of the land by faults and claims this occurred in pre-Tertiary time (ibid.:73). Two years after Fraas, Louis Lartet
explicitly interpreted the Jordan Valley in terms of faulting, using the
word *faille,* still the word for fault in French.[6] Whether Doughty's failure
to refer to Lartet as well was intentional or accidental may possibly be
verified. A footnote of Hogarth's (H, 33) refers to the Royal Geographical
Society's reaction to Doughty's written request from Vienna for financial
support for his proposed Arabian journey. One of the grounds for refusal
was the fact that Lartet (mistakenly spelled "Larteb" in Hogarth) had
already examined and published on a part of the region. One wonders
whether the letter of rejection written to Doughty included a reference to
Lartet's work. If so, he could not plead ignorance of Lartet.

Doughty's various errors are not uncommon among the geologists of his
period, but sometimes they are explicitly caused by his lack of knowledge
of Fraas and Lartet and other contemporaries. An error common to his
period concerns the quality of cross-sections, which provide the severest

test of the accuracy of any geologist's map. Poorly conceived and con-structed cross-sections are typical of the great majority of nineteenth-cen-tury geologic maps, and indeed only within the last twenty-five years has there been great improvement in this area. A major deficiency of Dough-ty's cross-sections is the great exaggeration of the thickness of sedimentary rock units. In the bottom cross-section on the map sheet Doughty implies thickness of sandstones in excess of fifty kilometers, while the correct value is closer to three kilometers! He was, of course, intent on emphasiz-ing the position of the sandstones in the geologic cake—above the plu-tonic crystalline rocks and below the limestone/flint formations—and did not concern himself with their thickness. Part of the exaggeration stems from a greatly expanded vertical scale compared to the horizontal, which requires in turn a corresponding exaggeration in the angle of inclination of the layering. In that cross-section, the vertical scale in the Dead Sea area is exaggerated about fifty times the horizontal scale (see figure 7a).

But other sources of error are less condonable and arise directly from his ignorance of the pertinent literature. Most important, the word "fault" and the concept of crustal blocks being displaced with respect to their neighbors—ideas used frequently in the work of both Fraas and Lartet, as noted above—are totally absent from *Arabia Deserta*. Clearly, a series of vertical earth fractures along which the left (northwest) side had moved upward relative to the right would permit one to traverse enormous dis-tances across a given rock unit and see endless repetitions of the same layers of rock; this explanation would yield a far more rational cross-sec-tion than Doughty gives us. The absence of faults in his sections becomes particularly serious in the cross-sections of the Jordan Rift—the bottom section on Doughty's map and the uppermost (Diagram 1) in the appendix (2:576). The bottom section on the map sheet attempts to show the rela-tionships in the rift in terms of down-folding of rock layers despite Fraas's clear evidence (figure 7a) for faulting and the absence of evidence for sig-nificant folding. The diagram in the appendix (figure 7b) lacks evidence of faulting and has a widely exaggerated vertical scale, which causes Doughty to depict a marked unconformity between the limestone/flints and the Petra Sandstone where none exists. (He does not acknowledge this unconformity in the text.) There is in addition the previously discussed granite intrusion shown in the uppermost section (figure 6). One particularly serious result of the exaggerated vertical scale is a depiction of steep inclination in the basal unconformity which in reality is almost horizontal.

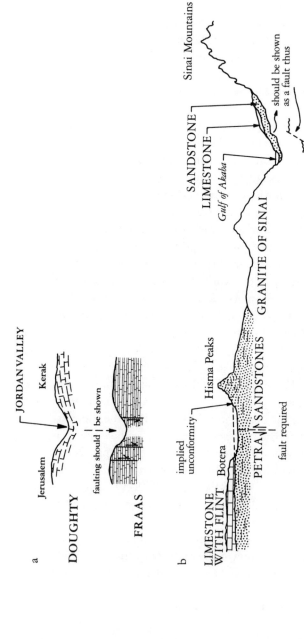

FIGURE 7. Renditions of portions of Doughty's cross-sections. a: Downfolding is clearly implied as the explanation for the Jordan Valley as shown on the bottom cross-section on his map sheet. Below it is the correct explanation involving downfaulting of horizontal layers as recognized and described by Fraas (see text for details). b: A portion of Doughty's Diagram 1 (2:576) with minor modifications. On the east (left) side the cross-section implies unconformity between the limestone/flints and the Petra Sandstone as indicated by our dashed line and arrow. The relationships cannot be explained by folding since the layering in the Hisma Peaks is in the reverse sense for such a solution. The only possible expla-

nation requires a vertical fault (shown symbolically) in the area between the Hisma Peaks and Botera with displacement of the right side upwards with respect to the left. The relationships at the western (right) end correspond to those illustrated in figure 2. Doughty clearly depicts the basal unconformity (but never acknowledged it in his text); however, the pronounced change in slope indicated by the arrow is not an original feature of the unconformity but represents displacement along a fault. Note that no faults are shown underlying the Gulf of Akaba, the southern extension of the Jordan Rift.

DOUGHTY AND NINETEENTH-CENTURY GEOLOGY

In reviewing Doughty's contributions to geology, our primary concern is to judge him against the background of his own time, and not to view him with the hindsight of a century.

Nineteenth-century earth science achieved quite a high level of sophistication, much of which seems to have passed Doughty by. For instance, Sir George Airy, following the measurements of British surveyors in India near the Himalayas, in 1855 suggested that the earth's crust floats on denser material. This floating equilibrium determines the high elevation of the relatively light continents with respect to sea level. Yet Doughty went down to the sub–sea level elevation of the Dead Sea (the lowest point of all the continents) twenty years after Airy's suggestion without any comment on or expression of curiosity about the mass balance (isostasy) problem posed by that remarkable depression. Perhaps the concept of floating equilibrium on a continental scale was too esoteric for Doughty's relatively weak geologic grasp.

On the other hand, in fairness to Doughty it must be noted that certain research tools and concepts vital to geologic processes and history were not yet developed. One enormous gap in nineteenth-century geology existed with regard to the whole conception of geologic time. Radioactivity was first recognized in 1896 and the first ages of minerals determined soon after the turn of the century. Only around 1945, however, did a steady flow of dates begin to appear in the geologic literature. This ability to date more accurately has led to the current view of the formation of a molten earth at about 4,500 million years ago and crustal solidification by about 4,000 million years ago. In Doughty's period, it was thought that a molten earth cooled and crystallized in an uncalculatable time, and subsequent cool-earth history was estimated by most at less than 100 million years ago! Thus Doughty, Fraas, and others might (wrongly) have viewed the plutonic rocks as representing some initial Hadean phase of earth history and the rocks above the basal unconformity as revealing the geologic history of the cooled earth. In such a framework the unconformity becomes an element that does not rate mention, much as one might describe a man without having to note that he had feet. If such was the case, then Doughty should have questioned the validity of the granite in Harrat el-Moahib which he showed intruding through the unconformity into the overlying formations (figure 6). Or, if such late granitic intrusion was unequivocal he was obliged to point out the nature and significance of the unconformity in distinguishing between different ages of granite emplacement. But he does neither.

A FINAL ASSESSMENT

Now we can step back and view Doughty's entire geologic canvas. Concerning the plutonic Precambrian basement, he contributed nothing. Surprisingly, the description of the Sinai plutonics by the "soft rocker" (a geologist interested in life history and cold earth processes such as sedimentation and glaciation) Fraas is much superior to that of the "hard rocker" (a geologist interested in hot processes such as plutonism and volcanism) Doughty. Fraas notes several varieties of rocks, their component materials, and their structural characteristics. And although we might understand Doughty's failure to comment on the basal unconformity, he should have recognized its value as a reference plane in crustal deformation.

Doughty's comments on the sandstone and limestone/flint formations above the unconformity are largely trivial. Only for the *harra* basalt is there adequate description, but here too we get no hypothesis. These basalts, extending over 7° of latitude (approximately five hundred miles), occur through an area only slightly smaller than that of the whole Italian peninsula, and certainly deserved some deeper comment by Doughty.

Although the concept of absolute time was not yet developed, a relative time scale dividing the earth into a sequence of eras and their subdivisions had long been established. But in contrast to Fraas, for instance, Doughty never refers to the Tertiary period or the Mesozoic and Paleozoic eras. In fact, only in the preface to the third edition of *Arabia Deserta* does he refer to any geologic time period at all (the Cretaceous). He must certainly have recognized the Cretaceous age of most of the limestones from their fossils, in which case the sandstones had to represent part or all of the Paleozoic era and possibly part of the lower two-thirds of the Mesozoic era. Yet when he finds fossils he does not ponder their age, and his grouping of marine invertebrates as "cockle shells" may be likened to grouping all paintings from the *Mona Lisa* to Picasso's *Guernica* as "colored pictures." Fraas by contrast gives an orderly description, phylum by phylum, with the proper Latin scientific names, and some plates of illustration of such quality that they would be instantly acceptable for publication in the most demanding modern journals of paleontology.[7] While we may not demand of Doughty, given his hard field conditions, the same technical precision characteristic of Fraas, we can expect a much higher level of scientific detail and expertise than we get in *Arabia Deserta*.

Doughty's grasp of structural or tectonic setting is equally poor. As we have noted, he failed to use the concept of faulting and he did not perceive the mass balance problem posed by the Dead Sea area. This only weakens his explanation that the relationships in the Rift Valley are the result of down-folding. The sub-horizontal layering of the sandstones and lime-stones bespeaks long-term stability of the crust; what then happened to initiate the sudden outpouring of basalt lavas? Doughty does not ponder this question.

Although Alfred Wegener had published in 1912 the first serious hy-pothesis of continental drift,[8] we cannot blame Doughty, perhaps, for his failure to refer to it in the second full edition of *Arabia Deserta*, published in 1921. Still, by 1921 we might certainly have expected an expanded version of the geologic appendix; yet it remains unchanged from the 1888 edition.

Doughty's role as geologist is questionable elsewhere, too. In his re-peated use of the adjective "horrid" he seems to intend "desolate" rather than "dreadful," but we find no accompanying sense of ecstasy. Desolation to a geologist is like nectar to a bee, for in desolate areas he will find pristine rock outcrop. Desolation, however, inspires in Doughty only the following sentiments:

what uncouth blackness and lifeless cumber of vulcanic matter!—an hard-set face of nature without a smile for ever, a wilderness of burning and rusty horror of unformed matter. What lonely life would not feel constraint of heart to trespass here! the barren heaven! the nightmare soil! where should he look for comfort?—There is a startled conscience within a man of his *mesquin* [pitiful] being, and profane, in presence of the divine stature of the elemental world! (1:452)

This passage is certainly powerfully written, but it expresses religious awe and an explorer's loneliness rather than a scientist's delight.

And Doughty's interminable religious squabbles with his illiterate nomad hosts might be seen as only an extension of his general lack of thoughtful perception. Doughty's impatience with a particularly xeno-phobic type of Islam might be understandable, but good relations with the native inhabitants of a region are paramount, especially for the geol-ogist who must travel to out-of-the-way areas. Lawrence in his preface praises Doughty for belonging to the "cleaner class" of Englishmen abroad; namely, those who retain their English manners come what may (1:20). But he learned from Doughty's social failures and thirty-odd years later he invariably managed to avoid confrontations of the kind which brought Doughty so much unnecessary and dangerous trouble.

Some readers with humanities backgrounds may minimize our literal measure of Doughty's contribution as a geologist—what the literary scholar Richard Bevis deprecates as "geology in a narrow, scientific sense." Certainly, *Arabia Deserta* has more dimensions than the purely scientific; the passage we quoted to illustrate Doughty's religious awe is also quoted by Bevis, who comments: "it has other aspects . . . whose common denominator is elusiveness"; "Each time we sense it approaching some familiar mode of thought our expectations are violated"; "this was a moment of deep religious . . . feeling for Doughty, a kind of epiphany"; "here is a suffocating tyranny of the material world."[9]

Bevis's inferences are perspicacious and well put, but they are impervious to concrete testing and demonstration. Doughty himself, in his preface to the second edition of *Arabia Deserta,* points up in his first paragraph his interest in "the Story of the Earth . . . and Her ancient rocks" (1:31). And he did stress to Hogarth that he was "as much Geologist as Nasrany [Christian]" (H, 130) in Arabia. For the scientist, Doughty's actual scientific results prove a far more solid, rational, and objective measure of how well he told that "story of the earth" than his vague and obliquely expressed sentiments. Although Doughty embraced some nineteenth-century advances in geology as expounded in Lyell's *Principles* of 1830,[10] and although he claims a major interest in geology for himself, the maximum that his work amounts to is that he was able to show (albeit without being aware of it) that the geologic relationships described by Fraas in Sinai and the Levant also hold for Arabia. In retrospect, his overall publication record also condemns his claim to distinction as a practicing geologist. Aside from the geologic notes in *Arabia Deserta,* we have only the monograph on Norwegian glaciers published the year after he graduated from Cambridge, although he lived almost fifty years after leaving Arabia.

How can we reconcile the journeyman geologist with the great writer? We have only to refrain from emphasizing that Doughty was a geologist. In fact, many of his superficial comments on Arabia's geology mesh nicely with what is basically a work of poetic ethnology; only taken by themselves as scientific observations do they cause trouble. In the end, the blurb on the Dover edition puts it precisely: "By training [not "profession," notice!] geologist, by inclination itinerant scholar." Doughty's pen was mightier by far than his hammer.

NOTES

Note: We thank Barry Kohn for the photograph of the basal unconformity. Hermann W. Pfefferkorn provided the translation of and advice on the geologic contributions of Fraas. We are grateful to Stephen E. Tabachnick for advice and for his tolerance and tenacity in extracting the manuscript from us. Margaret Fanok assisted with word processing.

1 There is no standard reference for the geology of Arabia. For the nonprofessional, a useful outline of the geology appears in Hugh Scott et al., *Western Arabia and the Red Sea*, B.R. 527, Geographical Handbook Series (London: Naval Intelligence Division, 1946). The Precambrian plutonics are treated at the professional level in *Evolution and Mineralization of the Arabian-Nubian Shield*, proceedings of a symposium convened by Ahmad M. S. Al-Shanti, Institute of Applied Geology, King Abdulaziz University, Jeddah, vols. 1, 2 (1979), 3, 4 (1980) (Oxford and New York: Pergamon). A detailed survey of sedimentary formations above the basal unconformity appears in R. W. Powers, L. F. Ramirez, C. D. Redmond, and E. L. Elberg, Jr., *Geology of the Arabian Peninsula: Sedimentary Geology of Saudi Arabia*, U.S. Geological Survey Professional Paper 560-D (Washington: U.S. Government Printing Office, 1966).

2 *Geologic Map of the Arabian Peninsula*, map I-70 A, scale 1 : 2,000,000 (Washington: U.S. Geological Survey and Arabian-American Oil Company, 1962).

3 Charles M. Doughty, *Travels in Arabia Deserta* (New York: Random House, 1936).

4 Oscar Fraas, *Aus dem Orient. Geologische Beobachtungen am Nil, auf der Sinai-Halbinsel und in Syrien* (Stuttgart: Verlag von Ebner & Seubert, 1867).

5 On this point, see Ta, 29–30, 157.

6 Louis Lartet, "Essai sur la géologie de la Palestine et des contrées avoisinantes, telles que l'Egypt et l'Arabie, comprenant les observations recueillies dans le cours de l'expédition du Duc de Luynes à la Mer Morte," part 1, Doctorat ès Sciences Naturelles thesis, University of Paris, 1869.

7 Hermann W. Pfefferkorn (letter to authors of 7 July 1985, from Heidelberg) notes apropos his translation of Fraas's work for us, that "Fraas was an excellent geologist and his treatment of fossils is among the best of his time. He also wrote a book on fossils which is still used by fossil hunters for first identifications. It has recently been reprinted."

8 Alfred Wegener, "Die Enstehung der Kontinents," *Geologische Rundschau* 3 (1912): 276–92.

9 Richard Bevis, "Spiritual Geology: C. M. Doughty and the Land of the Arabs," *Victorian Studies* 16, no. 2 (December 1972): 163–81.

10 Charles Lyell, *Principles of Geology* (London: Murray, 1830).

BAYLY WINDER

Arabia Deserta as a Historical Source for Nineteenth-Century Arabia

In assessing *Travels in Arabia Deserta* as a source for the history of Arabia in the nineteenth century, and especially of northern and western Arabia where Doughty travelled, one must perforce examine other sources. One of these is other travellers. A recent study of Chevalier Laurent d'Arvieux,[1] who lived and travelled in Syria in the late seventeenth century and who left a lengthy account of his sojourn, opines that since many travellers were generally ignorant of the area in which they travelled, "it is reasonable to question the value of European travel works as historical sources and to point to the dangers of too great a faith in them." The author does concede that some may have a qualified value and even that "the best of them give interesting physical descriptions of towns, villages and countryside and sometimes of ancient sites. In general travellers' accounts can also be of interest in reflecting European knowledge of and attitudes towards the area during the period concerned."[2] Interestingly, such faint praise does not even allude to the travellers' contributions to the history of their own times in the lands travelled, an attitude characteristic of those who have studied Arabian travellers.[3] At the other end of the spectrum is Stephen Ely Tabachnick's enthusiastic suggestion that "we remain indebted to Doughty almost alone for our present knowledge of the Ibn Rashid family."[4] The truth no doubt lies between the two views. In any case, an important issue is directly addressed.

In trying to consider this issue for *Arabia Deserta,* one may first consider the point that in general the background and motivations of those unusual people who travelled from Western Europe to the Middle East and especially to the vast fastnesses of forbidding Arabia were major determinants of what they could contribute to the history of their times. One would not expect much from a commercially motivated traveller like the Italian nobleman Carlo Guarmani, who in 1863 was commissioned by

Napoleon III as well as by King Victor Emmanuel II to go to Nejd in order to purchase Arab stallions for the respective royal stud-farms. Guarmani was not an illiterate in matters Arab, for he had long lived in Jerusalem and had travelled widely in Egypt, Palestine, and Syria. He was in fact something of an expert on tribes and Arab horseflesh and hence was a logical choice to seek Arabia's most famous and important export commodity (along with coffee) in the pre-petroleum era. Nor is Guarmani's account of his trip without any historical interest.[5] He visited Teyma, Kheybar, Aneyza, Hayil, and other places where Doughty passed a dozen years later. Guarmani's report on the political, social, and religious situation in the area under the Nejd Shammar would constitute a minor primary source for any historian of the period, but his relatively brief account of a four-month trip, basically motivated by business considerations, could in no way compare in historical importance with the monumental contributions of another type of traveller such as Alois Musil, the Czech Orientalist and intelligence officer who travelled throughout much of the Syrian desert and north Arabia in the years 1908–15.[6] The Arabian works of Musil, who ended his career as professor of Oriental studies at Charles University, Prague, were magnificently published by the American Geographical Society following World War I.[7] Musil's meticulous route notes (e.g., "From 7.00 to 7.19 our camels grazed on luxuriant *raẓa*. . . . At 8.08 the sand knoll Ṭuʿeys al-Weʿêl was some two kilometers away in front of us"[8]), his exhaustive citation of sources in various Semitic and other languages, and his numerous appendices on a wide variety of subjects including nineteenth-century history—all these mark him as a major scholar. His essays on the Houses of Rashid and of Saud (appendices to *Northern Neğd*) constitute perhaps the major studies of these two dynasties up to the time of their publication. Musil states, "For more than thirty years I have been collecting the material for [these appendices]. This material has consisted not solely of manuscripts and printed publications. Much of it has been gathered from personal conversations with participants in the events recorded, as well as from my own observations made in Arabia."[9] Clearly, Musil, freighted as he was with all the intellectual resources at the command of late nineteenth century professional Orientalist scholarship and highly interested in the recent history of his area, is a more important source for nineteenth-century Arabia than is Guarmani. Exactly the same positive appraisal would apply to the work of C. Snouck Hurgronje, the Dutch scholar, who lived in Mecca for a number of months in 1885.

Another major source for the history of the century is primary and secondary materials written in Arabic and Turkish. The present chapter is not the place to analyze these in detail, but clearly they are of major importance. Dari Ibn Rashid's *Nubdhah Ta'rikhiyyah 'an Nejd* (Historical sketch of Nejd), although a somewhat confused work, is by a member of the House of Rashid.[10] Uthman ibn Abdullah ibn Bishr's *'Unwan al-Madj fi Ta'rikh Nejd* (Title of glory in the history of Nejd) constitutes a careful annalistic work which chronicles the House of Saud up to 1850–51.[11] Ibrahim Ibn Isa, in his *'Iqd al-Durar fima Waqa'a fi Nejd* (The pearl necklace of what happened in Nejd) continues Ibn Bishr's account up to 1885–86.[12] Still another continuation, ascribed to Abd al-Rahman Ibn Nasir, takes it to 1936.[13] These works, despite their "chronological" approach, must be considered as fundamental sources. Numerous secondary works, including early ones such as Abd al-Aziz al-Rashid's *Ta'rikh al-Kuweyt* (History of Kuweyt),[14] which reflects a Kuweyti view of north Arabian history, are valuable in their own right for the time and period that concern us. Later studies such as those by Hafiz Wahbah[15] and Fuad Hamzah,[16] which, although obviously written from a Saudi perspective (the authors were senior officials of the Saudi regime in the first half of the twentieth century), must also be considered. It is reasonably invidious to single out the last two authors; there are many others. In Turkish one would not want to neglect works like, for example, Mehmed Sureyya's *Sicilli-i Osmani* (The Ottoman register),[17] a major biographical dictionary, or Ahmed Cevdet Pasa's monumental *Tarih-i Cevdet* (Cevdet's history).[18] In short, Arabic and Turkish materials, whether primary sources or early secondary works, will have to figure largely in any consideration of sources for nineteenth-century Arabia.

Archival materials constitute the third major resource for the understanding of Arabia in the last century. There are two major sets of these, the British and the Ottoman, but others in or from Cairo, Paris, Vienna, Saint Petersburg, and other capitals are hardly negligible. It is difficult to over-estimate the value of the British archives for nineteenth-century Arabia. Concentrated today in the Public Record Office and the India Office Library, these records constitute an absolutely essential set of documents for understanding the recent past of the Middle East in general and of Arabia in particular. Many agencies of government were involved. The Government of Bombay (until 1873, subsequently, the Government of India), the Admiralty, the Colonial Office, the Foreign Office, and Parlia-

ment and its committees form but the core of the imperial apparatus
which was concerned with gathering information deemed useful for the
management of imperial affairs.[19] Officials with naval and military titles,
as well as ambassadors, consuls, residents, political agents, local-hire informants, governors, governors-general, viceroys, and dragomen all wrote
letters, reports, précis, gazeteers, diaries, biographies, handbooks, des-
patches, proceedings, minutes, and indeed every type of document that
can be imagined. These represent an archive of immeasurable richness
which is in our day being systematically mined by scholars from around
the world. The Ottoman archives, which constitute one of the richest
historical resources anywhere in the world, are likely to contain as much
material on nineteenth-century Arabia as do the British or more.[20]
However, they are much less accessible both because they are in Ottoman
Turkish and also more importantly because they are not organized and cataloged in an easily accessible manner. In fact, millions of these documents
are either not cataloged at all or are only categorized in a very general way.
In short, despite the tremendous potential value of the Ottoman archives
the present—and presumably long-term—practical difficulties of gaining
access to the material needed effectively reduce their value.

From the discussion above, a certain picture relevant to Doughty begins
to emerge: we have reached our present general level of understanding of
the history of nineteenth-century Arabia—whether we think of the Ibn
Rashid dynasty in Hayil, the colony of Aden, or social relations in Mecca
—with only small reliance on *Arabia Deserta*. Furthermore, any future
increase in our knowledge is likely further to diminish the importance of
Doughty since he is a fixed quantity whereas the Ottoman archives, are, so
to speak, not. What then is the value of *Arabia Deserta?*

A few suggestive examples drawn from the vast number that exist in
Doughty's masterwork will illustrate its contributions to political and
social history. In the former category one might single out for examination
the hostilities between the Saudi-Wahaby forces and the town of Aneyza.
A first phase of this dispute had taken place in 1854–55 and was later
dubbed {el-}harb el-awwel, the first war (2:459). In 1862, hostilities re-
sumed, but neither the relevant Arabian chronicles nor, surprisingly,
some later Western historians were able to cite any reason. Doughty alone
(2:459–60) supplies the reason. It was a most Arabian one—a host's responsibility for his guests. What had happened was that the rebellious
governor of Boreyda, nervous about the intentions toward him of the

nearby central Wahaby army, had briefly taken refuge in neighboring Aneyza. As he left Aneyza for the greater safety of distant Mecca, a number of Aneyza townfolk had escorted him out of town to speed him on his way. But the Wahaby commander had received word of what was happening and sent out a detachment which attacked and killed the governor. The presence of the Aneyza townfolk meant that the governor was still under the protection of the town and, "When this tiding [of the governor's death] was brought to Aneyza, the sheykhs sent out armed riders who overtook the servants of Ibn Saud, and fought with them in the Nefud, crying out, 'Ye have slain *eth-thaif* (the guest of) Aneyza!' . . . This honourable action of the town drew the Wahaby upon them again." Thus commenced *{el-}harb eth-thany,* the second war. Doughty alone has indicated the *casus belli.* One is reassured as to the accuracy of his version of these events by the realization that the account of Ibrahim Ibn Isa,[21] the Wahaby chronicler, corroborates the rest of Doughty's account of these events, not excluding his splendid account of "the capital feat of arms in their second warfare"; namely, the decisive battle fought on 8 December 1862.

Doughty as delineator of important personalities is also worth examining. Abeyd Ibn Rashid (d. 1869) may be chosen as an example. Although never the ruling emir, Abeyd was a leader of the House of Rashid under several emirs. It will be noted that he had died several years before Doughty reached Hayil, and thus Doughty had to sift what he heard. Furthermore, several other travellers commented on Abeyd and thus we are able to compare Doughty's accounts with theirs. The various references to Abeyd in *Arabia Deserta* stress the following: his ability as a poet (1:306; 2:42), his military prowess (2:41–42, 460, 462; but Doughty does not hesitate to relate Abeyd's set-backs [1:502, 652]), his country estate outside Hayil (1:636, 665, 667 [plan]), with its palms and gazelles, and his children and other relatives (1:636, 642, 647, 650; 2:42–44). Doughty also highlights some other interesting aspects of Abeyd's character: he was the importer to Hayil of skilled metal workers from Jauf (1:652–53) once it was captured, he was the builder of the fortifications at Ria Agda (1:669), and finally he had "upon his formal hand full of old bloodshed, and violence" (1:654) accepted the conversion of a Jew from Baghdad who subsequently flourished under Abeyd's patronage as Abdullah el-Moslemanny (1:653–54).

Doughty's summary of Abeyd's character may be quoted at some length:

Abeyd was conductor of the military power of J. Shammar, in Abdullah his brother and in his nephew Telâl's days. He was a martial man, and a Waháby more than is now [his son] Hamûd, born in easier times. He was a master of the Arabian warfare, a champion in the eyes of the discomfited Aarab. Abeyd . . . was an excellent kassâd [poet, composer of odes], he indited of all his desert warfare; his boastful rimes, known wide in the wilderness, were ofttimes sung to me, in the nomad booths. The language of the kasasîd [poets] is a language apart from the popular speech; but here I may remember some plain and notable verse of Abeyd, as that which says, "By this hand are fallen of the enemies ninety men. Smitten to death the Kusmân [people from Kasim, the district that includes Aneyza and Boreyda] perished before me, until the evening, when my fingers could not be loosed from the handle of the sword; the sleeve of my garment was stiffened with the blood of war." This he made of the repulse of an ill-commanded and worse starred expedition, sent out by the great Kasîm town Aneyza, against Ibn Rashîd. . . .

Abeyd could be generous, where the Arabs are so least, with an adversary: and clad in his hauberk of mail which they call Davidian, —for David, say they, first found the ringed armour, and Ullah made the crude iron easy to be drawn in his prophetic fingers—the jeopardy of the strong leader was not very great in the field of battle. One day in his bitter warfare with the Annezy *Ibn Mujállad,* Beduins of el-Kasîm . . . , the sheykh of the tribe espying this prince their destroyer in the battle, with a great cry defied him, and tilted desperately against him; but Abeyd (though nettled with his injuries, yet pitying a man whom he had sorely afflicted) let the Beduwy pass under his romhh [lance], calling to him 'that he would not kill a man [having upon him only a cotton tunic] who ran thus wilfully to his own destruction.'

Abeyd was in his latter days the old man of the saffron beard at home, a mild father of the Arabian household. (2:41–42)

G. A. Wallin, the first European to describe Abeyd, speaks of Abeyd's "roughness and cruelty."[22] W. G. Palgrave describes him in even darker, almost incarnately evil, terms.[23] He was a fanatical Wahaby, who although an excellent warrior was "versed in all the resources of deceit and violence, of bloodshed and perjury." He was dubbed the Wolf and "assuredly did his best to deserve his name; thirty years of peace have not sufficed to re-people several of the tracts which he then ravaged." Etc., etc.

On the other side of Abeyd's ledger, Lady Anne Blunt, who with her husband, Wilfred Scawen Blunt, had arrived in Hayil some nine months after Doughty, dismissed Palgrave's "evil tales" and wrote that Abeyd was "the principal hero of Shammar tradition" and that "he has left a great reputation among the Arabs for his hospitality, generosity, and courage."[24] If we compare these opposing views with the summary in *Arabia Deserta*, we can see that Doughty has in no way overlooked Abeyd's bloody hands and indeed dwells on them hardly less than Palgrave. Yet, without transmuting Abeyd into Sir Galahad as Lady Anne came close to doing, Doughty does also bring out Abeyd's good qualities: as a poet, as a military commander, as a person not devoid of compassion, and finally as an authentic hero—viewed perhaps as Field Marshal Rommel was by the men of the British Eighth Army—in the eyes of foe and friend alike. On the face of it at least, Doughty comes out as a judicious biographer and, mutatis mutandis, I believe that the same can be said of his portraits of even more important people such as Emir Mohammed Ibn Rashid.

A third area to examine is Ottoman administrative institutions and practice in those parts of Arabia subject to the empire's jurisdiction. In western Arabia the focus was on Mecca and Medina, which Doughty obviously did not visit. Also to be considered, however, are other aspects of Ottoman administration of which we may mention these: the organization of the Syrian *Haj* or more specifically a particular part of it, the *Jurdy*; the set-up at the forts along the way; and mail service. Doughty touches on all of them. Many have remarked on the superlative Chaucerian picture that Doughty paints of the *Haj* caravan—and they are right, but in addition we learn of practical aspects not easily available elsewhere. The returning pilgrim caravan is regularly met at Medain Salih by a special "flying" provision caravan, the *Jurdy*,[25] sent down from Damascus to resupply the returning *hajjies* (1:40); the *Jurdy* was commanded by a pasha and was guarded by forty army horse troopers under a Turkish lieutenant. There was also a secretary who was a Nejdi Ageyli. It also included a five-inch brass artillery piece which was fired in enthusiasm many times as the *Jurdy* reached Medain Salih. Nevertheless, the *Jurdy* paid a *surra* (tributelike gift) to the various Beduin tribes as did the *Haj* caravan itself. Private enterprise was the order of the day for the *Jurdy*, aside from protection by the soldiers. The actual supplies, consisting of olives, cheese, flour, leeks, and "caravan biscuit," were carried by private Damascene traders, and their market camp was augmented by local fruit sellers from el-Ally, who brought dates and lemons to sell. The Damascenes also sold coffee cups, ironware, and carpets. Notwithstanding the guard, this outdoor market was one day attacked by Welad Aly tribesmen, even as one of their leading sheykhs sat talking with the pasha of the *Jurdy*. The garrison and the *Jurdy* guard combined to drive the attackers off. Beduin from distant tribes such as Bishr, Billi, and Jeheyna had to pay one riyal apiece for the privilege of buying or selling in the *Haj* market (1:238–41). Occasionally, the nervous cannoneers fired into the night desert (1:243). When the returning *Haj* caravan finally reached Medain Salih (it was eight days late that year), a "canvas city of a day, in the Thamudite plain, full of traffic" miraculously arose. Nor was the trading a one-way affair, for the traders who had gone south with the *Haj* caravan also brought southern commodities, of which the most noticeable was Yemeni coffee, but which also included spices from South and Southeast Asia, perfumes from Mecca, and East Asian porcelain. For their part the Beduin sold *samn* (butter). This temporary town was laid out in streets and included bakers, cobblers, and other artisans as well as the merchants' tents. As for the exhausted pilgrims who had been travelling all night, they "are now reposing in the tents, and the pleasant water-pipe and the cups are made ready at a hundred coffee fires: but the large white faces of girded Damascenes, their heavy foreheads wound round with solemn turbans, their citizen clothing and superfluous slops, are now quaint to the eye disused a while in the wilderness" (1:247). Nor were buying and selling the only activities. Moghraby soldiers arrived from the forts on the road to Medina and Mecca to collect their wages for the coming year. They may have been the only servants of the sultan to receive advance wages, for as Doughty laconically comments, "all other men's wages of the Ottoman Dowla be as much or more in arrear" (1:249). Another transaction was the delivery of the gift of a Nejdi (i.e., Arab) horse to Mohammed Said, the *Haj* pasha, from Ibn Rashid ("or what you call him" as a Syrian sneeringly commented [1:249]). The return gift from the pasha to Ibn Rashid would be sent the following year from the southbound caravan by messenger to Hayil and normally would be a Western product such as a revolver or telescope. In short, the *Jurdy*, which was only an adjunct of the *Haj*, was an institution which with its related social, economic, political, and administrative activities formed an important part of the annual life of northwestern Arabia. Doughty is probably the main primary source for our knowledge of it.

Postal service, as well as unofficial message transmittal, represents another institution touched on here and there by Doughty. Fourteen days after the southbound *Haj* caravan had left Medain Salih for Medina the *nejjab,* or camel courier, arrived from Medina headed north with letters from the *hajjies* for Damascus. The "postmaster of the wilderness" (1:162) was a sheykh (on whom see also 1:552) of the Welad Aly (was he paid a salary?), and he had hired a tribesman of the Sherarat for the trip in question. The man agreed, for payment, to add Doughty's letters to his Damascus-bound saddle bags and hoped to reach the great city in eleven or twelve days. When he did, a signal gun was fired to announce the arrival of the mail from the Holy Cities. The next day the *nejjab* picked up a sealed "light mail bag" (1:164) for the return trip to Medina and Mecca. In the event the Sherary had a hard ride back beset by cold weather and fog. Arriving in Medain Salih, he turned his mail bag over to another of Welad Aly for the rest of the camel express to Medina (1:27). Doughty gives no indication of how frequent this service was or whether it functioned other than during the high *Haj* season. More than likely the service was on demand the rest of the year although one other regular use is mentioned (1:47–48) as occurring during the month of Ramadan (Doughty's *ramathan*), before the pilgrimage, to report as to whether or not the cisterns, *birkets,* along the way were full of water. Doughty also implies (2:225) that the position of postmaster in Medina was an important one. He reports that one Abu Bakkar, whose mother was a Beduin and whose father was probably a Turk, had occupied this post prior to his promotion to the dignity of *Bab-el-Aarab,* or director of Arab (i.e., Beduin) affairs. As such he was during Doughty's time the second officer of the Prophet's city. He negotiated between Sabry Pasha and Ibn Rashid, he was acting chief of Medina when no pasha was in residence, and he personally led the Ageyl in the field against the nomads. Evidently the formal postal services were important in the far-flung empire.

An example of postal service on demand is provided by the need of Abdullah es-Siruan, *agha* or commander of Ottoman forces at Kheybar. Abdullah was a Galla-looking (Somali) man whose father had been a Kurd and whose mother was a Somali woman. He was, whatever his looks, identified as a Kurd. His command consisted of some twenty men: Kasimis, poor Beduins, Somalis, Turks, Albanians, Egyptians, Kurds, and Negroes. Three weeks after Doughty arrived in Kheybar the "slave-spirited Abdullah" (2:146) wrote or, rather, being illiterate, dictated to a scribe a letter to his superior, Sabry Pasha, the Ottoman governor of Medina, indicating that a stranger, a Christian Englishman, was now detained in Kheybar and that the *agha* had seized his effects in which were books and a letter from Ibn Rashid. Abdullah asked for instructions and and a letter from Ibn Rashid. Abdullah asked for instructions and also plaintively noted in a postscript that his soldiers had received no pay for thirty-two months. The scribe, it is of some interest to note, was Salih, the sheykh of Kheybar. The postman, a local hunter named Dakhil, agreed for four riyals to take the letter to Medina. He walked, wearing the simplest possible clothes, in order to avoid attracting attention. After a long and worrisome delay, Dakhil returned from Medina with an indecisive letter from Sabry Pasha to Abdullah: "Send all the stranger's books, and the papers which he brought with him from Ibn Rashid" (2:181). Doughty wanted to send his passport and also write to the pasha, but Abdullah forbade it. However, Doughty's Kheybar friend Mohammed en-Nejumy privately told Khalil to write the letter; he would make sure that Dakhil, the postman, took it. Reassured that there were people in Medina who knew English, Doughty penciled his note in his native language (who he was and where he had been), asking that he be allowed to proceed; he also enclosed his passport. After the *agha* had dictated his second letter to the pasha, "Abdullah set his seal to the letters, and delivered them to Dakhîl, who departed before noon. Amm Mohammed [en-Nejumy], as he was going, put a piece of silver (from me) in Dakhîl's hand, and cast my letter, with my British passport, into the worthy man's budget, upon his back, who feigned thus that he did not see it: the manly villager was not loath to aid a stranger (and a public guest) whom he saw oppressed in his village by the criminal tyranny of Abdullah" (2:183–84). When Dakhil returned, the answer was still indecisive: Medina had replied, " 'We have now much business with the Haj; at their departure we will examine and send again the books: in the meanwhile you are to treat the Engleysy honourably and with hospitality' " (2:218). A few days later another message came from the pasha, sent this time with some Beduin not the postman. The order was for Abdullah to treat Khalil well and forward him back to Ibn Rashid. A few days later Doughty received a personal letter from Sabry Pasha in French. It had been brought by six of the camelry— Ageylies. Sabry approved Khalil's objectives but advised him to return to Ibn Rashid and from Hayil, "prenez le chemin dans ces jours à votre destination" (2:222). Doughty wrote him back. Soon afterward Doughty left Kheybar. Dakhil the postman had offered to take him to Hayil, but a cheaper *rafik* was in the end found. Dakhil's speciality was clearly not a full-time job but he *was* a postman. Doughty has established the interesting point that in the Hejaz in the nineteenth century there were postmen.

The *Derb el-Haj,* or pilgrim road, and its proper maintenance have always been an important responsibility, practically and symbolically, for any government which like the Ottoman was to be the protector of the Holy Cities. The protection of the Syrian pilgrims from attack was based on soldiers sent from Damascus, but the guarantee of water on route was based on a line of cisterns guarded by tower-forts or *kellas* (*qal'ah* in standard transliteration). By Doughty's time some of the *kellas* had been abandoned but most functioned, and he reported (1:47) that they were two to three hundred years old and "are of good masonry." They were built where there were wells, not on a basis of distance, and the well was typically in the middle of the *kella's* courtyard. The water was raised, twenty-six feet in the case of Medain Salih, by a mule turning around a simple mechanism and flowed through a small canal into a cistern located outside the *kella* walls. The cisterns, including some at abandoned *kellas,* were also fed on occasion by rainwater. Beduins were allowed in through the iron doors only if well known and were not allowed to water at the cisterns, although there were instances in which Beduin seized *kellas* following a cut in their right-of-passage subsidies. "The kellas stand alone, as it were ships, in the immensity of the desert" (1:47). In Medain Salih Doughty, who had already met Mohammed Aly, the *kella agha* or *kellajy,* was admitted and assigned to a room for his extended stay. The total garrison was pathetically small, consisting, aside from Mohammed Aly, of old Haj Nejm, originally from Fez, who was the *mohafuz* or governor of the *kella;* another Moroccan, Haj Hasan, who had just returned to the *kella* service at the urging of Haj Nejm; two other men; and finally a slave and a man who was to work on water problems. The *kella's* artillery "were two very small rust-eaten pieces, which for their crudeness, might have been hammered by some nomad smith" (1:133). The Medain Salih *kella* is pictured by Doughty (1:opp. 417). It was a square, seventy feet on a side with storage rooms and stables on the ground floor around the courtyard, a gallery on the second floor with rooms on two sides, and a third-floor parapet to be used in case of attack. Doughty feared that the cesspool polluted the well. The cistern at Medain Salih was not small—eighteen feet deep and some eighteen by twenty-two yards in area. Two mules worked four hours each per day to keep it in water, but the system was leaky and inefficient. The *Haj* caravan brought supplies for the well gear each year from Damascus. Apparently Christian masons from Syria had built the *kellas* in the first place and had repaired the one in Medain Salih only a few years before Doughty was there. Outside the *kella* was an enclosed orchard where Haj Nejm raised vegetables and spices, and there were also several fruitful palm trees. A number of poor Beduin families, "gate Arabs" Doughty calls them (1:135), habitually lived "before the iron gate of the kella." Regular Beduins were admitted to the *kella* only sparingly, a very few at a time.

Former rations for a *kella* had been three tons of wheat, thirty hundred weight of caravan biscuit, thirty of bulgar, and forty pounds of *samn*. Then rations were reduced to enough wheat for ten men and a salary of £8 per man for ten men. Doughty estimates the total cost to Damascus at £220 per year. The system was of course that the *agha* and *mohafuz* never hired the whole ten men. The difference covered hospitality for the Beduin and a windfall for the higher officials. According to Doughty (1:165), the *kella* garrisons had earlier been made up mostly of Kurds, at least south of Maan (in Jordan today), but that after the former Algerian resistance fighter, Abd el-Kader, reached Damascus in 1855, North Africans began to predominate in the *kellas*. The daily routine of the *kella* is detailed (1:167), and the reader also is not spared an account of a bitter intramural flare-up (1:417–19). One may wonder that the Ottoman system held together in these barren regions, but it did, and one will not easily find a more reliable guide to how it worked than in *Arabia Deserta*.

This essay is not the place to make a study of Doughty as social historian, especially as there is a separate chapter in this book on ethnography. But it may be worth opining that Khalil was a sensitive observer of those among whom he wayfared even though the "narrator" often was prejudiced.[26] And Khalil was a sharp observer who missed little and whose typically Pre-Raphaelite "concern with precise factual description of 'indiscriminate detail' "[27] had much in common with the new social history of the Annales school, founded by Lucien Febvre and Marc Bloch in 1929, which de-emphasized political history in favor of social history. Doughty was sensitive to the pluralistic elements, vertical as well as horizontal, which made up Arabian society, he noted "manners and customs" in a comprehensive manner, he analyzed motivations, and he described details of domestic life with a notable sense of immediacy. One can only agree with T. E. Lawrence: "They are told of to the life, with words and phrases fitted to them . . . perfectly. . . . There is no sentiment, nothing merely picturesque" (1:17). A passing point is that Doughty's descriptions of town life are of perhaps greater importance than that of Beduin life simply because Beduins have more often been interesting to observers than have townsmen. A comprehensive social history of Arabia has not been attempted, but when it is its author will discover that when he asks the right questions of *Travels in Arabia Deserta,* he will find answers—probably more than anywhere else.

In short, *Arabia Deserta* is one useful work, but only one of many, in establishing "facts" about Arabian politics, tribes, chronologies, and dynasties. Every historian since has attested to this usefulness by his or her citations. But if one wants the "land with its smells and dirt, as well as its nobility and freedom" (T. E. Lawrence in 1:17), then Khalil is perhaps indispensable. Lawrence is wrong when he says that "the book can never grow old" (1:17) because the Arabia of Doughty and Lawrence has been swept away in recent years by the most rapid change that human history has ever recorded; but no single work paints an overall picture of nineteenth-century Arabian society that tells us more than does *Travels in Arabia Deserta.*

NOTES

1 Elizabeth Sirriyeh, "The *Memoires* of a French Gentleman in Syria: Chevalier Laurent d'Arvieux (1635–1702)," *Bulletin of the British Society for Middle Eastern Studies* 11 (1984): 125–39.

2 Ibid., 125.

3 Major studies of this genre include D. G. Hogarth, *The Penetration of Arabia* (New York: Frederick A. Stokes Co., 1904); R. H. Kiernan, *The Unveiling of Arabia: The Story of Arabian Travel and Discovery* (London: George C. Harrap and Co., Ltd., 1937); Jacqueline Pirenne, *A la découverte de l'Arabie: Cinq siècles de science et d'aventure* (Paris: Le Livre Contemporain—Amiot-Dumont, 1958); Robin Bidwell, *Travellers in Arabia* (London: The Hamlyn Publishing Group, Ltd., 1976); Zahra Freeth and H. V. F. Winstone, *Explorers of Arabia from the Renaissance to the End of the Victorian Era* (London: George Allen and Unwin, 1978).

4 Ta, 165.

5 *Northern Najd—A Journey from Jerusalem to Anaiza in Qasim,* trans. Lady Capel-Cure (London: The Argonaut Press, 1938).

6 Musil (1868–1944) studied both in Vienna and Prague and served the Austro-Hungarian empire on the eve of and during World War I. That Musil made intelligence reports (as was perhaps also true of Guarmani) may have been "enough to confirm the

worst fears of those in the Middle East and elsewhere who have been inclined to see
European orientalists as spies and agents of imperialism" (Geoffrey Roper, "George
Percy Badger [1815–1888]," *Bulletin of the British Society for Middle Eastern Studies* 11
[1984]: 141), but it did not reduce Musil's contributions to history.

7   *Oriental Explorations and Studies,* nos. 1–6: *The Northern Ḥeǧâz, a Topographical Itinerary*
     (New York, 1926); *Arabia Deserta, a Topographical Itinerary* (New York, 1927); *The
     Middle Euphrates, a Topographical Itinerary* (New York, 1927); *Palmyrena, a Topographical
     Itinerary* (New York, 1928); *Northern Neǧd, a Topographical Itinerary* (New York, 1928);
     The Manners and Customs of the Rwala Bedouins (New York, 1928); plus, separately slip
     cased, *Map of Northern Arabia* (in four sheets).

8   *Northern Neǧd,* 15.

9   Ibid., xi.

10   As dictated to Wadi al-Bustani (Er-Riath: Manshurat Dar al-Yamamah li-al-Bahth
     wa-al-Tarjamah wa-al-Nashr, 1386/1966).

11   (Er-Riath: Kingdom of Saudi Arabia, Wizarat al-Maarif, 1391/1971).

12   Published as a supplement to Ibn Bishr's *'Unwan al-Majd;* see note 11 above.

13   *'Unwan al-Sa'd wa-al-Majd fima Ustuzrifa fi Akhbar al-Hijaz wa-Nejd* (manuscript
     [1949], photostatic copy in possession of the Arabian-American Oil Co.).

14   In 2 vols. (Bagdad: al-Matbaah al-Asriyah, 1344/1926).

15   *Jazirat al-'Arab fi al-Qarn al-'Ishrin* (The Arabian peninsula in the twentieth century)
     (Cairo: Matbaat Lajnat al-Ta'lif wa-al-Tarjamah wa-al-Nashr, 1365/1946).

16   *Al-Bilad al-'Arabiyah al-Su'udiyah* (Mecca: Matbaat Umm al-Qura, 1355/1936–37)
     and *Khamsun 'Am fi Jazirat al-'Arab* (Fifty years in the Arabian peninsula) (Cairo:
     Sharikat Maktabat wa-Matbaat Mustafa al-Baba al-Halabi wa-Awladih, 1380/1960).

17   Four vols. in 3 ([Istanbul], Matbaa-i Amire, 1308–[1315]/[1890?–97?]).

18   Twelve vols. in 6 (Istanbul: Matbaa-i Osmaniye, 1309/[1891–92]).

19   For a compact summary of British official sources, see J. B. Kelly, *Britain and the
     Persian Gulf, 1795–1880* (Oxford: Clarendon Press, 1968), 852–62.

20   For a thorough survey, see Stanford J. Shaw, "Ottoman Archival Materials for the
     Nineteenth and Early Twentieth Centuries: The Archives of Istanbul," *International
     Journal of Middle Eastern Studies* 6 (1975): 94–114.

21   *'Iqd al-Durar,* 40–42.

22   "Narrative of a Journey, from Cairo to Medina and Mecca, by Suez, Araba, Tawila, al-
     Jauf, Jubbe, Hail, and Nejd in 1854," *The Journal of the Royal Geographical Society* 24
     (1854): 115–207.

23   *Narrative of a Year's Journey through Central and Eastern Arabia (1862–63),* 2 vols.
     (London: Macmillan and Co., 1865), 203 ff.

24   *A Pilgrimage to Nejd,* 2 vols. (London: John Murray, 1881), 1:194.

25   According to the index of *Arabia Deserta,* s.v. *Jurdy,* the Arabic would be transliterated
     by modern scholars as *Jardah.* The word is not attested in obvious dictionaries, en-
     cyclopedias, and the like. For another discussion of this goods caravan, called therein
     jarde, see R. Tresse, *Le Pèlerinage syrien aux villes, saintes de l'Islam* (Paris: Imprimerie
     Chaumette, 1937), 245–50. Tresse's work, the most important on the subject, is based
     heavily on French archival materials such as consular reports from Damascus; but the
     frequent citations of Doughty, passim, are themselves an indication of his importance

for the author. It is curious in light of this fact to note that Tresse does not cite Doughty on the *Jurdy*. The best modern treatment of the *Jurdy* is Abdul-Karim Rafeq, *The Province of Damascus, 1723–1783*, 2d ed. (Beirut: Khayats, 1970), especially pp. 65–68.

26 For the elegantly presented distinction between Khalil and the "narrator" in *Arabia Deserta*, see Ta, 48–52.

27 Ta, 41.

ROBERT A. FERNEA

Arabia Deserta: *The Ethnographic Text*

"I am saying that every anthropological observer, no matter how well
he/she has been trained, will see something that no other such observer
can recognize, namely a kind of harmonic projection of the observer's own
personality. And when these observations are 'written up' in monograph
or any other form, the observer's personality will again distort any purported 'objectivity.' "[1]

Sir Edmund Leach, dean of British social anthropology, has in the above
quotation cast doubt on the major source of anthropological truth by de-
nying the objectivity which in the 1950s was the unquestioned standard
of good ethnography. He is not alone. The door has swung open to new
approaches in ethnographic texts and there is no longer universal agreement as to what defines a proper ethnography or grants authority to the
personal experience on which it is based. By the same token, we can no
longer be so sure who is and who is not an ethnographer. Against this
background, *Travels in Arabia Deserta* seems much closer to some types of
modern ethnographic writing today than would have been the case a few
years ago. Author Charles Doughty appears to have confronted two issues
of major concern among anthropologists today—the authority of fieldwork among "others" and the rhetoric of the ethnographic text—and to
have done both in an exceptionally effective and imaginative fashion.

In 1957 I read, or attempted to read, *Travels in Arabia Deserta* while
preparing to undertake my first anthropological research in southern Iraq.
The text quickly tried my patience and I put it aside as a Victorian curiosity, full of value judgments, written in an affected manner in order to
sound "biblical," lacking the objective style necessary to convey reality
and speak to my own interest in Arab tribal society. In 1983 I turned to
Doughty's work again, having spent four months in Hayil, one of the
cities in Saudi Arabia that Doughty had visited a hundred years before and

about which he had written at length. This time I found Charles Doughty's account of Hayil a fascinating view of a human scene, its descriptive
and evocative powers far exceeding anything else I had read about the
Arabia of his day.[2] My view of Doughty has altered, but my change of
heart is not simply a private affair. The field of cultural anthropology itself
has changed, as the quote from Leach suggests.

In 1957 ethnography was defined as "The study of individual cultures.
It is primarily a descriptive and noninterpretive study."[3] No questions
were asked as to whether "noninterpretive study" was really possible or
how an "individual" culture could be isolated for study. The ethnography
was the foundation of the discipline, the logical and obvious outcome of
work in the "field." Anthropologists were relied upon to bring back
"facts" of their own experience. Rarely were such "facts" questioned. It
was rather the analysis of ethnographic data, the ethnological interpretation, the product around which scientific controversy raged. What did it
and did it not prove? What were the proper models of analysis, the acceptable theoretical assumptions? "Armchair anthropology" was a pejorative
term in the fifties, used to refer to the work of scholars who did not live
among the subjects of their studies, participating in as well as observing
their social life. Secondhand accounts could not be trusted. It was fieldwork, "objectively" reported, which authenticated professional opinion.

For many of us who began our studies thirty years ago, it was Bronislaw
Malinowski, a British-trained Polish anthropologist interned during
World War I on his Trobriand island fieldwork site, who was the perfect
example of the practicing cultural anthropologist. His ethnographies, beginning with the classic *Argonauts of the Western Pacific*,[4] set a new standard
for richness of description and analytic insight. The narrative voice of
these ethnographies was one of seeming objectivity and sympathetic understanding: a calm and professional tone which inspired confidence in the
reader. It was more than forty years before the authority of this ethnographer's persona was questioned. His private diary was published in
English in 1967, revealing a very different sort of man—frustrated, full of
resentment toward the Trobriand islanders, angry to the point of demean-
ing them.[5] Subsequently, fieldwork by anthropologist Annette Weiner
showed Trobriand women contributing to the well-being of the community in ways which Malinowski overlooked.[6] If Malinowski's complex personal feelings about the women, revealed in his diary, had been part of his
ethnography, would we have waited so long to question his work? Re-

cently, Derek Freeman raised a great deal of controversy by suggesting
that Margaret Mead's *Coming of Age in Samoa* portrayed a much less problematic adolescence among Samoan teenagers than he believes can be sub-
stantiated by the records and other observers' reports.[7] For many professional anthropologists, Freeman was attacking Mead's honesty, not the
construction of her text. Both cases lend support to the contention that
much of our ethnographic literature has until recently been read, as well
as written, in terms of "genre conventions of ethnographic realism about
which there has been a tacit and artificial consensus in Anglo-American
anthropology during approximately the past 60 years."[8]

Thus, until recently, the general assumption has been that an ethnographer, speaking through his or her text, is an authoritative source of
information, and that the problem lies not in its authenticity, but in the
interpretation of the personal experience through analytic paradigm, or
theoretical issue. The contemporary reaction to these assumptions is well
expressed in the following quotations. James Clifford states,

> It is understandable, given their vagueness, that experiential criteria of
> authority—unexamined beliefs in the "method" of participant observa-
> tion, in the power of rapport, empathy, and so on—have come under
> criticism by hermeneutically sophisticated anthropologists. In recent
> years the second moment in the dialectic of experience and interpreta-
> tion has received increasing attention and elaboration. Interpretation,
> based on a philosophical model of textual "reading," has emerged as a
> sophisticated alternative to the now apparently naive claims for experi-
> ential authority. Interpretive anthropology demystifies.[9]

Further, in a review of the subject of ethnographies as texts, Marcus and
Cushman assert, "Anthropologists have finally begun to give explicit attention to the writing of ethnographic texts, a subject long ignored either
by conceiving of ethnography primarily as an activity that occurs in the
field or by treating it as a method, rather than a product, of research."[10]

In this different intellectual climate, the work of Charles Doughty assumes a new significance. Charles Doughty did not go to Arabia as an
anthropologist and, unlike Richard Burton, never tried to assume that
professional role. Nonetheless, Doughty was dedicated to communicating
his experiences in Arabia to the English readers of the late nineteenth
century and prepared himself to do so while living with the Arabs for
twenty-one months, participating and observing much as would an an-

thropologist, with a meticulous eye for detail and with powers of description far greater than those of many professional ethnographers. Furthermore, he had studied the language and spoke a dialect of Arabic. Yet Doughty has not found a place in current anthropological textbooks on the Middle East nor has *Travels in Arabia Deserta* been given serious consideration as an ethnography. Why? It is not lacking in detailed information and observation. The answer seems to be that Doughty failed to write with the objectivity of style and the cultural relativism which became the hallmark of anthropological monographs in the 1930s. It is his value judgments which mark his work as nonanthropological, particularly his often polemic defense of Christianity. But does this conceal the relation between experience and interpretation on which his account is based, or does it in fact help reveal it? Does not his approach in fact enhance our ability to understand his experience and that of the people he visited?

As mentioned above, my own interest in Doughty was reawakened by spending some months in Saudi Arabia in 1983, for the most part in and around Hayil. Doughty spent a month in Hayil and devoted 111 pages out of a total of 1,245 to his experience there; almost a tenth of his book is concerned with episodes which occupied only a twenty-first part of his time in Arabia. He does not explicitly tell us why he wanted to go to Hayil, but for a stranger travelling in northern Arabia in the late nineteenth century, a visit to Hayil was absolutely necessary to assure one's safe passage, for at that time the town was the undisputed center of political authority in the region.

Hayil had become the independent center of authority for northern Arabia when Abdullah Ibn Rashid succeeded in becoming a balancing force between the Turko-Egyptian governor, Khurshid Pasha, to the north and Prince Ibn Saud, who was at odds with the Egyptians, in Riyadh to the south. Abdullah's son, Mohammed, who ruled while Doughty was in Hayil, had begun his sovereignty in 1869. He had added to the city's revenues by offering Baghdadi and Iranian pilgrims protection from tribal attack on condition that they pass by Hayil and pay a toll both going to and coming from Mecca. This greatly enriched both Mohammed and the merchants of the city, which was growing and prosperous while Doughty was there. However, Mohammed had not succeeded his father directly. Rather, a series of assassinations within the Ibn Rashid family had followed Abdullah's natural death. Mohammed himself was one of the most murderous of the lot, as he killed all six sons of his eldest brother to secure

his position. The memory of this bloody history still lingered on in stories
told in Hayil in 1983. In Doughty's day, however, this was fresh news,
circulated among the desert tents by the men who paid homage to or
fought against the emir. Mohammed Ibn Abdullah Ibn Rashid, however,
was a man who faced perhaps the greatest tragedy of all, the inability to
father a child despite a series of wives and concubines.

A highly dramatic retelling of Emir Mohammed's violent rise to power
appears as a central part of Doughty's Hayil account. There is no conde-
scension in Doughty's narrative. Instead he shows a thorough understanding of why the killings occurred and compassion for those caught up in the
struggle. As a royalist, Doughty often used the title "prince" when speaking of Emir Mohammed and was very curious about Arab aristocracy. He
came to Hayil both fascinated and frightened by the emir's reputation. Soon
after Doughty describes his passage through the gates of the walled city, we
are with him in the emir's audience room (*mejlis*). Although he was exhausted from his journey south over miles of sand dunes, across the Great
Nefud from Jauf to Teyma and Gofar, it was incumbent upon him to visit
the emir immediately and to make his presence known.

> The ruler Mohammed . . . was lying half along upon his elbow, with
> leaning cushions under him, by his fire-pit side, where a fire of the
> desert bushes was burning before him. (1:640)

Like many anthropologists, Doughty found it difficult to explain to the
emir exactly what he was doing in the area.

> "And well, well! but what could move thee . . . to take such a jour-
> ney?" I responded suddenly, "*El-elûm!* the liberal sciences;" but the
> sense of this plural is, in Nejd and the Beduin talk, *tidings*. The Ruler
> answered hastily, "And is it for this thou art come hither!" It was diffi-
> cult to show him what I intended by the sciences, for they have no
> experience of ways so sequestered from the common mouth-labours of
> mankind. (1:643)

As the interview progressed and the emir decided to see if his visitor
could read Arabic, Doughty seemed unable to improve upon his bad
beginning:

> the Emir Ibn Rashîd himself came over and sat down beside me.—
> "Where shall I read?"—"Begin anywhere at a chapter,—there!" and he

pointed with his finger. So I read the place, *'The king* (such an one) *slew all his brethren and kindred.'* It was *Sheytân* [satanic] that I had lighted upon such a bloody text; the Emir was visibly moved! and, with the quick feeling of the Arabs, he knew that I regarded him as a murderous man. (1:643)

Still, the emir seems to have welcomed his visitor in the beginning. Doughty had been a *hakim* (doctor) while with the Beduin and this is what he became in Hayil, setting up shop in his room in the emir's palace and receiving visits by day and sometimes by night. Doughty had taken pains to learn something about medicine and had brought with him a supply of useful drugs, including quinine, which was in constant demand. This is an experience familiar to many anthropologists. While most of us have little medical training, it is impossible to refuse requests for medicine which it is assumed one has. It becomes necessary to exercise some discretion in passing out such medicine to insure appropriate treatment and to prevent exhaustion of supplies. This involves attempts at diagnosis. It is not surprising, then, that many anthropologists have found themselves regarded as doctors by the people with whom they are living, an identity thrust upon them. However, Doughty went one step further. He charged for his doses. In this way he avoided appearing to patronize the people of Hayil. Instead, he involved himself with them by means of exchanges of his limited stock of drugs for small amounts of money as well as food and perhaps other supplies which he needed. He established relations of symmetrical exchange, not one-way favors. Also, Doughty refused to write charms. He was not, by his own standards, a charlatan. By working as a *hakim,* Doughty established a basis for meaningful participation in the life of the community. At the same time he did not try to conceal his interest in the town and countryside as he travelled about and took notes publicly; for instance, when the emir showed him around his garden:

He questioned me, between impatient authority and the untaught curiosity of Arabians, of his plants and trees,—palms and lemons, and the thick-rinded citron; then he showed me a seedling of the excellent potherb *bâmiya* and thyme, and single roots of other herbs and salads. All such green things they eat not! So unlike is the diet of Nejd Arabia to the common use in the Arabic border countries.

Gazelles were running in the further walled grounds; the Emir stood and pointed with his finger. . . . "*Uktub-ha!* write, that is portray, her!" exclaimed the Emir. (1:644)

Through the next 110 pages, the princely household is the center of Doughty's narrative and he develops a rich, full account of its manners and customs, executive functions, domain, and subjects. We are given demographic data on the size and population of the town and surrounding desert and oases as well as careful descriptions of the market and other points of interest. While an ethnographer might have used tables to present the quantitative data, a reader can obtain a good picture of the size and scope of the emir's kingdom from Doughty's figures. Undoubtedly, Doughty got much of his information from visitors to his room in the palace, where, as a *hakim,* he treated infected eyes and diarrhea with drops and herbs and stern advice, and also from the many visitors who gathered every day in the public rooms of the palace.

Travels in Arabia Deserta is not a journal. Doughty carefully worked through plentiful material, constructing descriptive passages with first-person conversations and maintaining dramatic tension by keeping his own often precarious position in Hayil at the forefront of his tale. This is not the style of most classic ethnographies, where the account is often organized according to such headings as "Kinship," "Religious Practices," "Political System," and the like. These accounts are most often written in the third person. Even if the voice is first person, the reader has little opportunity to read about the part played by the anthropologist, how he or she participated in the shaping of the conversations, of the actual responses of the informants. At the same time, informants rarely have identities as individuals located at a specific point in time and space; contradictions and misunderstandings disappear, along with any sense of the ethnographer-as-personality. In his account of Hayil, Doughty interacts with a wide variety of individuals and it is through his careful account of these encounters that the reader gets a sense of the people of the region. The modern anthropologist avoids trying to guess states of mind. Doughty, on the other hand, frequently speaks of "malignant young fanatics" (2:27) or talks of qualities being "natural even to Semitic souls" (2:23). But while his value judgments are disconcerting to the modern reader, an independent "sense of personality" of his hosts in Hayil transcends such remarks, thanks to the way in which Doughty situates his information.

The major element in this manner of presentation is Doughty's creation of the narrator-protagonist, Khalil, who is of course Doughty himself. *Travels in Arabia Deserta* is Khalil's tale; Doughty speaks to us directly only in the prefaces to the book and on other rare occasions, as when he refers to things that occurred after Khalil left Arabia or moments of subsequent reflection. Our knowledge of the people of Hayil is thus within the context of their conversations with Khalil and his thoughts about them. His comments about others are also a source of insight about himself. In describing a young deaf and dumb man, a member of the emir's entourage who had a very protective attitude toward the foreigner, Khalil comments, "Of his long sufferance of the malice of the world might be this singular resolution in him, to safeguard another manner of deaf and dumb person" (2:23).

Far from exhibiting a calm and unruffled manner with the "natives," Khalil reveals a shortness of temper and irritability often in excess of his hosts in Hayil. For example, when Hamud, the emir's cousin, who becomes Khalil's special friend in Hayil, looks at Khalil's white skin and asks if he might not be the son of a Circassian slave, Khalil replies "with some warmth, 'To buy human flesh is not so much as named in my country: as for all who deal in slaves we are appointed by God to their undoing. We hunt the cursed slave-sail upon all seas, as you hunt the hyena'" (1:655). He goes on to remark, "Hamûd was a little troubled, because I showed him some flaws in their manners, some heathenish shadows in his religion where there was no spot in ours, and had vaunted our naval hostility." Then Hamud says, "And Khalîl, the Nasâra [Christians] eat swine's flesh?" provoking Khalil to another round in which he says, "Do not the Beduin eat wolves and the hyena, the fox, the thób [lizard], and the spring-rat?—owls, kites, the carrion eagle? but I would taste of none such." It is Hamud who answers "with his easy humanity, 'My meaning was not to say, Khalîl, that for any filth or sickliness of the meat we abstain from swine's flesh, but because the Néby [Prophet] has bidden us.'" He adds that he has heard swine's flesh is very good meat. However, another companion cannot resist coming back at Khalil with, "And what . . . is the wedlock of the Nasâra? as the horse covers the mare it is said . . . the Nasâra be engendered, —wellah like the hounds!" (1:655–56). Doughty records no answer to this from Khalil. Did he rise in silence and stalk away? This exchange, like many others, has revealed as much about the personalities of the individuals involved as it has about the cultural mores of Hayil and of Victorian England.

The use of Khalil as the textual identity of Doughty was ethnographically analogous to his attempt to create an identity for himself as *el-hakim,* the doctor, while doing his fieldwork. In both cases, a diverse and often contradictory structure of attitudes and relationships was created which

reveals far more about the role of the fieldworker/traveler and eth-
nologist/writer than would otherwise have been apparent.

Of course, Khalil did not begin to exist merely as part of the text.
Doughty adopted this name for use among the Arabs. His own name was
difficult to pronounce by Arabic speakers. For this same reason, a *nom du
champ* is common among anthropologists. It was a more imaginative step,
beyond contemporary practice, to take Khalil back from the field and
make him a major persona in *Travels in Arabia Deserta*. Though a number
of ethnographies have recently been written in the first person or in the
form of dialogues between the ethnographer and the informant(s), it is
significantly different to distance the writer from his literary persona as
Doughty did. We learn a great deal from Khalil because we see him in
many situations and listen to him speak in the many conversations which
are part of the narrative structure of the text. Khalil reveals his bad temper, his pride, his pettiness, his chauvinism as well as his fatigue, compassion, fears, and hopes. He becomes a combination of human qualities
which both annoy us and attract our admiration, thereby involving the
reader in the construction of the ethnographic text. We are given an opportunity to judge for ourselves whether the Arabs are what Khalil says
they are in specific situations because we can put ourselves in both Khalil's
position and in the position of his counterparts, a radical departure from
conventional ethnographic styles. As a result, many times we find ourselves more sympathetic with the Arabs of Hayil than we are with Khalil,
and perforce we are left to wonder exactly what Doughty thought of
Khalil's (his own) behavior as he spent four years writing about him
(self) in action. For example, see what is said to Khalil after he has rudely
dismissed a young gentleman of Hayil who had accosted him:

> "Khalil," said the friendly Beduwy, "I speak it of fellowship, deal not so
> plainly with this townspeople; believe me they will take up thy words,
> he also that you now sent away will not cease to hate thee extremely."
> (2:16)

Is Doughty not criticizing his own behavior here by including this
conversation in the book? His bad temper and stubborn insistence on the
glories of his religion and his country are there to be admired by his
contemporaries and disapproved of by us. Both generations of readers have
an equal opportunity to come to their own conclusions. The creation of
Khalil is a literary device which adds an important distance between the

creative writer and the fieldwork, through which the anthropologist must reveal him- or herself in a deliberate fashion.

Doughty's insistence on his identity as a Christian (*Nasrany*) is another feature of *Travels in Arabia Deserta* which troubles modern readers with ethnographic interests. We must remember that other European travelers were busy trying to pose as Moslems so as to reach the holy city of Mecca and write books, for there was a growing European market for accounts of such Middle Eastern adventures. While in Hayil, Doughty meets an Italian camped on the outskirts of town who is on his way to Mecca with a group of Persian pilgrims. Posing as a Moslem, the young man is gathering experiences for a book on the city. Doughty, speaking directly to the reader instead of through Khalil, says that he looked for news of the Italian after he left Arabia but never heard of him again. He also mentions that other European travelers posing as Moslems in order to enter Mecca had been decapitated (2:68). It is conceivable that Doughty was moved to emphasize his Christianity (at least at first) to make sure he was not taken for such an imposter. After all, he was traveling in the style and costume of a Beduin. It was necessary that he be clear about his identity in order not to be mistaken for a Beduin. (These days the anthropologist stresses his academic calling in order not to be taken for a spy.) So Doughty is publicly known as the *Nasrany*, the Christian, though he is Khalil to his friends.

> In the early days of my being in Hâyil, if I walked through their sûk, children and the ignorant and poor Beduw flocked to me, and I passed as the cuckoo with his cloud of wondering small birds, until some citizen of more authority delivered me, saying to them, 'Wellah, thus to molest the stranger would be displeasing to the Emir!' Daily some worthy persons called me to coffee and to breakfast; the most of them sought counsel of the hakîm for their diseases, few were moved by mere hospitality, for their conscience bids them show no goodness to an adversary of the saving religion; but a Moslem coming to Hâyil, or even a Frankish stranger easily bending and assenting to them, might find the Shammar townspeople hospitable, and they are accounted such. (1:652)

Judging from the text, it is not the *Nasrany* who opens the subject of religious differences. Rather, it is a subject of conversation that others cannot resist and Doughty develops a number of conciliatory responses along with sharp replies.

Today, the exhibition of our religious identities has become largely irrelevant and it is a matter of simple good manners for the Western traveller to indicate respect for religious practices and beliefs in foreign lands.
For the ethnographer, making moral or ethical judgments about the behavior of "others" is professionally questionable. However, the Victorian
gentleman was not expected to exhibit such relativistic, much less approv-
ing attitudes. Richard Burton, Doughty's contemporary, suffered much
criticism for his discovery of the praiseworthy in Islam.[11] Doughty's attitudes were in tune with British public opinion of the day when he states
about a meal: "The devil is not in their dish; all the riot and wantonness of
their human nature lies in the Mohammedan luxury of hareem" (1:650).
Or again, "the Moslem religion ever makes numbness and death in some
part of the human understanding" (2:21) just because the people of Hayil
were not ready to import grain from some distance in the face of a local
shortage.

Doughty was evidently not a stupid man and simply to view him as a
religious fanatic seems inconsistent with his ability to exhibit so much
sympathetic insight about other aspects of Beduin culture. What led
Doughty to his religious declarations? Was it a preoccupation he brought
with him to Arabia? Was it an irrepressible dislike for Islam which he
developed there? Both views have been presented by critics (see Ta, 64–
83). However, not enough importance has been given to the special pressures that a person in Doughty's position faced.

To achieve professional legitimacy, the ethnographer must live among
the people being studied and become defined as a person to them in the
course of participating and observing. Doughty *had* to have a religious
identity; there was no opportunity to leave his religious affiliation ambiguous. Daily life in a Beduin camp or a small town like Hayil is Islamic,
punctuated by regular prayers, universally observed five times a day. Anyone who does not pray constantly reminds his neighbors and friends of a
difference between them which, were it to remain purely ideological,
might well be overlooked. It soon became clear that if the *Nasrany* did not
wish to follow the example of Abdullah el-Moslemanny, an "apostate Isra-
elite," as Doughty calls him, and convert to Islam, he had better move on.
If, on the other hand, he would follow the example of the Jew from
Baghdad and convert to Islam, he would receive from the emir the neces-
sities to start a new life for himself in Hayil.

Why did Doughty not accept conversion as a possible solution? Was it out of strong Christian belief? Fear of hypocrisy? Uncertainty that his knowledge of Islamic theology and of classical Arabic were great enough to allow him to pass as a Moslem in the way Richard Burton had done? For whatever reason, the fact that there was no neutral religious ground on which Doughty might have found a peaceful basis for coexistence cannot be understood as the outcome of Victorian fanaticism. Once Doughty took a stand and refused to pretend to be a Moslem, he was in a polemic position of having to defend his faith and of having to accept his Christianity as the major portion of his identity. Try as he would to establish himself as a *hakim,* or an explorer or scientist (which was understood by the Arabs to mean polemicist or propagandist), it was as a *Nasrany* (literally, a person from Nazareth) that he was known. This was an uncomplimentary term for Christian, a form of insult. Also, Doughty was the guest of the emir. He was totally dependent on the generosity of his hosts for housing and for much of his food. Yet Doughty refused to pray with his hosts and troubled them by using ritual forms of Arabic speech which have Islamic significance. His constant nonconformity was a red flag to many sincere believers who could not accept that a person in Doughty's position could continue to fail to see the error of his ways. Finally, a coffee server is provoked to the point of attacking Doughty.

> Then holding the large blade aloft, and turning himself upon me, he said, *Sully aly en Nêby,* 'Give glory to the apostle,' so I answered, "we all worship the Godhead. I cannot forsake my name of Nasrâny, neither wouldst thou thine if thou be'st a worthy man"—But as he yet held the knife above my breast, I said to him "what dagger is that? and tell these who are present whether thy meaning be to do me a mischief?" Then he put it down as if he were ashamed to be seen by the company savagely threatening his coffee guest. (2:53)

What seems to us fanatic about Doughty clearly was perceived by Doughty to be characteristic of his Arab hosts: the field notes labeled "Fanaticism" are some of the most extensive of his materials for *Travels in Arabia Deserta* (Ta, 45).

Doughty several times was told by well-meaning Arab friends that the practice of Islam would have been quite sufficient, his beliefs and behavior after he left Arabia being his own business. This was really his only alternative to "being a Christian" as the major part of his public identity. But Doughty puts this temptation behind himself with alacrity. His problem was not how to be taken for a Moslem, but how not to be misunderstood as one. With his Arab clothes and reddish beard (the Beduin often reddened their beards with henna), Doughty could easily be taken for an Arab and therefore for an imposter.

The upshot of Doughty's religious position in Hayil was his expulsion. Though the simple-minded servant was severely chastized for his behavior by the emir, this experience really ended Doughty's visit. He felt he could never return to the emir's coffee room over which his attacker presided. This was the room where the men visited and where he probably learned much about the community and region from the nomadic visitors. To be cut off from this social meeting-place was to be cut off from a major center of local communication.

Khalil expresses some bitterness about his expulsion from Hayil by the emir after only one month's stay. But he tells us enough to let us understand that the emir may well have felt he could no longer protect Doughty from the religious feelings of many townspeople or risk the criticism which stemmed from keeping Doughty so long as a guest. Doughty had long exceeded any customary period of welcome required by local Beduin rules of hospitality. But it is more important to remember that the people of Hayil were Wahabies, members of the movement which arose in the eighteenth century and had as its clearly stated purpose the purging of Islam of alien influence and practice. Wahaby fundamentalism stressed that Islam was not simply the right way to believe but, more important, the only way to live. Therefore, Doughty's religion was not only perceived as foreign but as threatening to pollute public life.

The spread of the Wahaby movement in Central and Eastern Arabia under Ibn Saud had been a major factor in the consolidation of the king's power over the often factious tribes under his rule. The town of Hayil was full of people with Wahaby convictions and the emir was certainly aware of the risks of appearing in any way slack in his own religious fervor. Moreover, a Moslem state, Turkey, was at this time at war with Christian Russia and Doughty has told us how his own explanation of his activities made him sound like an intelligence agent. Making inexplicable trips around Hayil with a notebook increased suspicions about him. Nor did he have any papers indicating his legitimacy; his own consul in Damascus had refused to give him any form of *laissez-passer*.

In making his own problems the theme of his account Doughty not only manages to convey a wide range of information and observations, but also reveals a great many of the contradictions and ambiguities which were part of his hosts' and his own feelings and behavior. Other accounts of European visitors often contain long paeans of praise about Arab hospitality and conventional descriptions of religious belief and practices. But Arab culture is no more a smooth, unruffled cloth than our own culture. Doughty's stance was not a product of "fanaticism" but of historical circumstances. Indeed, there is an opinion among some anthropologists that an adversarial position is more likely to reveal the nature of things than the idealized version transmitted in the warmth of friendly relations. The papering over of disagreement, the avoidance of matters of conflict help conceal a great deal about daily life.

Finally, a word about Doughty's style, the "new English style" he announced he was developing in *Travels in Arabia Deserta,* for it has a direct bearing on his ethnographic legitimacy. Ethnography is as much the way things are said as what is said. It is impossible to escape the particularizing nature of the experience of writing or the subjective nature of personal interaction with others. Ethnographers cannot totally transcend the historic specificity of field work experiences by attempting to relate them in an abstract fashion. Allowing the "others," the subjects of our ethnography, a voice for themselves in fact is a more honest replication of our own intellectual experience, for in most cases our understandings arise out of discussions with informants who understand what interests us, what is significant according to our framework of understanding. Thus, it is characteristic of "experimental ethnographies" that the informants speak directly. There are problems with this, however, since we edit and select what is said. It is similar to ethnographic film which, however relentlessly accurate what is filmed may be, a selection is still necessary to conform to the limitations of the presentation.

In the past, the movement from the ethnographic fieldnotes to the final book was governed by theoretical issues. Information was organized around a conception of the nature of the phenomena under study: social organization, irrigation, etc. To recognize the unsatisfactory nature of these paradigms is to admit to the weakness in such ethnographies, since today they are no longer read for their theoretical importance but instead to find information which may fit into new interests of our own. In the case of *Travels in Arabia Deserta* we see a text in which something of the dialectic (which is essential to extended fieldwork) remains intact, the conversational exchanges, the unresolved differences in viewpoint, the acts of reconstruction which are embedded in the fieldwork of the anthropologist. However, with Doughty, we must still confront Leach's challenge: ethnographies are but the "harmonic projections" of the ethnographer—a personal statement, not an objective truth.

So why is it in reading Doughty that I have a continual sense of familiarity with what he says? Why do I find his descriptions so apt? Why do his reflections on his experiences contain so much that enlightens aspects of my own experience in Hayil? Given the differences in our personal and intellectual outlook, it would seem highly unlikely that his "harmonic projections" would have anything to do with my own. Perhaps the answer lies in the fact that he went one step further than most experimental ethnographers by turning himself into one of the personages in the text, revealing personal sides to himself as intimate as those of his informants. We know who and where he is. By so doing he maintains an open quality to his text, allowing understandings and judgments to flow back and forth across the characters and their behavior. Doughty has restored the discourse missing from theoretically governed ethnographies by exposing himself, and so also the authority of his statements, which we can disagree with and yet learn from as we read of his experiences.

A second problem exists for the ethnographer in turning fieldwork into a text, a problem which certainly receives little formal attention. For the ethnographer who would let the subjects of his or her study speak for themselves through interviews or recorded conversations, the biggest obstacle is translation. Not that some version of meaning cannot be conveyed; the problem is the way in which such meaning is expressed. Speech connotes much through the way in which something is said. Idioms, metaphors—all the figures of speech—provide much more insight about the intentions of the speaker and the nature of his or her cultural tradition than a literal translation could provide. How can such features of verbal communication be successfully moved across linguistic boundaries, especially if the foreign language is outside the Indo-European domain, where a common heritage makes translation somewhat easier? Even more important, how can the ethnographer transform meaningful utterances into written text, moving from a language which often has no written form into the conformity of written, academic prose? It is extremely difficult not to make one's informants into distorted reflections of themselves, into pedants or fools or both. This was the problem which Doughty faced in the four years he took to write *Travels in Arabia Deserta* from his collection of notes and memories.

Doughty's remarkable ingenuity in approaching the problem of translation in *Travels in Arabia Deserta* may have been a by-product of the search for a purer form of English to which most of his critics attribute his stylistic efforts. However, I suggest that it was speech, not written text, which initiated this interest in the first place. Doughty had a speech defect, one serious enough to keep him from passing the entrance exam for the Royal Navy, which was a great disappointment to him (H, 3). I would guess that this speech problem was behind his preoccupation with language or at least preceded the development of more intellectualized concerns. I say this because I have come to realize that the language of *Travels in Arabia Deserta* is strongly vocal in style and content. It is this quality which, after thirty years of speaking Arabic dialects, makes the text seem familiar to me and exceptionally evocative, whereas when as a student I tried to read the book I found it as alien and uninviting as did the several British publishers who first turned it down. When I read *Travels in Arabia Deserta* today I hear Arabic being spoken, not the formal Arabic of the Quran or even that of the educated urbanite, but rather the country speech which is all Doughty and I have ever learned. Doughty refers in a number of places to his limited knowledge of the language, to "an unflattering plainness of speech" which he felt was suitable for a "wandering anchorite" like himself (2:59). His antipathy toward the Quran (he always spelled it "koran," with a lowercase *K*) may well stem in part from his lack of ability to understand it, for unlike Richard Burton, Doughty was not a brilliant student of languages, at least in spoken form. It was only when he wrote that Doughty could have been free of his speech disability and perhaps it is relevant that he wrote English poetry for publication only after having written *Travels in Arabia Deserta*.

On any page Doughty's transcription of the speech of the people of Hayil sounds like the way they would have expressed themselves in their dialect of Arabic, and this is reinforced by the interjection of Arabic words, often without benefit of direct translation. For example, after he is expelled from Hayil, he meets two women on the way to the village of Gofar who greet him thus:

"Ah! thou,—is not thy name Khalîl?—they in yonder town are *jab-âbara,* men of tyrannous violence, that will cut off a man's head for a light displeasure. Eigh me! did not he so that is now Emir, unto all his brother's children? Thou art well come from them, they are hard and cruel, *kasyîn.* And what is this that the people cry, '*Out upon the Nasrâny!*' The Nasâra be better than the Moslemîn." *Eyad:* "It is they themselves that are the Nasâra, wellah, *khubithîn,* full of malignity." (2:284)

With a knowledge of Arabic the connotative meanings of the dialogues become almost unsettling because unlike other contemporary ethnographic attempts one really seems to hear Arabs speaking. In this way Doughty has given the Arab people who fill his pages a far better opportunity to represent themselves in an authentic fashion than would a more standard form of prose, all the while placing a heavier burden on the reader, especially those with no knowledge of a Semitic language. Even when Khalil himself is talking or describing the environment, it is easier to read out loud and follow the meanings through the natural phrasings of speech than it is to scan the page as with ordinary texts. Doughty accomplished on the page what he could not manage vocally. While the present ethnographic fashion is to provide long statements from "native" speakers, no one in recent times has approached the success of Doughty in translating the emotive and the semantic properties of conversation. Of course, it may be argued that there is no need for the emotive aspect of others' speech, that rational discourse is all that is necessary. But then, why bother with translations? Why not be content with more analytic summations?

Doughty is very conscious of Arabic speech, contrasting the language of the nomadic Beduin with that of the sedentary people of Hayil, or that of learned men with ordinary conversation. His own speech problems must have put him at a considerable disadvantage in mastering the subtleties of Arabic speech and perhaps contributed to his inability to accept and be comfortable with the people of Hayil and Arabia in general. However, this personal disadvantage may well have sharpened his attention and helped him capture so well the speech of others, serving in some degree the function of the theoretical issues which the modern ethnographer uses to focus attention on specific problems while doing fieldwork. Certainly

Doughty's use of written language and powers of description are far beyond the ordinary and Khalil's own trials and tribulations are used to enhance the ethnographic effort. Again, the contrast with Richard Burton is interesting, for Burton's superb ability to speak Arabic allowed him to become part of the Arab setting. Doughty's more limited ability was the material counterpart to the religious ideology which maintained a certain distance between him and his hosts, no matter how he may have longed for a more intimate and less problematic relationship. Yet Burton did not succeed half so well in conveying Arab speech and character in English. Surely Doughty himself never realized the future of his "new English style" in terms of ethnographic documentation. In fact, it was a sad failure when used in the epic poems which he wrote after *Travels in Arabia Deserta*.

In *Orientalism* Edward Said dismisses Doughty as an Orientalist writer who sees "every detail through the device of reductive categories (the Semites, the Muslim mind, the Orient, and so forth)."[12] To be sure, *Travels in Arabia Deserta* is full of remarks which reflect such categories and they offend the contemporary reader. But Said doesn't seem to consider the implications of the fact that this ethnocentrism and stereotyping, when it occurs, tells us about Khalil/Doughty, not the people of Arabia. Such remarks are a product of tendencies toward super-patriotism, perhaps. However, *Travels in Arabia Deserta* is saved from being *only* this precisely because it is an ethnography in which the personality which is projected is far from the "harmonic" one Leach describes above. Instead, it is confrontational. As readers a hundred years later, we have the chance to see how the observer's personality has distorted the "purported objectivity" of which Leach speaks, a far more revealing circumstance than we know from texts which paper over the relation between the fieldworker and his or her "others" with a tone of sympathetic understanding.

Furthermore, in the construction of his text, Doughty attempts to deal with the subtle ethnocentrism involved in using "our" language to describe the "other" and with the double bind of translation. "Our" language carries a heavy freight of connotations, of commonsense associations which turn the "other" into something comfortably plausible. English translations of native statements, if in any way made to sound "foreign," can make the speaker sound stupid or queer, but when rendered in standard English can "impose our logic upon them."[13] Doughty struck a middle ground in creating a special language for his account, an English full of the rhythms and words of Arabic speech. It is not an easy language for the average reader. But after many years of trying to communicate in various dialects of Arabic, I find it unmistakably authentic. Doughty's twenty-one months of fieldwork were not easy for him; through his textual use of language he would make us work part of the way into Arab culture ourselves if we would wander with him in Arabia Deserta.

NOTES

1 Edmund R. Leach, "Glimpses of the Unmentionable in the History of British Social Anthropology," *Annual Review of Anthropology* 13 (1984): 22.

2 See Philip Ward, *Ha'il: Oasis City of Saudi Arabia* (Cambridge: The Oleander Press, 1983), which is a collection of accounts of Hayil written by Europeans from 1844 to 1983.

3 Charles Winick, ed., *Dictionary of Anthropology* (London: Peter Owen, Ltd., 1957).

4 Bronislaw Malinowski, *Argonauts of the Western Pacific* (New York: E. P. Dutton, 1922).

5 Bronislaw Malinowski, *A Diary in the Strict Sense of the Term* (New York: Harcourt, Brace, World, 1967).

6 Annette B. Weiner, *Women of Value, Men of Renown* (Austin: University of Texas Press, 1976).

7 Derek Freeman, *Margaret Mead and Samoa: The Making and Unmaking of an Anthropological Myth* (Cambridge: Harvard University Press, 1983); Margaret Mead, *Coming of Age in Samoa* (New York: William Morrow, 1928).

8 George E. Marcus and Dick Cushman, "Ethnographies as Texts," *Annual Review of Anthropology* 11 (1982): 25.

9 James Clifford, "On Ethnographic Authority," *Representations* 1, no. 2 (Spring 1983): 130.

10 Marcus and Cushman, "Ethnographies," 25.

11 A, 40–41.

12 Edward W. Said, *Orientalism* (New York: Pantheon Books, 1978), 239.

13 Marcus and Cushman, "Ethnographies," 46.

Bibliographies

PHILIP M. O'BRIEN

Charles M. Doughty's *Travels in Arabia Deserta* and Its Abridgments: A Descriptive Bibliography

In 1884 when Doughty submitted his manuscript relating the story of his sojourn among the Beduin in inner Arabia from November 1876 to August 1878 to the first of four commercial publishers, little did he know that it would be four long years before the book would finally be published by Cambridge University Press. The story of his efforts is told by Hogarth (H, 115–26). The 1888 edition of five hundred copies in two volumes did not sell well and indeed as late as 1907 the last copies were remaindered by Cambridge. An unknown young man named Robert Bridges commented in one of the two letters written to Doughty about his book in the first year of publication that "Your book is too good for the many, too just and too poetic" (H, 128). Prophetic words, still true today.

Between 1907 and 1921, except for a 1908 abridgment, this monolithic monument of travel literature, adventure, and dedication to style was out of print. This has remained the longest period since it was first published that the few willing readers seeking it could not purchase it new. In a letter written in 1920, T. E. Lawrence complained of how dear it was in the antiquarian market (*Letters of T. E. Lawrence,* ed. David Garnett, London: Cape, 1938, p. 303). In January 1921 he was instrumental in having the book reprinted jointly by the new firm of Jonathan Cape Ltd. and the Medici Society in an edition of five hundred copies with six large paper copies in a special issue.

The fledgling firm wished to have the added security of Lawrence's name directly associated with the book and obtained an introduction from him for that purpose. This first Cape edition and a reprint did well. In 1923 the third English edition was published without Lawrence's introduction; this edition in its turn was reprinted. In a one-volume edition published in 1926 the introduction was restored and the book has remained in print ever since either in England or America, a tribute to the lasting recognition given this difficult-to-read work.

Before and between publication dates of the complete edition there have also been a number of abridgments and selections published, including two German, one Swedish, one French, and one Hebrew, reflecting further the esteem in which this book is held (although I fail to see how the majesty of the style can survive in translation). These selections and abridgments are included in the following bibliography in which some thirty editions—to my knowledge all that exist—are described. Descriptions of *Travels in Arabia Deserta* are followed by those of the abridgment *Wanderings in Arabia* and the selections *Passages from Arabia Deserta*. It will be noted that some publishers used the title of the unabridged work for their abridgments, sometimes adding to the confusion. In the process of locating copies of the editions for the present listing it became obvious that catalogers of the book had need of a guide to the various editions and states. Any number of later editions were erroneously cataloged as the 1921 edition, an error stemming from the date on the frontispiece and the fact that they frequently lack copyright or issue dates.

Now follows an explanation of the abbreviations used in this bibliography. The designations following the binding color are the ISCC-NBS (Inter-Society Color Council—National Bureau of Standards) *Color-Name Designations*. Items within square brackets are supplied by the compiler. The figures within parentheses beginning the collation are leaf measurements. The entry "Text:" gives the type measurements for the number of lines indicated, usually twenty, and the middle set within parentheses is the same number of lines but including the running title. Abbreviations used for locations of materials are: AC = author's collection; HL = Huntington Library; Cal = a private collection in California; UC = University of California, Berkeley; USC = University of Southern California. Other locations are spelled out sufficiently. One additional abbreviation perhaps needing comment is that of "prp." under "contents." This refers to preliminary page sequences before any "pp." section which is the main sequence of pagination.

The small issue of the early editions makes them difficult to locate. While as many copies as possible have been examined in most cases, the numbers have been small for others. Given the limited numbers for some it is very possible that some major variant or state has been overlooked. Any reader noting such omissions is encouraged to correspond with me.

SECTION I: *Travels in Arabia Deserta,* UNABRIDGED

Travels in Arabia Deserta, Cambridge University Press, 1888
FIRST ENGLISH EDITION

Title page desc: TRAVELS | IN | ARABIA DESERTA | BY | CHARLES M. DOUGHTY | VOL. I. {II.] | CAMBRIDGE: | AT THE UNIVERSITY PRESS | 1888 | [*All Rights Reserved*]

Collation: (22.7 × 14.5 cm): Vol. I: [a]^2 b^8 1–39^8 1^{16}, 338 leaves, pp. [i–v] vi–vii [viii–ix] x–xx 1–[624] [1–32]; Vol. II: π^8 1–42^8 43^{10}, 354 leaves, pp. [1–2] [i–v] vi–xiv 1–690 [1–2].

Contents: Vol. I: prp. [i] bastard title, [ii] printer's colophon, [iii] title page, [iv] [Old English type] "Cambridge: | PRINTED BY C. J. CLAY, M. A. AND SONS, | AT THE UNIVERSITY PRESS," v–vii preface, [viii] correction, [ix–xx] contents, pp. 1–619 text, 620–623 appendix, [624] blank, 1–32 catalog of books printed by Cambridge University; Vol. II: prp. [1–2] blank, [i] bastard title, [ii] printer's colophon, [iii] title page, [iv] printer's credit, [v]–xiv contents, pp. 1–539 text, 540–542 appendix, [543]–690 index and glossary of Arabic words, [1–2] blank.

RT: On verso TRAVELS IN ARABIA DESERTA. On recto [according to subject of page].

Plates: Vol. I: 4 fold out plates following pp. 106, 108, 112, 176, fold. map in pocket inside rear cover.

Typography and paper: $ 1,2 signed D.T. 6, 6–2.

   Text: 20 lines 7.3 (7.6) × 9.7 cm.

   Paper: White, wove, unwatermarked, top edges trimmed, sheets bulk Vol. I 3.8 cm, Vol. II 4 cm.

Binding: Dark green cloth 126 d. 01 G. On front cover [blind rules along all edges, gilt illus. different for each volume]. On spine [gilt] [triple rule] | ARABIA | DESERTA | [university coat of arms] | CAMBRIDGE | UNIVERSITY | PRESS | [triple rule]. On back cover [blind rules along all edges]. Black endpapers.

Published at: 3 gns.

Notes: 500 copies printed. Last copies remaindered early in 1900s. Last paragraph of preface consisting of acknowledgments omitted from subsequent editions. HL, AC.

Travels in Arabia Deserta, Warner, Medici Society, Cape, 1921
SECOND ENGLISH EDITION

Title page desc: TRAVELS IN | ARABIA DESERTA | BY CHARLES M. DOUGHTY, WITH A NEW PREFACE BY THE AUTHOR, INTRODUCTION | BY T. E. LAWRENCE, FELLOW OF ALL SOULS | AND ALL ORIGINAL MAPS, PLANS AND CUTS | [Medici Society seal] | VOLUME I [II] | PHILIP LEE WARNER, PUBLISHER TO THE | MEDICI SOCIETY, LTD., AND JONATHAN | CAPE, LONDON: AND AT BOSTON, U.S.A. 1921

Collation: (22 × 14.5 cm): Vol. I: [a]^2 b–c^8 1–39^8, 330 leaves, pp. [i–iv] v–xxxvii, 1–624; Vol. II: [a]^8 1–42^8 43^{10}, 354 leaves, pp. [1–2] [i–iv] v–xiv 1–690 [1–2].

Contents: Vol. I: prp. [i] bastard title, [ii] blank, [iii] title page, [iv] *"First published by the Cambridge University Press 1888 | new edition, type reset, 1921* | PRINTED IN GREAT BRITAIN BY WILLIAM CLOWES AND SONS, LIMITED | DUKE STREET, STAMFORD STREET, S.E.1, AND GREAT WINDMILL STREET, W.1," v–xi prefaces of first two editions, [xii] correction note, [xiii]–xxiv contents, xxv–xxxv introduction by T. E. Lawrence, [xxxvi] blank, pp. [1]–619 text, [620]–623 appendix to Vol. I, [624] blank; Vol. II: prp. [1–2] blank, [i] bastard title, [ii] blank, [iii] title page, [iv] issue statement, printer's credit, [v]–xiv contents, pp. [1]–539 text, 540–542 appendix to Vol. II, [543]–690 index and glossary of Arabic words, [1–2] blank.

Plates: Vol. I: following pp. [ii], 106, 108, 112, 176, 384, 400, 404, 416, fold. maps 106, 110; Vol. II: fold. map in pocket inside rear cover.

Typography and paper: $ 1,2 signed D.T. 2, 2–2.

 Text: 20 lines 7.3 (7.9) × 10.1 cm.

 Paper: White, wove, unwatermarked, top edge trimmed, sheets bulk Vol. I 3.3 cm, Vol. II 3.2 cm.

Binding: Green cloth 151 d. gy G. On front cover [blind stamped rules along outer edges, gilt cuts]. On spine [double rules] | ARABIA | DESERTA | VOL. I [II] | *C.M.* | *DOUGHTY* | LEE WARNER &. | JONATHAN CAPE | [double rules]. T.e. gilt. Black endpapers.

Published at: 9 gns Jan. 1921.

Notes: 500 copies, Cape's first book. Six large paper copies of this second edition were printed in Jan. 1921. These differ from the above in the following: Collation]: (26.5 × 20 cm); Plates]: 8 plates following pp. 106, 108, 112, 176 fold, 384, 402, 404, 416 fold.; Paper]: white, laid, watermarked, top edges trimmed, sheets bulk Vol. I: 6.5 cm, Vol. II: 7.5 cm; Binding]: Tan buckram 76 1 y Br., red and gold head and tail bands. Linen backed colored map in pocket inside rear cover of Vol. II. These six copies were distributed as follows: 1 Doughty, 2 Lawrence, 3 Medici Society, 4 Jonathan Cape, 5 Emir Feisal, 6 William H. Lee-Warner. UTA Reprinted Sept. 1921 (trade issue). HL.

Travels in Arabia Deserta, Cape and Medici, 1923

THIRD ENGLISH EDITION

Title page desc: TRAVELS IN | ARABIA DESERTA | BY CHARLES M. DOUGHTY, WITH A NEW | PREFACE BY THE AUTHOR, AND ALL | ORIGINAL MAPS, PLANS AND CUTS | VOLUME ONE [TWO] | JONATHAN CAPE AND | THE MEDICI SOCIETY LIMITED | LONDON

Collation: (22 × 14.5 cm): Vol. I: [a]⁸ b⁴ c² 1–39⁸, 326 leaves pp. [1–2] [i–v] vi–xxvi 1–623 [1]; Vol. II: π^8 1–43⁸ 44¹, 361 leaves, pp. [1–2] [i–v] vi–xiv 1–690.

Contents: Vol. I: prp. [1–2] blank, [i] bastard title, [ii] blank, [iii] title page, [iv] *"First published by the Cambridge University Press 1888 | New edition, type reset, January 1921 | Reprinted September 1921 | New and Cheaper edition September 1923 |* MADE AND PRINTED IN GREAT BRITAIN BY WM. CLOWES AND SONS, LIMITED | DUKE STREET, STAMFORD STREET, LONDON S.E.1," [v]–xv prefaces to first three editions, [xvi]–xxvi contents, pp. 1–619 text, [620]–623 appendix to Vol. I, [1] blank; Vol. II: prp. [1–2] blank, [i] bastard title, [ii] blank, [iii] title page, [iv] issue statement, printer's credit, [v]–xiv contents, pp. 1–539 text, 540–542 appendix to Vol. II, [543]–690 index and glossary of Arabic words.

RT: On verso *TRAVELS IN ARABIA DESERTA.* On recto [in italics according to subject of opening].

Plates: Vol. I: 9 b/w plates following pp. [ii], 106, 108, 112, 176, 384, 402, 404, 416, fold. map in pocket inside rear cover.

Typography and paper: $ 1,2 signed D.T. 12,12–2; D.T. 5,5–2; [-D.T.II 34].

Text: 20 lines 7.4 (7.7) × 10.2 cm.

Paper: White, wove, unwatermarked, top edge trimmed, sheets bulk Vol. I: 3 cm, Vol. II: 4 cm.

Binding: Red cloth 16 d. red. On front cover [blind stamped rules along all edges]. On spine [gilt] [Oxford rule] I ARABIA I DESERTA I VOL. I [II] I *C.M.* I *DOUGHTY* I JONATHAN CAPE & I THE MEDICI SOCIETY LTD I [Oxford rule]. T.e. gilt.

Published at: 65s   Sept. 1923.

Notes: Reprinted May 1924, same as above. One copy examined with this binding, title page, and issue statement 'New and cheaper edition, September, 1923,' contains the sheets of the second edition without the preface to the third edition and includes the T. E. Lawrence introduction which was withdrawn in the two impressions of this third edition. Were remaining sheets of the second edition bound and sold as the third edition? Or is this a stray variant? [Bates College]. University of Missouri St. Louis.

Travels in Arabia Deserta, Cape & Medici, 1926
FOURTH ENGLISH EDITION

Title page desc: TRAVELS IN I ARABIA DESERTA I BY CHARLES M. DOUGHTY, WITH I A NEW PREFACE BY THE AUTHOR, I INTRODUCTION BY T. E. LAWRENCE, I AND ALL ORIGINAL MAPS, PLANS I & ILLUSTRATIONS I THIN-PAPER EDITION IN ONE VOLUME I COMPLETE AND UNABRIDGED I JONATHAN CAPE LTD. & I THE MEDICI SOCIETY LIMITED I LONDON

Collation: (22 × 14 cm): [a]^{10} b^{16} 1–40^{16} 41^{18} (b and 40 are two gatherings of 8s, one inserted within the other, the second gathering is signed b*, etc.; 41 is composed of 41^2 41**^{8} each inserted within the other), 684 leaves, pp. [i–vii] viii–lii [1] 2–623 [3] [1] 2–690.

Contents: Prp. [i] half-title, [ii] blank, [iii] title page, [iv] *"First published by the Cambridge University Press 1888* I *New edition, type reset, January 1921* I *Reprinted September, 1921* I *New and Cheaper edition, September 1923* I *Reprinted May 1924* I *One volume edition March 1926.* MADE AND PRINTED IN GREAT BRITAIN BY BUTLER AND TANNER LTD., FROME AND LONDON," [v] pub. note, [vi] blank, [vii]–xvi prefaces, [xvii–xxviii] introduction by T. E. Lawrence, [xxix] blank, [xxx]–xl contents to Vol. I, [xli]–l contents to Vol. II, [li] section title, [lii] blank, pp. [1]–623 text, [1] blank, [2] section title, [3] blank, 1–539 text, 540–542 appendix, 543–690 index and glossary of Arabic words.

RT: On recto TRAVELS IN ARABIA DESERTA. On verso [according to page contents].

Plates: 9 line drawings by author of varying sizes tipped in. Frontis. on coated paper, following pp. ii, 106, 108, 112, 176, 384, 402, 404, 416.

Typography and paper: $ 1,5 signed 4,4*, 41 41* 41** (1,2,5).

   Text: 20 lines 7.8 (8.2) × 10.1 cm.

   Paper: Thin, white, wove, unwatermarked, all edges trimmed, sheets bulk 4 cm.

Binding: Black cloth. On spine [gilt] [triple rule] | ARABIA | DESERTA | *C.M.* | *DOUGHTY* | JONATHAN CAPE & | THE MEDICI SOCIETY Ltd | [triple rule].

Published at: 30s Mar. 1926.

Notes: Reprinted July 1926 identical to above. Reprinted Sept. 1926 identical to above. Reprinted Oct. 1927 identical to above. Reprinted May 1928. AC.

Travels in Arabia Deserta, Cape, 1930
FIFTH ENGLISH EDITION

Title page desc: TRAVELS IN | ARABIA DESERTA | BY CHARLES M. DOUGHTY, WITH | A NEW PREFACE BY THE AUTHOR, | IN-TRODUCTION BY T. E. LAWRENCE, | AND ALL ORIGINAL MAPS, PLANS | & ILLUSTRATIONS | THIN-PAPER EDITION IN ONE VOLUME | COMPLETE AND UNABRIDGED | JONATHAN CAPE LTD. | THIRTY BEDFORD SQUARE LONDON | AND AT TORONTO

Collation: (22 × 14 cm): [a]^{10} b^{16} 1–40^{16} 41^{18} (b and 40 are two gather-ings of 8s, one inserted within the other, the second gathering is signed b* etc.; 41 is composed of 41^2 41*^{8} and 41**^{8} each inserted within the other), 684 leaves, pp. [i–vii] viii–li [1] 2–623 [3] [1] 2–690.

Contents: Prp. [i] half-title, [ii] blank, [iii] title page, [iv] *"First published by the Cambridge University Press 1888* | *New edition, type reset, January 1921* | *reprinted September, 1921* | *New and Cheaper edition, September 1923* | *Re-printed May 1924* | *One volume edition, March 1926* | *Reprinted, July 1926* | *Reprinted, September 1926* | *Reprinted, October 1927* | *Reprinted, May 1928* | *Reprinted, October 1930* | JONATHAN CAPE LTD. 30 BEDFORD SQUARE LONDON | & 91 WELLINGTON STREET WEST, TORON-TO | JONATHAN CAPE & HARRISON SMITH INC. | 139 EAST 46TH STREET NEW YORK | PRINTED IN GREAT BRITAIN BY | BUTLER & TANNER LTD," [v] pub. note, [vi] blank, [vii]–viii pref-

ace, [xvii]–xxvii introduction by T. E. Lawrence, [xxix] blank, [xxx]–xl
contents to Vol. I, [xli]–l contents to Vol. II, [li] section title, [lii] blank,
pp. [1]–623 text, [1] blank, [2] section title, [3] blank, 1–539 text,
540–542 appendix, 543–690 index and glossary of Arabic words.
RT: On recto TRAVELS IN ARABIA DESERTA. On verso [according to
subject of opening].
Plates: 9 plates, of varying sizes, tipped in. Frontis. on coated paper,
following pp. [ii], 106, 108, 112, 176, 384, 402, 404, 416.
Typography and paper: $ 1,5 signed 4,4*, 41 41* 41** (1,2,5).
   Text: 20 lines 7.8 (8.2) × 10.1 cm.
   Paper: Thin, white, wove, unwatermarked, all edges trimmed, sheets
   bulk 4 cm.
Binding: Black cloth. On spine [gilt] ARABIA | DESERTA | *C.M.* |
DOUGHTY | JONATHAN CAPE. Top and fore edge trimmed. Boxed as
issued.
Notes: Oct. 1930. This is really only a reprint of the previous edition with
a new title page and spine imprint. Reprinted Sept. 1933. HL.

Travels in Arabia Deserta, Cape, 1936
SIXTH ENGLISH EDITION

Title page desc: TRAVELS IN | [in red] ARABIA DESERTA | By |
CHARLES M. DOUGHTY | [pub. device] | With an Introduction by | T.
E. LAWRENCE | New and | definitive edition | VOLUME I [II]. | LON-
DON | JONATHAN CAPE 30 BEDFORD SQUARE | 1936
Collation: (25.3 × 19.3 cm): Vol. I: [a]–TT⁸, 336 leaves, pp. [1–6] 7–
674; Vol. II: [A]⁸ B*⁸ C2–NN2⁸ OO*–UU*⁸ XX*⁴, 348 leaves, pp. [1–
4] 5–696.
Contents: Vol. I: pp. [1] bastard title, [2] list of author's works, [3] blank,
[4] frontispiece, [5] title page, [6] 14-line issue statement ending with
"NEW AND DEFINITIVE EDITION IN TWO VOLUMES 1936 |
PRINTED IN GREAT BRITAIN IN THE CITY OF OXFORD | AT
THE ALDEN PRESS | PAPER MADE BY JOHN DICKINSON & CO.
LTD. | BOUND BY A. W. BAIN & CO. LTD.," 7–16 contents, 17–28
introduction by T. E. Lawrence, 29–35 prefaces to first three editions,
[36] blank, [37] section title, [38] blank, 39–672 text, 673–674 appendix to Vol. I; Vol. II: pp. [1] bastard title, [2] list of author's works, [3]
title page, [4] issue statement, credits, 5–11 contents, [12] blank, 13
section title, [14] blank, 15–574 text, 575–576 appendix Vol. II, 577
section title, 578 blank, 579–696 index and glossary of Arabic words.

RT: On verso TRAVELS IN ARABIA DESERTA. On recto [according to subject of page].

Plates: Vol. I: 9 plates, frontis. pp. [3–4], others following pp. 148, [149], [152], 218 fold., 430, 448, 452, 462 fold. Fold maps inside both rear covers.

Typography and paper: $ 1 signed TT.

   Text: 20 lines 9.8 (9.9) × 13.1 cm.

   Paper: Buff, wove, unwatermarked, top edges trimmed, unopened. Sheets bulk Vol. I: 3.8 cm; Vol. II: 3.8 cm.

Binding: Brown buckram 46 gy r Br. On spine [gilt] ARABIA | DESERTA | [cut] | C.M. | DOUGHTY | VOLUME I [II] | JONATHAN CAPE. T.e. brown, endpapers white. Each vol. has fold. map pasted inside back cover.

Published at: £3 15s.

Notes: Dec. 1943 reprint as above with following differences: Plates]: poorer quality paper; Paper]: poorer quality, sheets bulk 3.5 cm both vols. Jan. 1944 reprint as above. Jan., Mar. 1949 reprint as above with following differences: Contents]: papermaker's credit replaced by illustrator's credit; Paper]: poorer quality. AC, HL.

Travels in Arabia Deserta, Cape, 1964
SIXTH ENGLISH EDITION (SMALLER FORMAT)

Title page desc: CHARLES M. DOUGHTY | Travels in | Arabia Deserta | With an Introduction by | T. E. LAWRENCE | VOLUME I [II] | JONATHAN CAPE | THIRTY BEDFORD SQUARE LONDON

Collation: (19.7 × 12.2 cm): guillotined sheets, Vol. I: 339, Vol. II: 348 leaves, Vol. I: pp. [4] 7–674 [4], Vol. II: 696 [4].

Contents: Vol. I: pp. [1] series and bastard titles, [2] blank, [3] title page, [4] "FIRST PUBLISHED BY THE CAMBRIDGE UNIVERSITY | PRESS 1888 | NEW EDITION PUBLISHED BY PHILIP LEE WARNER AND | JONATHAN CAPE 1921 | NEW AND DEFINITIVE EDITION IN TWO VOLUMES 1936 | THIS PAPERBACK EDITION FIRST PUBLISHED IN 1964 | *Condition of Sale* | For copyright reasons this | book may not be issued on loan | or otherwise except in | its original soft cover | *Printed in Great Britain by* | *Fletcher & Son Ltd, Norwich* | *and bound by* | *Richard Clay and Company Ltd, Bungay, Suffolk,*" 7–16 contents, 17–28 introduction by T. E. Lawrence, 29–35 prefaces to first three editions, [36] blank, [37] section title, [38] blank, 39–672 text, 673–674 appendix to Vol. I, [1–4] ads; Vol. II: pp. [1] series and bastard titles, [2] blank, [3] title page, [4] issue and copyright statements, printer's credit, 5–11 contents, [12] blank, [13] section title, [14] blank, 15–574 text, 575–576 appendix to Vol. II, [577] section title, [578] text, 579–696 glossary and index to Arabic words, [1–4] ads.

RT: On verso TRAVELS IN ARABIA DESERTA. On recto [according to page].

Plates: Vol. I: following pp. 218, 448, 462.

Typography and paper:

   Text: 20 lines 7.3 (7.5) × 10.1 cm.

   Paper: White, wove, unwatermarked, all edges trimmed, sheets bulk Vol. I: 3 cm, Vol. II: 3 cm.

Binding: Pictorial paper covers. On front cover CHARLES M. DOUGHTY 25s I Travels in [in pink] JONATHAN CAPE I [in pink] CAPE I Arabia Deserta [in pink] PAPERBACK I INTRODUCTION BY T. E. LAWRENCE I ILLUSTRATED I VOL. II. On spine JCP 20 I [running down] CHARLES M. DOUGHTY I Travels in Arabia Deserta I [across at bottom] Jonathan I CAPE I PAPERBACK. On back cover: [front cover repeated and two excerpts from reviews].

Published at: 25s.

Notes: Hardbound issue: Brown buckram 57 l. Br. On spine ARABIA I DESERTA I [cut] I C. M. I DOUGHTY I VOLUME I [II] I [pub. device]. T.e. tan. Gold and brown striped head bands. Pub. at]: 50s. Univ. of Mo. at St. Louis. HL.

Travels in Arabia Deserta, Boni & Liveright, 1923
FIRST AMERICAN EDITION

Title page desc: TRAVELS IN I ARABIA DESERTA I BY CHARLES M. DOUGHTY, I WITH A NEW I PREFACE BY THE AUTHOR, AN INTRO- I DUCTION BY T. E. LAWRENCE, AND ALL I ORIGINAL MAPS, PLANS AND CUTS I VOLUME ONE [TWO] I BONI & LIVE-RIGHT, Inc., NEW YORK I JONATHAN CAPE & THE MEDICI I SOCIETY LTD. :: :: LONDON I 1923

Collation: (23 × 14.2 cm): Vol. I: π^8 [a]^6 b^4 c^2 1–39^8, 332 leaves, pp. [2] [i–v] vi–xxvi 1–624; Vol. II: π^8 1–43^8 44^1, 352 leaves, [2] [i–v] vi–xiv, 1–690.

Contents: Vol. I: prp. [1–2] blank, [i] half-title, [ii] blank, [iii] title page, [iv] *"All Rights Reserved* I by I BONI AND LIVERIGHT, INC. I NEW

YORK I PRINTED IN ENGLAND," [v]–xiv prefaces, xv–xxv introduction by T. E. Lawrence [xxvi] blank, [xv]–xxvi [*sic*] contents, pp. 1–623 text, [624] blank; Vol. II: prp. [1–2] blank, [i] half-title, [ii] blank, [iii] title page, [iv] copyright statement, [v–xiv] contents, pp. 1–542 text, 543–690 index and glossary of Arabic words.

RT: On verso TRAVELS IN ARABIA DESERTA. On recto [according to subject of page].

Plates: Vol. I: following pp. 107, 108, 112, 176, 385, 402, 405, 416, fold. linen backed map (55.9 × 73.4 cm) loosely inserted in pocket inside rear cover.

Typography and paper: $ 1,2 D.T. 7, D.T.II 7.

   Text: 20 lines 7.4 (7.7) × 10.2 cm.

   Paper: White, wove, unwatermarked, all edges trimmed, sheets bulk Vol. I: 4.5 cm, Vol. II: 4 cm.

Binding: Black linen. On spines [all gilt] [Oxford rule] I ARABIA I DESERTA I I [II] I *C.M.* I *DOUGHTY* I [cut] I BONI & LIVERIGHT I [Oxford rule]. Yellow head and tail bands. Black endpapers. Boxed as issued.

Published at: $17.50.

Notes: May 1924 identical to above with following differences: title page date change; Contents]: prp. [iv] issue statement, printer's credits added. May 1925 identical to immediately above. AC.

Travels in Arabia Deserta, Boni & Liveright, 1926

FIRST AMERICAN EDITION (THIN PAPER EDITION)

Title page desc: TRAVELS IN I ARABIA DESERTA I BY CHARLES M. DOUGHTY, WITH I A NEW PREFACE BY THE AUTHOR, I INTRODUCTION BY T. E. LAWRENCE, I AND ALL ORIGINAL MAPS, PLANS I & ILLUSTRATIONS I THIN-PAPER EDITION IN ONE VOLUME I COMPLETE AND UNABRIDGED I NEW YORK I BONI & LIVERIGHT

Collation: (21.7 × 14 cm): a^{10} b^{16} $1–40^{16}$ 41^{18} (b–40 are made up of two gatherings, one inserted inside the other; 41 is made up as follows: 41^2 42^{*8} 42^{**8} each inserted within the other), 684 leaves, pp. [i–vii] viii–lii [1] 2–623 [3] [1] 2–690.

Contents: Prp. [i] half-title, [ii] blank, [iii] title page, [iv] "MADE AND PRINTED IN GREAT BRITAIN BY I BUTLER & TANNER LTD., FROME AND LONDON," [v] pub. note, [vi] blank, [vii]–xvi prefaces,

[xvii]–xxvii introduction by T. E. Lawrence, [xxix] blank, [xxx]–1 contents, [li] section title, [lii] blank, pp. 1–623 text, [1] blank, [2] section title, [3] blank, 1–539 text, 540–542 appendix to Vol. II, 543–690 index and glossary of Arabic words.

RT: On recto TRAVELS IN ARABIA DESERTA. On verso [according to contents of page].

Plates: 9 line drawings by author on paper same weight as sheets except for frontis. varying sizes all in Vol. I following pp. 106, 110, 112, 176, 384, 402, 416, fold. map inside rear cover.

Typography and paper: $ signed 1,2 b,b* 1,1* 41, 41*,41**.

   Text: 20 lines 7.3 (7.8) × 10.2 cm.

   Paper: Thin, white, wove, unwatermarked, all edges trimmed, sheets bulk 3.8 cm.

Binding: Dark blue cloth 187 d. gy. B. On front cover [gilt cut]. On spine [gilt] [Oxford rule] | ARABIA | DESERTA | *C.M.* | *DOUGHTY* | BONI & LIVERIGHT | [Oxford rule]. Dark blue endpapers.

Published at: $10.00.

Notes: AC.

Travels in Arabia Deserta, Random House, 1934

SECOND AMERICAN EDITION (THIN PAPER EDITION)

Title page desc: TRAVELS IN | ARABIA DESERTA | BY CHARLES M. DOUGHTY, WITH | A NEW PREFACE BY THE AUTHOR, | INTRODUCTION BY T. E. LAWRENCE, | AND ALL ORIGINAL MAPS, PLANS, | & ILLUSTRATIONS | THIN-PAPER EDITION IN ONE VOLUME | COMPLETE AND UNABRIDGED | [pub. device] | RANDOM HOUSE | NEW YORK

Collation: (21.7 × 14 cm): a^{10} b^{16} 1–40^{16} 41^{18} (b–40 are made up of two gatherings, one inserted inside the other; 41 is made up as follows: 41^2 42*^{8} 42**^{8} each inserted within the other), 684 leaves, pp. [i–vii] viii–lii [1] 2–623 [3] [1]–690.

Contents: Prp. [i] half-title, [ii] blank, [iii] title page, [iv] "PRINTED IN GREAT BRITAIN," [v] pub. note, [vi] blank, [vii]–xvi prefaces, [xvii]–xxvii introduction by T. E. Lawrence, [xxviii] blank, [xxix]–1 contents, [li] section title, [lii] blank, 1–623 text, [1] blank, [2] section title, [3] blank, 1–539 text, 540–542 appendix to Vol. II, 543–690 index and glossary of Arabic words.

Rt: On recto TRAVELS IN ARABIA DESERTA. On verso [according to

Plates: 9 drawings by author on paper same as sheets except for frontis. varying sizes, Vol. I: following pp. 106, 110, 112, 176, 384, 402, 416, fold. map inside rear cover.

Typography and paper: $ signed 1,2 b,b* 1,1* 41,41*,41**.

Text: 20 lines 7.3 (7.8) × 10.2 cm.

Paper: Thin, white, wove, unwatermarked, all edges trimmed, sheets bulk 3.8 cm.

Binding: Dark blue cloth 187 d. gy. B. On front cover [gilt cut]. On spine [gilt] [Oxford rule] | ARABIA | DESERTA | *C.M.* | *DOUGHTY* | RANDOM HOUSE | [Oxford rule]. White endpapers. Blue head and tail bands.

Published at: $7.00.

Notes: Sheets are those of Boni & Liveright 1926 edition and identical to that edition except that spine imprint is RANDOM HOUSE at foot instead of BONI AND LIVERIGHT. White endpapers. AC.

Travels in Arabia Deserta, Random House, 1937
THIRD AMERICAN EDITION

Title page desc: TRAVELS IN | [in red] ARABIA DESERTA | BY | CHARLES M. DOUGHTY | With an introduction by | T. E. LAWRENCE | New and | definitive edition | VOLUME I [II] | [pub. device] | NEW YORK · RANDOM HOUSE · MCMXXXVII

Collation: (25.3 × 10.5 cm): Vol. I: [A]–TT⁸, 336 leaves, pp. 1–674, Vol. II: A–UU*⁸, 348 leaves, pp. 1–696. Frontispiece counted in pagination.

Contents: Vol. I: pp. [1] bastard title, [2] list of author's works, [3] blank, [4] frontispiece, [5] title page, [6] "PRINTED IN GREAT BRITAIN," 7–16 contents, 17–28 introduction by T. E. Lawrence, 29–35 prefaces to first three editions, [36] blank, [37] section title, [38] blank, 39–672 text, 673–674 appendix; Vol. II: pp. [1] bastard title, [2] list of author's works, [3] title page, [4] "PRINTED IN GREAT BRITAIN," 5–11 contents, [12] blank, [13] section title, [14] blank, 15–574 text, 575–576 appendix, [577] section title, [578] blank, 579–696 index and glossary of Arabic words.

RT: On verso TRAVELS IN ARABIA DESERTA. On recto [according to chapter].

Plates: Only in Vol. I: following pp. 148, 150, 152, 218, 430, 448, 452, 462.

Typography and paper: $ 1 signed Vol. I: C, Vol. II: C2.

Text: 20 lines 9.8 (10) × 13.3 cm.

Paper: Buff, laid, unwatermarked, top edge trimmed, sheets bulk Vol. I: 4 cm, Vol. II: 4 cm.

Binding: Tan oatmeal cloth. On front cover [in blue] [rule] | [Doughty's facs. signature] | [rule]. On spine [within rectangle of blue edged in gilt] TRAVELS IN | ARABIA | DESERTA | [cut] | C. M. DOUGHTY | I [II] [within blue rectangle] | [at foot, within blue rectangle edged in gilt] Random House. Boxed as issued. T.e. blue, white endpapers.

Published at: $15.00.

Notes: HL.

Travels in Arabia Deserta, Random House, 1937

FOURTH AMERICAN EDITION (ONE-VOLUME EDITION)

Title page desc: TRAVELS IN | [in red] ARABIA DESERTA | BY | CHARLES M. DOUGHTY | With an Introduction by | T. E. LAW-RENCE | New and | definitive edition | in one volume | [pub. device] | RANDOM HOUSE · PUBLISHERS · NEW YORK

Collation: (23.2 × 16.4 cm): [1–43]¹⁶, 688 leaves pp. [1–24] 17–674, 13–696.

Contents: Prp. [1] bastard title, [2] list of author's works, [3] blank, [4] frontispiece, [5] title page, [6] "MANUFACTURED IN UNITED STATES OF AMERICA," [7–16] contents of Vol. I, [17–23] contents of Vol. II, [24] blank, pp. [17]–28 introduction by T. E. Lawrence, 29–35 various prefaces, [36] blank, [37] section title, [38] blank, 39–674 text of Vol. I, [13] section title, [14] blank, 15–574 text of Vol. II, 575–576 appendix to Vol. II, [577] section title, [578] blank, 579–696 index and glossary of Arabic words.

RT: On verso TRAVELS IN ARABIA DESERTA. On recto [according to contents of page].

Plates: On sheets as part of gatherings in Vol. I only, following pp. 3, 148, 150, 152, 430, 448, 451, 462, printed on one side only.

Typography and paper: $ 1 signed Vol. I C, Vol. II C2 [not for this edition].

Text: 20 lines 9.7 (9.9) × 13.3 cm.

Paper: White, wove, unwatermarked, all edges trimmed, sheets bulk 4.7 cm.

Binding: Tan oatmeal cloth. On front cover [blue rule] | [Doughty's signature in facsimile] | [blue rule]. On spine [within blue rectangle with gilt border] TRAVELS IN | ARABIA | DESERTA | [cut] | C. M. Doughty | [at foot, within blue rectangle with gilt border] Random House, T.e. blue.

Notes: Another state with altered title page: same as above except that title page has been reset as below: TRAVELS IN | ARABIA DESERTA | BY | CHARLES M. DOUGHTY | With an Introduction by | T. E. LAWRENCE | [within rectangle of single rules with rows of decorated cuts outside left and right sides] [swash] Season's Greetings | A. C. VROMAN, INCORPORATED | [below rectangle] New and | definitive edition | in one volume | RANDOM HOUSE • PUBLISHERS • NEW YORK. Reprinted 1946 identical to above. Reprinted 1947 identical to above, $7.50. Reprinted 1949 as above but title page all in black. AC.

Travels in Arabia Deserta, Dover, 1979
FIFTH AMERICAN EDITION

Title page desc: TRAVELS IN | ARABIA DESERTA | BY | CHARLES M. DOUGHTY | With an Introduction by | T. E. Lawrence | IN TWO VOLUMES I [II] | DOVER PUBLICATIONS, INC. | NEW YORK

Collation: (23.3 × 16.5 cm): Vol. I: [1–22]^{16}, Vol. II: [1–22]^{16}, 352 leaves in each volume, pp. Vol. I: [1–6] 7–674 [10], Vol. II: [2] [1–4] 5–696 [6].

Contents: Vol. I: pp. [1–2] blank, [3] bastard title, [4] frontispiece, [5] title page, [6] [Canadian and Great Britain pub. credits], "This Dover edition, first published in 1979, is an | unabridged and unaltered republication of the definitive | version of the third edition published in London in 1936 | by Jonathan Cape Ltd. The work was originally published | in 1888 by Cambridge University Press. The second edi- | tion was published in London by P. Lee Warner in Jan- | uary, 1921, and the third edition was first issued by the | same publisher in October, 1921." ISBN, LC numbers, USA pub. credit, 7–16 contents, illustrations, 17–28 introduction by T. E. Lawrence, 29–35 prefaces to first three editions, [36] blank, [37] VOLUME I, [38] blank, 39–672 text, 673–674 appendix, [1–10] ads; Vol. II: prp. [1–2] blank, pp. [1] bastard title, [2] blank, [3] title page, [4] issue statement, printer's credit, 5–11 contents, [12] blank, [13] VOLUME II, [14] blank, 15–574 text, 575–576 appendix, [577] section title, [578] blank, 579–696 index and glossary, [1–6] pub. ads.

RT: On verso TRAVELS IN ARABIA DESERTA. On recto [according to chapter].

Typography and paper:

   Text: 20 lines 9.7 (10.5) × 13.1 cm.

   Paper: White, wove, unwatermarked, all edges trimmed, sheets bulk 3.1 cm.

Binding: Pictorial paper covers Vol. I: brown, Vol. II: blue. On front cover [all in white] Charles M. Doughty | TRAVELS IN | ARABIA DESERTA | With an Introduction by T. E. Lawrence | In Two Volumes | Volume I [II]. On spine [all in white] Doughty | [running down] TRAVELS IN | ARABIA DESERTA | [across] Volume I [II] | Dover | [running down, ISBN number] | [across, pub. device]. On back cover [blurb].

Published at: $8.95 per volume.

Notes: AC.

SECTION 2: *Wanderings in Arabia,* ABRIDGMENT

Wanderings in Arabia, Duckworth, 1908
FIRST ENGLISH EDITION

Title page desc: WANDERINGS IN | ARABIA | BY | CHARLES M. DOUGHTY | BEING AN ABRIDGEMENT OF | "TRAVELS IN ARABIA DESERTA" | ARRANGED WITH INTRODUCTION BY | EDWARD GARNETT | *IN TWO VOLUMES* | VOL. I. [II.] | LONDON | DUCKWORTH AND CO. | 3 HENRIETTA STREET, W.C. | 1908

Collation: (22.4 × 15 cm): Vol. I: π^{10} A–T^8 U^4, 166 leaves, pp. [i–v] vi–xx [1]–309 [1–3]; Vol. II: π^6 A–S^8 T^2 U^4, 156 leaves, pp. [1–2] [i–v] vi–x [1]–297 [1–3].

Contents: Vol. I: prp. [i] bastard title, [ii] blank, [iii] title page, [iv] blank, [v]–xi introduction by Edward Garnett, [xii] blank, [xiii]–xx contents, pp. [1]–309 text, [1–3] blank; Vol. II: prp. [1–2] blank, [i] bastard title, [ii] blank, [iii] title page, [iv] blank, [v]–x contents, pp. [1]–297 text. "Printed by Ballantynes & Co. Tavistock, London," [1–3] blank.

RT: On verso WANDERINGS IN ARABIA. On recto [according to subject of opening].

Plates: Vol. I: b/w plate following prp. [iv]; Vol. II: [frontispiece on same paper as text, tipped in] following prp. [iv], single fold map following p. 292.

Typography and paper: $ 1 signed VOL. I [II] B.

Text: 20 lines 7.3 (7.9) × 9.7 cm.

Paper: White, thick, wove, unwatermarked, all edges trimmed, sheets bulk 2.5 cm each volume.

Binding: Green cloth 127 gy. Ol. G. On spine [gilt] [rule] | WANDER-INGS | IN | ARABIA | VOL. I. [II.] | CHARLES M. | DOUGHTY | DUCKWORTH & CO. | [rule]. Back cover [blind stamped, pub. device]. T.e. gilt.

Published at: 16s.

Notes: Reprinted 1908 same as above. Reprinted 1912 same as above. Reprinted 1923 same as above with following differences: Collation]: Vol. I: π^8, A–T^8 U^4, 164 leaves, pp. [1–2] [i–ii] [1–2] [iii–iv] v–xii [1]–309 [1–3]; Vol. II: π^6 A–S^8 T^2 U^4, 156 leaves prp. [1–2] [i–v] vi–x [1]–297 [1–3]; Contents]: Vol. I: prp. [1–2] blank, [i] bastard title, [ii] blank, pp. [1] blank, [2] frontispiece, [iii] title page, [iv] *"Published 1908 | Reprinted 1908 | Reprinted 1912 | Reprinted 1923 | Made and printed in Great Britain | by Turnbull & Spears, Edinburgh,"* v–xii contents, [1]–309 text, [1–3] blank; Vol. II: prp. [1–2] blank, [i] bastard title, [ii] blank, [iii] title page, [iv] printer's credit, [v]–x contents, [1]–292 text, [293]–297 glossary, [1–3] blank; Plates]: Vol. I: [on same paper as text, frontispiece (formerly frontispiece of Vol. II)], folded map following pp. [1] of last sequence; Binding]: green cloth 110 gy. Ol. T.e. not gilt, no. pub. device on back cover; Published at]: 20s. HL.

Wanderings in Arabia, Duckworth, 1926

SECOND ENGLISH EDITION (FIRST ONE-VOLUME)

Title page desc: WANDERINGS IN | ARABIA | BY | CHARLES M. DOUGHTY | BEING AN ABRIDGEMENT OF | "TRAVELS IN ARABIA DESERTA" | [pub. device] | DUCKWORTH | 3 HENRIETTA STREET, LONDON, W.C.2

Collation: (21.4 × 13.5 cm): π^{10} A–2P^8, 314 leaves, pp. [i–ii] [1–2] [iii–v] vi–xviii [1]–607 [1].

Contents: Prp. [i] bastard title, [ii] blank, [1] blank, [2] frontispiece, [iii] title page, [iv] *"Published in 2 vols. 1908 | Reprinted " 1908 | Reprinted " 1912 | Reprinted " 1923 | Reprinted in 1 vol. 1926 | With the Author's sanction the | abridgement of his narrative | here presented was made by | Mr. Edward Garnett | Made and Printed in Great Britain | by Turnbull & Spears, Edinburgh,"* v–xviii contents, pp. [1]–602 text, 603–607 glossary, [1] blank.

RT: On verso WANDERINGS IN ARABIA. On recto [according to subject of page].

Typography and paper: $ 1 signed K.

   Text: 20 lines 7.4 (7.5) × 9.7 cm.

   Paper: White, wove, unwatermarked, all edges trimmed, sheets bulk 3.5 cm.

Binding: Green cloth 110 gy. Ol. On spine [gilt] WANDERINGS | IN | ARABIA | CHARLES M. | DOUGHTY | DUCKWORTH. On back cover [pub. device, blind stamped].

Published at: 20s.

Notes: First one-volume issue. Reprinted 1927 same as above. Reprinted 1939 same as above. University of Arizona, LC.

Wanderings in Arabia, Duckworth, 1949

THIRD ENGLISH EDITION

Title page desc: WANDERINGS | IN ARABIA | BY | CHARLES M. DOUGHTY | An abridgment of *Travels in Arabia Deserta* | made with the author's sanction by | Edward Garnett | [pub. device] | DUCKWORTH | 3 HENRIETTA STREET, LONDON, W.C.2

Collation: (21.5 × 13.7 cm): [A]–T¹⁶U⁸, 312 leaves, pp. [i–iv] v–xvi 1–607 [1].

Contents: Prp. [i] bastard title, [ii] frontispiece, [iii] title page, [iv] "*Published in 2 vols. 1908 | Reprinted" 1908 | Reprinted" 1912 | Reprinted" 1923 | Reprinted in 1 vol. 1926, 1927, 1939, 1949* | PRINTED IN GREAT BRITAIN BY | THOMAS NELSON AND SONS LTD," v–xvi contents, pp. 1–602 text, 603–607 glossary, [1] blank.

RT: On verso WANDERINGS IN ARABIA. On recto [according to subject of page].

Plates: Fold. map inside rear flyleaf.

Typography and paper: $ 1,5 signed B,B*.

   Text: 20 lines 7.3 (7.4) × 9.6 cm.

   Paper: White, wove, unwatermarked, all edges trimmed, sheets bulk 2.7 cm.

Binding: Green cloth 164 m. b G. On spine [gilt] [double rule] | WANDERINGS | IN ARABIA | [short rule] | C. M. DOUGHTY | [double rule] | DUCKWORTH. T.e. bluegreen.

Notes: Second impression 1953. Tarleton State College.

Wanderings in Arabia Deserta, Scribners, 1908

FIRST AMERICAN EDITION

Title page desc: WANDERINGS IN | ARABIA | BY | CHARLES M. DOUGHTY | BEING AN ABRIDGMENT | OF | "TRAVELS IN ARABIA DESERTA" | ARRANGED WITH INTRODUCTION BY | EDWARD GARNETT | *IN TWO VOLUMES* | VOL. I. [II.] | NEW YORK | CHARLES SCRIBNER'S SONS | 1908

Collation: (22.3 × 15 cm): Vol. I: π^2 b^8 A–T^8 U^4, 166 leaves, pp. [i–v] vi–xx 1–309 [3]; Vol. II: π^8 A–S^8 T^2, 158 leaves, pp. [1–8] [i–v] [1]–297 [3].

Contents: Vol. I: prp. [i] bastard title, [ii] blank, [iii] title page, [iv] blank, [v]–xi introduction by Edward Garnett, [xii] blank, [xiii]–xx contents, pp. [1]–309 text, [1–3] blank; Vol. II: prp. [1–4] paste down and free endpapers, [5–6] blank, [7] bastard title, [8] blank, [i] blank, [ii] frontispiece, [iii] title page, [iv] blank, [v]–x contents, pp. [1]–292 text, pp. [293]–297 glossary, [1–4] blank.

RT: On verso WANDERINGS IN ARABIA. On recto [according to subject of page].

Plates: Vol. I: frontispiece following prp. [ii]; Vol. II: map following p. 292.

Typography and paper: $ 1 signed VOL. II D.

  Text: 20 lines 7.3 (7.5) × 9.8 cm.

  Paper: White, wove, thick, unwatermarked, untrimmed, sheets bulk Vol. I 3 cm; Vol. II 3 cm.

Binding: Green buckram 127 gy. Ol G. On spine [gilt] [rule] | WANDERINGS | IN | ARABIA | VOL. I [II] | CHARLES M. | DOUGHTY | SCRIBNERS. T.e. gilt.

Published at: $4.50.

Notes: 1909 reprint same as above. Cal. Inst. Tech.

Wanderings in Arabia, Seltzer, 1924

SECOND AMERICAN EDITION

Title page desc: WANDERINGS IN | ARABIA | BY | CHARLES M. DOUGHTY | BEING AN ABRIDGMENT | OF | "TRAVELS IN ARABIA DESERTA" | *IN TWO VOLUMES* | VOL. I [II] | NEW YORK | THOMAS SELTZER | 1924

Collation: (22.5 × 15 cm): Vol. I: π^8 [A]–T^8 U^4, 164 leaves, pp. [1–4] [i–iv] v–xii [1]–309 [3]; Vol. II: π^6 [A]–S^8 T^2 U^4, 156 leaves, pp. [1–2] [i–v] vi–x [1]–297 [1–3].

Contents: Vol. I: prp. [1–2] blank, [3] bastard title, [4] blank, [i] blank, [ii] frontispiece, [iii] title page, [iv] printer's credit, v–xii contents, pp. [1]–309 text, [1–3] blank; Vol. II: prp. [1–2] blank, [i] bastard title, [ii] blank, [iii] title page, [iv] "Made and Printed in Great Britain | by Turnbull & Spears, Edinburgh," v–xii contents, pp. [1]–309 text, [1–3] blank; Vol. II: prp. [1–2] blank, [i] bastard title, [ii] blank, [iii] title page, [iv] printer's credit, [v]–x contents, [1]–292 text, [293]–297 glossary, [1–3] blank.

RT: On verso WANDERINGS IN ARABIA. On recto [according to opening].

Typography and paper: $ 1 signed VOL. I. [II.] Q.

  Text: 20 lines 7.2 (7.5) × 9.6 cm.

  Paper: White, wove, thick, unwatermarked, all edges trimmed, sheets bulk 3 cm each volume.

Binding: Green paper-covered boards 151 d. gy. G. Natural buckram spine. On spine [in green] Wanderings | in | Arabia | Charles M. | Doughty | *Vol.* I [II] | THOMAS | SELTZER. Fold map inside last leaf Vol. II.

Published at: $7.50.

Notes: Univ. of San Francisco.

Wanderings in Arabia, Boni, 1927

THIRD AMERICAN EDITION

Title page desc: WANDERINGS IN | ARABIA | BY | CHARLES M. DOUGHTY | BEING AN ABRIDGMENT | OF | "TRAVELS IN ARABIA DESERTA" | NEW YORK | ALBERT & CHARLES BONI | 1927 *Collation:* (21.6 × 14.3 cm): π^{10} A–2sP^8, 314 leaves, pp. [i–ii] [1–2] [iii–iv] v–xviii [1]–607 [1].

Contents: Prp. [i] bastard title, [ii] blank, [1] blank, [2] frontispiece, [iii] title page, [iv] "With the Author's sanction the | abridgment of his narrative | here presented was made by | Mr. Edward Garnett | Made and Printed in Great Britain | by Turnbull & Spears, Edinburgh," v–xviii contents, [1]–602 text, 603–607 glossary, [1] blank.

RT: On verso WANDERINGS IN ARABIA. On recto [according to subject of opening].

Typography and paper: $ 1 signed P.

Text: 20 lines 7.2 (7.4) × 9.7 cm.

Paper: White, wove, unwatermarked, top and bottom edges trimmed, sheets bulk 3.3 cm.

Binding: Brown cloth 58 m. Br. On front cover [blind stamped pub. device]. On spine [within pale green paper label pasted to spine] [red wavy Oxford rule] | [all lettering in green] Wanderings | in | Arabia | [red wavy rule] | CHARLES M. | DOUGHTY | [red Oxford rule]. T.e. pale yellow.

Notes: Cal. Institute of the Arts.

Travels in Arabia Deserta, Limited Editions Club, 1953

FOURTH AMERICAN EDITION

Title page desc: [Double page spread, within double rule frame, multi-colored map of Northwestern Arabia showing Doughty's route, handlettered all in red] Travels in | Arabia Deserta | BY Charles M. Doughty | THE TEXT AS ABRIDGED AND ARRANGED BY EDWARD GARNETT, WITH | A PREFATORY NOTE BY MR. GARNETT, A GENERAL INTRODUCTION BY | T. E. LAWRENCE, AND ILLUSTRATIONS BY EDY LEGRAND | NEW YORK The Limited Editions Club 1953

Collation: (26.6 × 19.1 cm): $[1]^6 [2]^8 [3-4]^{10} [5]^{12} [6]^{10} [7]^{12} [8]^{10} [9]^{12} [10]^{10} [11]^{12} [12]^{10} [13]^{12} [14]^8 [15-18]^{10} [19]^{12} [20]^{10} [21]^{12} [22]^{10} [23]^{12}$, 240 leaves, pp. [i–viii] ix–xvi [xvii–xviii] xix–xxi [xxii] [1–2] 3–455 [1–3].

Contents: Prp. [i] cut, [ii] blank, [iii] cut, [iv] blank, [v] bastard title within arabesque frame, [vi–vii] title pages, [viii] "THE SPECIAL CONTENTS OF THIS EDITION ARE | COPYRIGHT 1953 BY THE GEORGE MACY COMPANIES INC.," ix–xvi introduction by T. E. Lawrence, [xvii] illustration, [xviii] contents, xix–xxi editor's preface, [xxii] blank, pp. [1] half–title, [2] illustration, 3–451 text, 452–455 glossary, [1] colophon, [2–3] blank.

RT: On both verso and recto [according to chapter].

Plates: Illustrations are full page, printed in gatherings and counted in pagination.

Typography and paper:

Text: 20 lines 8.5 (9) × 6.5 cm, double column.

Paper: White, wove, unwatermarked, all edges trimmed, sheets bulk 3 cm.

Binding: Rough natural linen of natural tone. On front cover [all in brown, arabesque frame, with drawing of rider on camel superimposed over Doughty's route in Arabia]. On back cover, [arabesque design over whole cover in brown]. Binding has fore edge flap that covers fore edge and extends back over part of front cover. On fore edge [swash, running down] Travels in Arabia Deserta. Illustrated endpapers.

Notes: 1,500 copies printed. AC, HL.

Travels in Arabia Deserta, Heritage Press, 1953

FOURTH AMERICAN EDITION (SECOND ISSUE)

Title page desc: [Double spread, all within double rule frame, all swash handlettered] Travels in | Arabia Deserta | By Charles M. Doughty | THE TEXT AS ABRIDGED BY EDWARD GARNETT, WITH | A PREFATORY NOTE BY MR. GARNETT, A GENERAL INTRODUCTION BY | T. E. LAWRENCE, AND ILLUSTRATIONS BY EDY LEGRAND | NEW YORK: [swash] The Heritage Press

Collation: (26.7 × 19 cm): π^4 [1]^{10} [2]^{12} [3]^{10} [4]^{12} [5]^{10} [6]^{12} [7]^{10} [8]^{12} [9]^{10} [10]^{12} [11]^{10} [12]^{12} [13]^8 [14]^{10} [15]^{10} [16]^{10} [17]^{10} [18]^{12} [19]^{10} [20]^{12} [21]^{10} [22]^{10} [23]^{12}, 240 leaves, pp. [i–ix] x–xxi [xxi] [1–2] 3–453 [5] includes pastedown endpapers.

Contents: Prp. [i–ii] pastedown endpaper, [iii–iv] free endpaper, [v] bastard title within arabesque frame, [vi–vii] title pages, [viii] "THE SPECIAL CONTENTS OF THIS EDITION ARE | COPYRIGHT 1953 BY THE GEORGE MACY COMPANIES, INC.," [ix] contents, x–xii editor's preface, [xiii] illustration, xiv–xxi introduction by T. E. Lawrence, [xxii] blank, pp. [1] half-title, [2] illustration, 3–449 text, 450–453 glossary, [1] blank, [2–3] free endpaper, [4–5] pastedown endpaper.

RT: On both verso and recto [according to chapter] printed in Civilite.

Plates: Illustrations are full page, printed in gatherings and counted in pagination.

Typography and paper:

    Text: 20 lines 8.5 (9.3) × 6.5 cm, double column Cloister Old Style.

    Paper: White, wove, unwatermarked, all edges trimmed, sheets bulk 2.7 cm.

Binding: Rough natural linen of natural tone. On front cover [all in brown, arabesque frame, with drawing of rider on camel superimposed on Doughty's route in Arabia]. On spine [swash, in brown running down] Travels in Arabia Deserta. On back cover [in brown, same arabesque frame enclosing drawing of points of the compass]. All edges brown. Head and tail bands red and gold. Illustrated endpapers.

Published at: $6.00.

Notes: Printed by offset lithography from Limited Editions Club issue of same book. AC, HL.

Travels in Arabia Deserta, Doubleday Anchor, 1955
FIFTH AMERICAN EDITION

Title page desc: CHARLES M. DOUGHTY | TRAVELS IN | ARABIA DESERTA | An Abridgment by Edward Garnett | DOUBLEDAY AN-CHOR BOOKS | Doubleday & Company, Inc., Garden City, New York, 1955

Collation: (17.6 × 10 cm): guillotined sheets glued to covers, 180 leaves, prp. [1–8] pp. 1–349 [1–3].

Contents: Prp. [1] bastard title, [2] brief biography of Doughty, [3] title page, [4] "Published by arrangement with | Liveright Publishing Corporation, New York | COVER AND TYPOGRAPHY BY EDWARD GOREY," [5] half-title, [6–7] map, [8] blank, pp. 1–337 text, [338] blank, 339–349 glossary, [1–3] ads.

Typography and paper:

Text: 20 lines 7.7 × 8.3 cm.

Paper: White, wove, unwatermarked, all edges trimmed, sheets bulk 2 cm.

Binding: Yellow pictorial paper covers 87 m. Y. On front cover ANCHOR A 50 $1.25 | In Canada $1.45 | *Travels in* | [brown] ARABIA | [brown] DESERTA | CHARLES M. DOUGHTY | *An Abridgment by* | Edward Garnett | A DOUBLEDAY ANCHOR BOOK [pub. device]. On spine [running down] *Travels in* CHARLES M. DOUGHTY | [brown] ARABIA DESERTA | [across at bottom] ANCHOR | A 50. On back cover [two quotes from review of book].

Published at: $1.25.

Notes: Univ. Calif. Irvine.

Travels in Arabia Deserta, Peter Smith, 1968
SIXTH AMERICAN EDITION

Title page desc: CHARLES M. DOUGHTY | TRAVELS IN | ARABIA DESERTA | An Abridgment by Edward Garnett | GLOUCESTER, MASS. | PETER SMITH | 1968

Collation: (20.3 × 13.5 cm) [1–10]^16 [11]^4 [12]^16, 180 leaves, [1–8] 1–349 [1–3].

Contents: Prp. [1] bastard title, [2] brief biography of Doughty, [3] title page, [4] "Copyright, 1931 | Reprinted, 1968 by Permission of | Liveright Publishing Corp.," [5] half-title [6–7] map, [8] blank, pp. 1–337 text, [338] blank, 339–349 glossary, [1–3] blank.

Typography and paper:

    Text: 20 lines 8 × 8.8 cm.

    Paper: White, wove, unwatermarked, all edges trimmed, sheets bulk 2 cm.

Binding: Gray-green cloth 105 gy. g Y. On spine [running down] TRAVELS IN ARABIA DESERTA - - - DOUGHTY | ABRIDGED BY EDWARD GARNETT.

Published at: $4.25.

Notes: USC.

Reisen in Arabia Deserta, DuMont, 1979

FIRST GERMAN EDITION

Title page desc: Charles M. Doughty | Reisen in Arabia Deserta | Wanderungen in der Arabischen Wüste 1876–1878 | Mit einer Einleitung von Lawrence von Arabien | [in white] DuMont Buchverlag Köln

Collation: (20.5 × 15 cm): guillotined sheets glued to paper covers, 128 leaves, pp. [1–6] 7–250 [6].

Contents: Pp. [1] series title, [2–3] double spread title page, all lettering on recto, [4] "HERAUSGEGEBEN UND UBERSETZT VON HANS-THOMAS GOSCINIAK | [CIP, 8 lines] | [ISBN] | Die Orginalausgabe erschein in Cambridge 1888 | © dieser Auswahl 1979 DuMont Buchverlag, Köln | © der Einleitung von T. E. Lawrence Jonathan Cape Ltd., London | Alle Rechte vorbehalten | Druck: Rasch, Bramsche | Buchbinderische Verarbeitung: Kleins Druck, Lengerich | Printed in Germany [ISBN]," [5–6] contents, 7–9 pub. notes, 10–16 introduction by T. E. Lawrence, [17] section title, [18] synopsis, 19–249 text, 250 postscript, [1–6] ads.

RT: On verso only [according to contents of page].

Typography and paper:

    Text: 20 lines 8.1 (8.7) × 12.1 cm.

    Paper: White, wove, unwatermarked, all edges trimmed, sheets bulk 1.7 cm.

Binding: pictorial paper covers. On front cover <u>DuMont-Reiseberichte</u> <u>Charles M. Doughty</u>| *Wanderungen in der* | *Arabischen Wüste 1876–1878* | *Mit einem Vorwort von* | *Lawrence von Arabien* | Reisen in | Arabia Deserta.

On spine [running up] Charles M. Doughty Arabia Deserta | [across at top in blue] ai | id. On back cover [illus].
Published at: DM 28.
Notes: Abridgment. AC.

SECTION 3: *Passages from Arabia Deserta,* SELECTED PASSAGES

Passages from Arabia Deserta, Cape, 1931

FIRST ENGLISH EDITION

Title page desc: THE LIFE AND LETTERS SERIES NO. 21 | [tapered rule] | CHARLES M. DOUGHTY | PASSAGES FROM | ARABIA DES-ERTA | Selected by | EDWARD GARNETT | London - JONATHAN CAPE - Toronto

Collation: (20 × 13.3 cm): [A]–K^{16}, 160 leaves, pp. [1–8] 9–320.

Contents: Pp. [1] series, bastard titles, [2] pub. note on series, [3] title page, [4] "First published by the Cambridge University Press 1888 | New edition Jonathan Cape 1921 | Second impression September 1921 | New and cheaper edition September 1923 | Second impression May 1924 | New edition in one volume March 1926 | Second impression July 1926 | Third impression September 1926 | Fourth impression October 1927 | Fifth impression May 1928 | Sixth impression April 1931 | These Passages first issued in | The Life and Letters Series | 1931 | JONATHAN CAPE LTD. 30 BEDFORD SQUARE LONDON | AND 91 WELLINGTON STREET WEST, TORONTO | JONATHAN CAPE & HARRISON SMITH INC. | 139 EAST 46TH STREET NEW YORK | PRINTED AND BOUND IN GREAT BRITAIN | BY THE GARDEN CITY PRESS LIMITED | LETCHWORTH HERTS AND LONDON | PAPER MADE BY JOHN DICKINSON & CO. | LTD.," [5–7] introduction by Edward Garnett, [8] note on glossary, 9–[309] text, 311–320 glossary.

RT: On verso PASSAGES FROM ARABIA DESERTA. On recto [according to selection].

Plates: B/w frontispiece following p. [2], map on coated paper following p. [8].

Typography and paper: $ 1 signed B.

   Text: 20 lines 8.6 (8.8) × 9.8 cm.

   Paper: White, wove, unwatermarked, all edges trimmed, sheets bulk 2 cm.

Binding: Green buckram 146 d. G. On front cover [gilt] PASSAGES
FROM I ARABIA DESERTA I [series device]. On spine [gilt] PASSAGES
I FROM I ARABIA I DESERTA I [series device] I C. M. I DOUGHTY I
JONATHAN CAPE. On back cover [blind stamped pub. device].
Published at: 4s 6p.
Notes: Reprinted 1935. Reprinted 1949 as above with following differences:
Title page]: PASSAGES FROM I ARABIA DESERTA I CHARLES M.
DOUGHTY I Selected by I EDWARD GARNETT I [pub. device] I
JONATHAN CAPE I THIRTY BEDFORD SQUARE I LONDON; Con-
tents]: pp. [1] no series device, [2] blank, [4] issue statement, printer's
credits; Plates]: fold map following p. 320; Binding]: Brown cloth 38 d. r
O. binding printing silver, no series device on binding, pub. device at foot
replacing name of publisher on spine. T.e. brown. Univ. of Miami. Cal.
State San Bernardino.

Passages from Arabia Deserta, Penguin, 1956
SECOND ENGLISH EDITION

Title page desc: CHARLES M. DOUGHTY I [Oxford rule] I PASSAGES
FROM I ARABIA DESERTA I SELECTED BY I EDWARD GARNETT I
PENGUIN BOOKS I IN ASSOCIATION WITH I JONATHAN CAPE
Collation: (17.5 × 10.5 cm): [A]–I^{16} K^8 L^{16}, 168 leaves, pp. [i–iv] v [vi–
viii] 1–327 [1].
Contents: Prp. [i] pub. name, book number in series, bastard title, pub.
device, [ii] partial list of author's works, [iii] title page, [iv] "Penguin
Books Ltd, Harmondsworth, Middlesex I AUSTRALIA: Penguin Books
Pty Ltd, 762 Whitehorse Road, I Mitcham, Victoria I [short rule] I First
published 1931 I Published in Penguin Books 1956 I Made and printed in
Great Britain I by Spottiswoode, Ballantyne and Co. Ltd I London and
Colchester," v–[vi] introduction by Edward Garnett, [vii] pub. statement
on glossary, map notice, [viii] blank, pp. 1–312 text, 313–327 glossary,
[1] blank.
RT: On verso PASSAGES FROM ARABIA DESERTA. On recto [accord-
ing to subject of opening].
Typography and paper: $ 1 signed K.
  Text: 20 lines 7.6 (7.8) × 8.9 cm.
  Paper: White, wove, unwatermarked, all edges trimmed, sheets bulk
  1.5 cm.
Binding: Red and white paper covers. On front cover [all within white

rectangle centered on cover running full length] [in red] PENGUIN BOOKS | [long rule running across entire cover] Passages from | Arabia Deserta | [wood engraving of Doughty] | Charles M. Doughty | Selected by Edward Garnett | [long rule across entire cover] | COMPLETE [in red] 3/6 UNABRIDGED. On spine [rule] | [running up] Charles M. Doughty | [across, pub. device] | [running up] Passages From Arabia Deserta | 1157 | [rule]. On back cover [in red] PENGUIN BOOKS | [rule] | CHARLES M. DOUGHTY | [brief biography] | [rule] | NOT FOR SALE IN THE U.S.A. | [pub. device to right of brief biography]. Pub. ads inside both covers.

Published at: 3s 6p.

Notes: Reprinted 1983, 1984; see next entry. Univ. of Texas, El Paso.

Passages from Arabia Deserta, Penguin, 1983
SECOND ENGLISH EDITION

Title page desc: CHARLES M. DOUGHTY | PASSAGES FROM | ARABIA DESERTA | SELECTED BY | EDWARD GARNETT | [pub. device] | PENGUIN BOOKS

Collation: (19.8 × 12.8 cm): guillotined sheets glued to covers, 68 leaves, pp. [1–6] 1–327 [1–3].

Contents: Prp. [1] brief biography of author and pub. history of book, [2] blank, [3] title page, [4] [5 lines of addresses for Penguin] | "First published 1956 | Reprinted 1983 | All rights reserved | Made and printed in Great Britain by | Richard Clay (The Chaucer Press) Ltd, | Bungay, Suffolk | Set in Monotype Garamond" | [9-line conditions-of-sale statement] | [5] pub. note, [6] blank, pp. 1–312 text, 313–327 glossary, [1] blank, [2] blurb on publisher, [3] blank.

RT: On verso PASSAGES FROM ARABIA DESERTA. On recto [according to chapter].

Typography and paper:
  Text: 20 lines 8 (8.10) × 9.3 cm.
  Paper: White, wove, unwatermarked, all edges trimmed, sheets bulk 2 cm.

Binding: Pictorial paper covers. On front cover [all except last line in white] C. M. DOUGHTY | [rule] | PASSAGES FROM | ARABIA DESERTA | [rule] | SELECTED BY EDWARD GARNETT | [rule] | A BOOK SO MAJESTIC, SO VITAL, OF | SUCH INCOMPARABLE BEAUTY OF THOUGHT, | OF OBSERVATION, AND OF DICTION,

| AS TO OCCUPY A PLACE APART—*OBSERVER* | {Oxford rule} | PEN-GUIN TRAVEL LIBRARY. On spine {pub. device} | {Oxford rule} | {running down} C. M. DOUGHTY PASSAGES FROM ARABIA DESERTA | ISBN 0 14 | 00.9508 X. On back cover {blurb, cover design credit, prices, ISBN}.
Published at: $5.95.
Notes: 1984 reprint same as above. Cal.

Passages from Arabia Deserta, Liveright, 1931
FIRST AMERICAN EDITION

Title page desc: CHARLES MONTAGU DOUGHTY | {tapered rule} | PASSAGES FROM | ARABIA DESERTA | Selected by | EDWARD GARNETT | NEW YORK - HORACE LIVERIGHT, INC. | LONDON - JONATHAN CAPE
Collation: (19.2 × 13 cm): [A]–K^{16}, 160 leaves, pp. [1–8] 9–320.
Contents: Pp. [1] bastard title, [2] blank, [3] title page, [4] "First published by the Cambridge University Press 1888 | These Passages first issued in | 1931 | PRINTED IN GREAT BRITAIN | BY THE GARDEN PRESS LIMITED | LETCHWORTH HERTS AND LONDON," [5–7] introduction by Edward Garnett, [8] credit for glossary, 9–[309] text, [310] blank, 311–320 glossary.
RT: On verso PASSAGES FROM ARABIA DESERTA. On recto {according to contents of page].
Plates: One b/w plate on coated paper frontispiece. Map following p. [8].
Typography and paper: $ 1 signed B.
  Text: 20 lines 7.7 (7.9) × 9.8 cm.
  Paper: White, wove, unwatermarked, all edges trimmed, sheets bulk 1.8 cm.
Binding: Black cloth. On front cover {gilt} PASSAGES FROM | ARABIA DESERTA. On spine {gilt} PASSAGES | FROM | ARABIA | DESERTA | C. M. | DOUGHTY | LIVERIGHT.
Published at: $2.50.
Notes: San Francisco State Univ.

Arabia deserta, Payot, 1949
FIRST FRENCH EDITION

Title page desc: BIBLIOTHÈQUE HISTORIQUE | {long rule} | CHARLES M. DOUGHTY | {short rule} | ARABIA DESERTA | TEXTES CHOISIS

PAR EDWARD GARNETT I ET TRADUITS PAR JACQUES MARTY I [short rule] I *PRÉFACE DE T. E. LAWRENCE* I AUTEUR DES ≪SEPT PILIERS DE LA SAGESSE≫ I [short rule] I [pub. device] I PAYOT PARIS I 106, BOULEVARD SAINT-GERMAIN I [short rule] I 1949 I Tout droits de traduction de reproduction et d'adaption resérvés pour tous pays. I *Passages from Arabia Deserta,* selected by E. Garnett Jonathan Cape, 30, Bedford Square, London

Collation: (22.3 × 14.3 cm): [1]–21^8, 168 leaves, pp. [1–6] 7–334 [335–336].

Contents: Pp. [1] blank, [2] list of series titles, [3] title page, [4] quotes from reviews, [5–6] 7–18 preface by T. E. Lawrence, [19]–21 advertisement by Garnett, [22] blank, [23]–327 text, [328]–334 glossary, [335] contents, [336] blank.

RT: On both verso and recto [according to section].

Typography and paper: $ 1 signed 3.

Text: 20 lines 8.2 (8.3) × 10.4 cm.

Paper: White, wove, unwatermarked, untrimmed, sheets bulk 2.5 cm.

Binding: Tan paper covers 73 p. OY. On front cover [within rule frame] *BIBLIOTHÈQUE HISTORIQUE* I [long rule] I Charles M. Doughty I [short rule] I [in red] ARABIA I [in red] DESERTA I *PRÉFACE DE T. E. LAWRENCE* I [cut] I Textes choisis par Edward Garnett I et traduits par Jacques Marty I PAYOT, PARIS. On spine [rule] I CHARLES I M. DOUGHTY I [rule] I Arabia I Deserta I [rule] I 780fr. I [rule] I PAYOT I PARIS I [rule]. On back cover [list of works by publisher, within single rule frame].

Published at: 780 fr.

Notes: AC, HL.

Die Offenbarung Arabiens, List, 1937

FIRST GERMAN EDITION

Title page desc: CHARLES M. DOUGHTY I DIE OFFENBARUNG I ARABIENS I *(ARABIA DESERTA)* I [pub. device] I PAUL LIST VERLAG LEIPZIG

Collation: (21.2 × 13 cm): [1]–38^8 39^4, 308 leaves, pp. [1–5] 6–612 [1–4].

Contents: Pp. [1] bastard title, [2] blank, [3] title page, [4] "Aus dem Englischen von H. Federmann I Titel der Orginalausgabe: Travels in Arabia Deserta I Umschlag und Einband von Prof. H. Hussman I Mit einen

Titelbild und der Orginalkarte Arabiens von Doughty | Alle Rechte, be-
sonders die des Nachdrucks, der Übersetzung, Dramatisierung, Ver-
filmung und Radioverbreitung vorbehalten | Copyright 1937 by Paul List
Verlag Leipzig. Printed in Germany | Druck und Bindearbeiten der
Spamer A.-G. in Leipzig," [5]–9 translator's foreword, [10]–16 prefaces,
[17]–32 introduction by T. E. Lawrence, [33]–594 text, [595] translator's postscript, [596]–598 chronology and English measures, [599]–
612 name and place index, [1] contents, [2–4] ads.

RT: On both verso and recto [according to chapter].

Plates: Frontispiece on coated paper printed on one side only following p.
[2]. Fold map inside rear cover.

Typography and paper: $ 1,2 signed Doughty, Die Offenbarung Arabiens
2,2*.

   Text: 20 lines 8.2 (8.5) × 10 cm.

   Paper: White, wove, unwatermarked, all edges trimmed, sheets bulk
   3.8 cm.

Binding: Green cloth 164 m. b. G. On front cover (gilt & swash) DIE
OFFENBARUNG | ARABIENS. On spine [gilt] [within gilt rectangle,
lettering green] CHARLES | M. DOUGHTY | [below rectangle] [swash]
DIE | OFFEN /| BARUNG | ARABIENS | [gilt sword] | [pub. device].
T.e. green. Gold and white head and tail bands.

Notes: Selected chapters. AC.

Al pene arav, N. Tabarsky, 1945/46
FIRST HEBREW EDITION

Title page desc: CHARLES M. DOUGHTY | AL PENE ARAV | TUR-
GAM MAYANGLIT | A. REUVENI | HOTSAAT SFARIM N. TAB-
ARSKY, CHEVRAH BA'AM | TEL-AVIV, TAVSHINVAV

Collation: (19 × 13 cm): [1–9]^{16}, 144 leaves, [1–4] 5–288.

Contents: Pp. [1] bastard title, [2] blank, [3] title page, [4] note on glossary, copyright, printer's credit, 5–6 Edward Garnett's introduction,
7–281 text, [282] blank, 283–288 glossary.

Plates: Frontispiece before p. [1].

Typography and paper:

   Text: 20 lines 10.8 × 10 cm.

   Paper: Newsprint, wove, unwatermarked, all edges trimmed, sheets
   bulk 1.3 cm.

Binding: Tan paper covered boards 90 r gy. Y, brown cloth spine. 63 l. br.

GY. On front cover [in brown] CHARLES M. DOUGHTY | AL PENE
ARAV. On spine CHARLES | M. | DOUGHTY | AL | PENE | ARAV |
HOTSAAT | N. TABARSKY. Map end papers [in green].
Notes: Passages from Arabia Deserta 1931 edition. LC.

Arabisk resa, Berghs, 1959
FIRST SWEDISH EDITION

Title page desc: CHARLES M. DOUGHTY | Arabisk resa | ÖVER-
SATTNING FRÅN ENGELSKAN | AV H. S. NYBERG | SVEN-ERIK
BERGHS FORLSL | STOCKHOLM LONDON NEW YORK
Collation: (22.1 × 14.2 cm): [1]−22⁸, 176 leaves, pp. [1−4] 5−352.
Contents: Pp. [1] pub. device, [2] blank, [3] title page, [4] "Orginalets
titel: Passages from Arabia Deserta | Sven-Erik Berghs Bokforlag | ©
Jonathan Cape, London | Box 7273, Stockholm 7 | Sven-Eric Berghs As-
sociates, Inc | 545 Fifth Avenue, New York 17, N.Y. | Printed in Sweden
NR 5963 | Klara Civiltryckeri AB, Stockholm 1959," 5−10 prefaces, 11−
23 introduction by T. E. Lawrence, 24 map, 25−337 text, 338−352
glossary and index.
Typography and paper: $ 1 signed 2,2- Arabisk resa.
   Text: 20 lines 9 × 10.4 cm.
   Paper: White, wove, unwatermarked, untrimmed, sheets bulk 2 cm.
Binding: Orange 50 s.O paper covers. On front cover [swash] Arabisk | resa |
av Charles M. Doughty | *In ledning av* T. E. LAWRENCE | BERGHS. [all
in white printed over line drawing of figure riding camel]. On spine
[running up] *Charles M. Doughty* ARABISK RESA | [at foot, pub. device] |
BERGHS. On back cover [blurbs and pub. note].
Published at: 26:50 SKR paper bound; 29:50 SKR hardbound.
Notes: Hardbound issue: Binding]: Brown cloth 61 gy. Br. On front cover
[gilt cut]. On spine [gilt, running up] *Charles M. Doughty* - ARABISK
RESA. White head and tail bands. AC.

STEPHEN E. TABACHNICK

A Selected Bibliography of Works about Travels in Arabia Deserta

BOOKS

Assad, Thomas J. *Three Victorian Travellers: Burton, Blunt, Doughty.* London: Routledge and Kegan Paul, 1964.

Fairley, Barker. *Charles M. Doughty: A Critical Study.* London: Jonathan Cape, 1927.

Hogarth, David G. *The Life of Charles M. Doughty.* London: Oxford University Press, 1928.

Tabachnick, Stephen Ely. *Charles Doughty.* Boston: Twayne, 1981.

Treneer, Anne. *Charles M. Doughty: A Study of His Prose and Verse.* London: Jonathan Cape, 1935.

DISSERTATIONS

Deledalle-Rhodes, Janice. "*Arabia Deserta* de Charles M. Doughty et les récits des voyageurs anglais au Moyen-Orient de 1809 à 1896: Mythes, réalités et transformation des mentalités." Doctorat d'État dissertation, Université Paul Valéry, 1981.

Kaddal, M. "Charles Montagu Doughty, His Life and Works." Ph.D. dissertation, Glasgow University, 1962.

McCormick, Annette. "The Origins and Development of the Styles of Charles M. Doughty's *Arabia Deserta.*" Ph.D. dissertation, Bedford College, University of London, 1952.

Rogers II, William N. "Arabian Involvement: A Study of Five Victorian Travel Narratives." Ph.D. dissertation, University of California, Berkeley, 1971.

Safady, Issam. "Attempt and Attainment: A Study of Some Literary Aspects of Charles Doughty's *Arabia Deserta* as the Culmination of Late-Victorian Anglo-Arabian Travel Books to the Levant." Ph.D. dissertation, University of Kentucky, 1968.

PARTS OF BOOKS

Bidwell, Robin. *Travellers in Arabia*. London: Hamlyn, 1976.
Brent, Peter. *Far Arabia*. London: Weidenfeld and Nicolson, 1978.
Freeth, Zara, and H. V. F. Winstone. *Explorers of Arabia from the Renaissance to the End of the Victorian Era*. London: Allen & Unwin, 1978.
Hogarth, David G. *The Penetration of Arabia*. New York: Frederick A. Stokes, 1904.
Kiernan, R. H. *The Unveiling of Arabia: The Story of Arabian Travel and Discovery*. London: Harrap, 1937.
Meyers, Jeffrey. *The Wounded Spirit: A Study of "Seven Pillars of Wisdom"*. London: Martin Brian & O'Keeffe, 1973.
Nasir, Sari J. *The Arabs and the English*. London: Longman's, 1976.
Pirenne, Jacqueline. *A la découverte de l'Arabie: Cinq siècles de science et d'aventure*. Paris: Amiot-Dumont, 1958.
Said, Edward. *Orientalism*. New York: Pantheon, 1978.
Sykes, Percy. *A History of Exploration*. London: Routledge and Kegan Paul, 1949.
Tabachnick, Stephen Ely. *T. E. Lawrence*. Boston: Twayne, 1978.
Tidrick, Kathryn. *Heart-Beguiling Araby*. Cambridge: Cambridge University Press, 1981.
Wilcox, Desmond. *Ten Who Dared*. Boston: Little, Brown, 1977.

ARTICLES AND PAMPHLETS

A.H.S. Review. *Nature* 38, 28 June 1888, 195–96.
Anon. Review. *Times* (London), 6 April 1888, 13.
———. Obituary. *Times* (London), 22 January 1926, 14.
Babinger, Franz. Obituary. *Islam* 16 (1927): 122–25.
Bevis, Richard. "Spiritual Geology: C. M. Doughty and the Land of the Arabs." *Victorian Studies* 16 (December 1972): 163–81.
Bishop, Jonathan. "The Heroic Ideal in Doughty's *Arabia Deserta*." *Modern Language Quarterly* 21 (March 1960): 59–68.

Burton, Richard Francis. "Mr. Doughty's Travels in Arabia." *The Academy* 34 (28 July 1888): 47–48.

Cartwright, J. "Charles M. Doughty and 'Travels in Arabia Deserta,'" *Papers of the Manchester Literary Club* 64 (1940): 141–60.

Cunninghame-Graham, R. B. Review of *Wanderings in Arabia. The Nation and Athenaeum,* 7 March 1908, 844–45.

Dibben, Eric. "Doughty the Man." *Cornhill Magazine* 72 (1932): 618–26.

Douglas, Norman. "Arabia Deserta." *London Mercury* 4 (May 1921): 60–70.

Eliot, T. S. "Contemporary English Prose." *Vanity Fair* 20 (July 1923): 51–98.

Fedden, Robin. *English Travellers in the Near East.* Writers and Their Work, no. 97. Ed. Bonamy Dobrée. London: Longman's, Green, 1958.

Foss, Michael. "Dangerous Guides: English Writers and the Desert." *The New Middle East* 9 (June 1969): 38–42.

Freeman, John. Obituary. *London Mercury* 14 (August 1926): 368–82.

Garnett, Edward. "Books Too Little Known." *The Academy and Literature,* 24 January 1903, 86–87.

Gay, Ruth. "Charles Doughty: Man and Book." *American Scholar* 50 (Autumn 1981): 527–35.

Grant, Douglas. "Barker Fairley on Charles Doughty." *University of Toronto Quarterly* 26 (1967): 220–28.

Hess, Jean Jacques. "Bermerkungen zu Doughty's Travels in Arabia Deserta." *Wiener Zeitschrift f. d. Kunde d. Morgenlandes* 16 (1902): 45–62.

Hogarth, David G. Obituary. *Geographical Journal* 67 (April 1926): 381–84.

Hogarth, W. D. "Doughty, Charles Montagu." *Dictionary of National Biography 1922–1930.* London: Oxford University Press, 1937.

Leavis, F. R. "Doughty and Hopkins." *Scrutiny* 4 (December 1935): 316–17.

Lowenstein, Solomon. "Travels in Arabia Deserta." *Papers.* New York: Quarto Club, 1930, pp. 55–77.

McCormick, Annette. "Hebrew Parallelism in Doughty's *Travels in Arabia Deserta.*" *Studies in Comparative Literature.* Humanities Series, no. 11. Ed. Waldo McNeir. Baton Rouge: Louisiana State University Press, 1962, pp. 29–46.

———. "An Elizabethan-Victorian Travel Book: Doughty's *Travels in Arabia Deserta*," *Essays in Honor of Esmond Linworth Marilla*. Ed. Thomas Kirby and William Olive. Baton Rouge: Louisiana State University Press, 1970, pp. 230–42.

Murry, John Middleton. Obituary. *Times Literary Supplement*, 11 February 1926, 85–86.

———. "*Arabia Deserta*." *The Adelphi* 3 (March 1926): 657–65.

Pastner, C. M. "Englishmen in Arabia: Encounters with Middle Eastern Women." *Signs* 4 (Winter 1978): 309–23.

Robbins, Ruth M. "The Word Notes of C. M. Doughty." *Agenda* 18 (1980): 78–98.

Rogers, William N., and S. E. Tabachnick. "British Literary Responses to the Near East: C. M. Doughty and T. E. Lawrence." Taped one-hour colloquium. San Diego State University, 18 April 1979. Doughty by W. N. Rogers, Lawrence by S. E. Tabachnick.

———. Review of S. E. Tabachnick, *Charles Doughty*. *Victorian Studies* (Spring 1983): 358–59.

Storrs, Sir Ronald. "The Spell of Arabia: Charles Doughty and T. E. Lawrence." *Listener* 38, 25 December 1947, 1093–94.

Sullivan, Anthony T. "The Obstinate Mr. Doughty." *Aramco World Magazine* 20 (January/April 1969): 2–5.

Tabachnick, Stephen E. "Two 'Arabian' Romantics: Charles Doughty and T. E. Lawrence." *English Literature in Transition: 1880–1920* 16 (1973): 11–25.

———. "Adam Cast Forth: The First Sentence of Doughty's *Arabia Deserta*." *The Pre-Raphaelite Review* 1 (May 1978): 49–63.

Taylor, Walt. *Doughty's English*. S. P. E. Tract, no. 51. Oxford: Clarendon Press, 1939.

Woolf, Leonard. Review. *The Nation and the Athenaeum*, 27 October 1923, 155.

CONTRIBUTORS

Richard Bevis is the compiler of *Bibliotheca Cisorientalia: An Annotated Checklist of Early English Travel Books on the Near and Middle East.* He has taught at the American University of Beirut and is now with the English Department at the University of British Columbia, Vancouver.

Janice Deledalle-Rhodes received a Doctorat d'État in 1981 at the Université Paul Valéry with a dissertation on *Arabia Deserta.* She has taught in Europe and Africa and is presently maître-de-conférences at the University of Avignon.

Carol Faul is an associate in the Geology Department at the University of Pennsylvania and has co-authored *It Began with a Stone: A History of Geology from the Stone Age to the Age of Plate Tectonics.*

Robert Fernea is the author of *Shaykh and Effendi: Changing Patterns of Authority among the El-Shabana of Southern Iraq* and other works on the Middle East. He has most recently co-authored *The Arab World: Personal Encounters,* and he teaches in the Anthropology Department of the University of Texas, Austin.

Philip C. Hammond teaches in the Anthropology Department at the University of Utah, Salt Lake City, and is the author of *Petra, The Excavations of the Main Theater* and *The Nabataeans—Their History, Culture and Archaeology.*

Edward A. Levenston has taught in the English Department of the Hebrew University since 1958. He is the co-compiler of *The New Bantam-Megiddo Hebrew and English Dictionary* and enjoys a good game of *Scrabble.*

Philip O'Brien is director of the Whittier College Library and an avid collector of children's books and T. E. Lawrence and Charles Doughty materials. He is the author of the mini-book *T. E. Lawrence and Fine Printing* and has contributed an article on collecting Lawrence to *The T. E. Lawrence Puzzle.*

William N. Rogers II is the editor of *Exploration* and the author of a dissertation and several articles on nineteenth-century Anglo-Arabian travel writers. He teaches in the English Department at San Diego State University.

Reginald Shagam, of the Ben-Gurion University, Israel, Geology Department, is the author of numerous publications on South American geology in particular, and has served in the geology departments of Princeton and the University of Pennsylvania.

Stephen E. Tabachnick, formerly of the Ben-Gurion University, is now chairman of the English Department at Tennessee Technological University. He is the author of *T. E. Lawrence* and *Charles Doughty* and co-author of *Harold Pinter.* Most recently, he has edited *The T. E. Lawrence Puzzle* (Georgia, 1984).

J. M. Wagstaff, senior lecturer in geography at the University of Southampton, England, is the co-author of *The Middle East: A Geographical Study,* author of *The Development of Rural Settlements,* and editor, with C. Renfrew, of *An Island Polity: The Archaeology of Exploitation in Melos.*

Bayly Winder is the author of *Saudi Arabia in the Nineteenth Century* and holds a joint appointment in the History and Near Eastern Departments and directs the Kevorkian Center for Near Eastern Studies at New York University. His most recent published works include articles on Mecca and Medina in the *Encyclopedia of Islam* and a translation from the Arabic.

INDEX

Abercrombie, Lascelles, 92, 94
Abu Bakkar, 194
Abu Nejm, Abdullah, 67, 79
Académie des Inscriptions et Belles-Lettres (Paris), 148
Adams, Percy, 12; bibliography of travel literature, 12; *Travel Literature and the Evolution of the Novel*, 12
Adams, Robert Martin, 63, 67; *Nil*, 64, 67
Addison, Joseph, 63–64, 65; concept of "the Great," 63–64
Aden, 189
Admiralty (British), 188
Aesthetic movement: and *TAD*, 49, 59–60
Africa: sundered from Arabia, 164
Africans, 115
Ageyl (Beduin tribe), 118, 119, 192, 194, 195
Airy, Sir George: and isostasy theory, 181
Akaba, 155
al-Rashid, Abd al-Aziz, 188; *Ta'rikh al-Kuweyt*, 188
Albanians, 194
Alexandria, 149
Alfred (Saxon king), 47
Algeria, 167
Allah (Ullah), 73, 90, 91, 99, 103
Allat temple (Petra), 157
Alps: and the "Sublime," 63, 64
Alt, Albrecht, 152
Aly, 83
Aly, Mohammed (*kella* commandant), 3, 70, 82, 86–87, 88, 196
America, 224
American Geographical Society: publishes Musil's work, 187

Aneyza, 5, 66, 70, 82, 103, 122, 143, 145, 168, 172, 176, 187, 189, 190, 191
Anglo-Arabian travel tradition, 19, 20, 63, 111–29 passim, 143–46
Annales historical school: and Doughty, 197
Anthropology, 72; and travel writers, 19; in nineteenth century, 46; in twentieth century, 201–4; *TAD's* importance for, 201–19. See also *TAD*: Anthropology in
Arabia, 3–6 passim, 11, 15, 18, 33, 46, 52, 53, 54, 59, 62, 64, 65, 66, 67, 68, 72, 75, 79, 83, 84, 88, 90, 92, 114, 125, 172, 175, 210, 217; geological history of, 15, 163–67, 177; history of, 16, 178, 186–200; geography of, 18, 62, 133–47, 178; and bareness, 74; ancient map of, 135; archaeology in, 148; in twentieth century, 154, 157, 159, 198; sundered from Africa, 164; anthropology of, 201–19
Arabia Felix, 155
Arabian Nights, 121
Arabian-American Oil Company, 169; 1962 map prepared by, 169, 171, 172, 173, 174
Arabian peninsula, 4, 91, 101, 133, 140, 146, 149; Doughty explored only a small part of, 135
Arabic language, 10, 90, 188, 205, 209, 212; as recorded in *TAD*, 91–110 passim; authenticity of Doughty's use of, 215–19
Arabs, 19, 20, 32, 50, 59, 67, 68, 70, 71, 72, 74, 82, 92, 192; attack Doughty, 80; fear Doughty, 84; Doughty's relations with, 87, 111–29,

—Anthropology in, 18–19, 46, 69, 72, 140, 159, 201–19; Doughty's contribution to, 18–19, 218–19

—Archaeology in, 17, 148–62; Doughty's contribution to, 17, 150–51, 160; lack of ceramic knowledge, 152, 161 (n. 13), 162 (n. 26); appendix, 150; ancient travel, 155–56; desert life, 156–57; town and village life, 157; institutions, 157–58; hydrology, 158; natural history, 158–59. *See also* Nabataeans

—Architecture in, 26–27

—Art and science combined in, 1, 2, 3, 9, 13, 23, 25, 43, 44, 60, 62, 77, 88, 136–37, 146, 160, 184–85, 207–10, 214–19

—Attitudes in: toward the past, 16–17, 45–48, 52, 148–62 passim, 186–200 passim; toward the Arabs, 20, 87, 111–29 passim, (not systematic) 117, 201–19; toward friendship, 20, 121–24, 140; awe, 22; toward the reader, 43, 94, 117, (treats reader as bilingual) 31, 97, 217, 219; religion-science controversy absent, 46; toward duty, 49, 50–51; toward slave trade, 50, 208; toward Beduin, 69–70, 73–76, 81–82, 111–29 passim, 201–19 passim; toward cultural relativism, 88–89, 111–29 passim, 211; toward Arab hospitality, 118, 158, 213, 214; toward Negroes, 125. *See also* Arabs; Beduin; Doughty: Attitudes of

—British bureaucracy in, 5

—Cartography in, 16–17, 35, 62, 135, 143, 168–75, 175–77, 183–85

—Centenary of, 6, 12, 62

—Characterization in: of Arabs, 30–31, 70–71, 86–88, 116, 214–19; of Khalil, 32–36, 200 (n. 26), 209–10, 215

—Christianity in, 2, 4, 5, 20, 32, 35, 43, 47, 49–51, 59, 69–70, 80, 81, 83, 84, 85, 210–14

—Composition of, 6, 32, 39 (n. 51), 140, 212, 216

—Conflict in, 3–5, 19–20, 35, 52, 59, 70–71, 80, 82, 83, 84, 86–87, 111–29 passim, 123, 183–84, 201–19 passim, esp. 211–14

—Consciousness in, 21–23

—Contradictions in, 73, 75, 82, 117–20

—Diary for, 135, 140, 143

—Disease in, 3, 10, 26, 83, 173

—Eating habits in, 81, 84, 208

—Editions of, 6–7, 37 (n. 8), 175, 183, 184, 185, 223–53; first (1888) edition worth $300. See also *Passages from Arabia Deserta; Wanderings in Arabia*

—Ethnography in, 18–19, 154–55, 184, 197, 201–19

—Factual elements in, 15–19, 73, 132–46, 133–47, 148–62, 163–85, 215; factual accuracy of, 14, 15–19, 24, 143–46; used by intelligence in W.W.I and W.W.II, 18, 38 (n. 39), 153, 161 (n. 14)

—Flora and fauna in, 17, 77–89, 152, 153, 158–59

—Genre of: autobiography of travel, 13–36, 39 (n. 50)

—Geography in, 10, 16–17, 43–44, 62, 133–47, 133, 135, 136, 178; historical geography in, 17, 133, 142–46; topography in, 18, 24, 62, 135, 136, 141, 146; humanistic and perception geography, 133, 139–42; Doughty's contribution to geography summarized, 135, 137, 138, 145–46; Arabian regionalization in, 136–39; problem of subjectivity, 136, 140, 142; and nineteenth-century geography, 136–37; arranged unsystematically, 136; Doughty's description of Hayil compared to that of other travellers, 143–46

—Geology in, 1–2, 6, 7, 10, 15, 18, 47, 136, 146, 153, 159, 163–85; lack of interpretation, 163, 175–77; contribution to geologic mapping, 168–75; errors, 172, 174–75, 178–79; quality of observations assessed, 176; unfavorably compared to Fraas's contribution, 177–80; Doughty's ignorance of contemporaries' work, 177–80; geologic appendix, 177, 179, 183; and nineteenth-century geology, 181–82; failure to classify fossils, 182; final assessment, 182–85

—Gestures in, 99–100, 107–8, 109 (n. 8)

—Gothic atmosphere in, 4, 10, 85–87